W9-BGL-064

BIBLICAL
ARCHAEOLOGY

LIBRARY OF JEWISH KNOWLEDGE

Geoffrey Wigoder, General Editor of the Series

The Jews of the United States
What Does Judaism Say About . . . ?
Bible and Civilization
Biblical Archaeology
Kabbalah

𝕿𝖍𝖊 𝕹𝖊𝖜 𝖄𝖔𝖗𝖐 𝕿𝖎𝖒𝖊𝖘
Library of Jewish Knowledge

BIBLICAL ARCHAEOLOGY

Edited by SHALOM M. PAUL
and WILLIAM G. DEVER

QUADRANGLE/THE NEW YORK TIMES BOOK CO.

Copyright © 1974 by Keter Publishing House Jerusalem Ltd.
P.O. Box 7145, Jerusalem, Israel
All rights reserved, including the right to reproduce
this book or portions thereof in any form.

Published in the Western Hemisphere by
QUADRANGLE/THE NEW YORK TIMES BOOK CO.
10 East 53 Street, New York, N.Y. 10022.
Distributed in Canada by Fitzhenry & Whiteside, Ltd., Toronto.

ISBN 0–8129–0351–X
Library of Congress Catalog Card Number 73–77034

Manufactured in the United States of America

CONTENTS

EDITORS' INTRODUCTION

Archaeology is the scientific study of the material remains of antiquity. The term is derived from two Greek words *archaios* ("ancient") and *logos* ("knowledge"). Biblical archaeology hence pertains to all those remains which shed light on the life, customs, history, literature, language, and architecture of early Israel and its neighbors.

Prof. G. Ernest Wright of Harvard, founder and editor of the journal *The Biblical Archaeologist,* defined it as a "special 'armchair' variety of general archaeology." In this view, biblical archaeology is largely an amateur affair, in which non-archaeologists utilize the results of the professional field archaeologist, in this case for purposes of biblical illustration. (We should not, of course, disparage the work of the "amateur," for etymologically the word simply means "lover," one who pursues a subject not as a means of making a living but for the pure love of learning; every branch of archaeology needs such friends.) However, more recently, with the expansion of the archaeological enterprise, there has grown up a school of *professional* biblical archaeologists — people who are both competent biblical scholars *and* trained field archaeologists. Thus "biblical archaeology" must now be defined in a sense broad enough to include informed laymen such as the readers of this volume, as well as scholars who work full-time at excavation, research, and publication.

The coupling of archaeology with the Bible is not surprising. In fact, the exploration of the ancient Near East began, more than a century ago, precisely when Western scholars were drawn to the Fertile Crescent in the search for the sources of their own Judeo-Christian heritage. The "Lands of the Bible" were among the first to be opened up in the archaeological revolution that followed, and biblical scholars were a majority among the first generation of explorers, collectors of antiquities, and somewhat later, excavators. This combination of interests has been especially characteristic in America, where Near Eastern archaeologists have typically come out of biblical backgrounds, from Edward Robinson, whose work in the 1830s made him the first modern Palestinologist, to W.F. Albright, whose towering

scholarship in this century established the discipline on scientific foundations. Of course, there has been a parallel, secular tradition of Near Eastern
archaeology, both in America and in Europe. This approach is more fully
developed in the burgeoning "Israeli school," where archaeologists are not
only professional biblical scholars but also may be cultural historians,
anthropologists, or even specialists in the natural sciences. Nevertheless, all
Near Eastern archaeologists, when they work in the lands or in the periods
where the Bible is relevant, must employ it, if for no other reason than the
fact that it looms as our largest, and no doubt as our most influential,
surviving literature from the ancient Near East. The study of the Bible and
the pursuit of archaeology belong together.

However, the essence of Prof. Wright's definition must be recalled:
"biblical archaeology" is only *one* among many legitimate specializations
within the broader field of Near Eastern archaeology. For instance, the
biblical archaeologist usually begins with the same phenomenon as any Near
Eastern archaeologist: the *tell* (from an ancient Semitic root meaning "ruin-
heap"). These artificial mounds, which are peculiar to the Near East with its
long history of continuous occupation at strategic, well-watered sites, may
contain as many as two dozen superimposed strata, representing as many
successive, buried civilizations. The untangling of the complex threads of
man's story at such a site requires the most meticulous stratigraphic excavation, carefully separating each stratum and attempting to reconstruct from
the surviving artifacts the material culture of a given era. The objects from
everyday life, the architecture, and especially the pottery which is so
durable and so reliable an indicator of cultural and chronological change, all
must be analyzed from the standpoint of technology, classified typologically, studied in the light of comparisons elsewhere, and dated as closely as
possible. If the archaeologist is fortunate enough to turn up any written
material, these must be deciphered and studied in similarly exhaustive
fashion. Plant and animal remains must be studied by paleo-ethno botanists
and zoologists as well as physical anthropologists; samples of sedimentary
deposits, clay sources, and pottery tempers must be analyzed by geologists;
and all this and much other evidence must be brought into a synthesis by
environmental experts and other specialists in the effort to reconstruct the
total pattern of culture and behavior in an extinct society.

This bare listing of the tasks before the archaeologist makes it clear that
the biblical archaeologist may no longer be able to command all the
technical and interpretive skills required. But he must at least be able to
appreciate and to make use of the work of specialists. He himself will

probably be an experienced field excavator, a member of a multi-disciplinary team; his own speciality may be stratigraphy or ceramic typology. And to an acquaintance with the many languages and literatures of the ancient Near East, he will necessarily add a particular competence in the biblical literature.

It must be stressed that there are no "special" methods or aims for biblical archaeology. It works with the same materials and techniques, it presupposes the same standards of objectivity, it strives for the same total reconstruction of the past, that characterize all archaeology. Biblical archaeology simply confines itself – not arbitrarily but deliberately – to those areas which are of direct relevance for the Bible. Its geographical scope extends to all of the "Lands of the Bible," which means the entire Eastern Mediterranean as far as Iraq and Iran, but with primary focus on ancient Syria-Palestine, comprising parts of modern Israel, Jordan, Syria, and Lebanon. The chronological scope of biblical archaeology dealt with in this volume extends until the Persian period. (What is sometimes called "New Testament Archaeology," which covers the Hellenistic, Roman, and Byzantine periods, may be considered a separate specialization.) The biblical archaeologist deliberately specializes in certain areas, both because these best suit his own scholarly interests and because he recognizes the limits of his own archaeological competence. Yet he acknowledges the broad context of Near Eastern archaeology as the general framework for his own research. Parallel to his own specialization, he recognizes the legitimacy of another approach, i.e., that of "Syro-Palestinian archaeology" conceived as an independent, secular discipline, not dominated primarily by biblical interests but pursued by cultural historians for its own sake. Finally, the biblical archaeologist defends his own particular enterprise by stressing that one of the many values of archaeology, and the one he happens to be interested in, is its usefulness in illustrating the Bible.

Until about 150 years ago the biblical lands were virtually mute. Interest in their sites began in the 19th century, entered into the first decades of the 20th century with the beginnings of the modern method of excavation, and advanced remarkably with increasing improvement of new scientific techniques during the periods between the two world wars. From the end of World War II until the present it has resulted in a plethora of riches uncovered in the finely executed exploration of countless sites.

The relationship between archaeology and the Bible has often been misunderstood. The most dangerous error – albeit one often committed in innocence by religious persons – is to suppose that the task of archaeology is to "prove the Bible." Thus well-meaning attempts have been made to see evidence of the flood of Genesis in silt-layers of mounds in Mesopotamia; to locate Noah's ark in the ice-bound glaciers of Soviet Armenia; to recover Moses' tomb on Mount Nebo; to relate the collapsed walls of Jericho (long before the biblical period) to the "walls of Joshua"; to find the treasure of the "Copper Scroll" from Qumran; or to authenticate the innumerable "holy places" which claim to memorialize Old and New Testament events.

Biblical faith is based on history, to be sure, and if we wish to share that faith it is important for us to recover as much of the historical background as we can. But essentially biblical faith is beyond history: it is a way of viewing the result of God's action in history which *interprets* events through the "eyes of the faith." A single illustration will show the unique nature of this faith. It might be supposed that archaeology could "prove" the Israelite conquest of Canaan about 1200 B.C.E. We could excavate destruction levels at various sites mentioned in the Bible, and with the modern means at our disposal could easily show whether they date to the period in question. If we found evidence of a new occupation and material culture about the ash levels, and especially if we found Hebrew inscriptions in the new building levels, we would probably be safe in concluding that the destruction was indeed due to the Israelites. Would this not prove the biblical account of Joshua's conquest? Hardly, for the fundamental point of the biblical writers' claim is not that Israel *took* the Land, but that God *gave* the Land to Israel. That claim is simply not open to archaeological investigation! We may be able to show the likelihood of certain events described in the Bible happening in such a way as to make the claim possible. But acceptance of the claim itself is a matter of faith, since it cannot be proved – nor for that matter disproved – by archaeology.

There seems to be no shortage of works which attempt to satisfy the fascination of the public with biblical archaeology. There are authoritative handbooks like Prof. Wright's *Biblical Archaeology*. The *National Geographic* and other journals have run excellent series on discoveries in Bible Lands. Some popular novels, like James Michener's *The Source*, have even become bestsellers.

What justifies yet another book on the subject? In the first place, archaeology, while dealing with antiquities, is one of the fastest-moving fields of contemporary research. New discoveries are made literally every day, not only fascinating in themselves but often upsetting old theories. It is the very unpredictableness of archaeology that makes it continuously fascinating – and requires the story of man's past to be constantly rewritten. The present volume is welcome precisely because it incorporates the latest findings and interpretations. Furthermore, the new discoveries reported here have been made mostly in Israel, where so much of the significant archaeological activity going on currently in the Middle East is concentrated. The research is not only competent but is also partially based on unpublished material or on original works in Hebrew, which are inaccessible to most Western readers.

A further feature of this book is its broad, humanistic approach to the Bible, remarkably free of the sectarian bias or tendentious argument which has marred so many treatments of biblical archaeology. The work is based on the research of secular historians and biblical scholars, both in Israel and elsewhere. It is thus a unique venture and one which should commend itself to enlightened readers of whatever background or religious persuasion.

Still another interesting feature of this volume is its topical approach. Instead of presenting the material by a listing of sites excavated or by following chronological criteria, it diachronically examines the plethora of finds by subject matter so that a total picture evolves for each topic under study.

The resources of the recently published *Encyclopaedia Judaica* have been at the disposal of the editors and writers. Acknowledgements are due particularly to Naftali Winter (especially for his research for the first two parts) and to Yuval Kamrat, Yaara Eisenberg, and Priscilla Fishman, for their help in assembling the material.

As this volume shows, the result of archaeological activity has produced a revolutionized attitude toward the traditions, memories, stories and facts recounted within the Bible. For the archaeological finds, being contemporary to the events recorded, recover the setting and background of the times, places, and even occasionally, though rarely, of the personalities, mentioned in the Bible. The history of Israel comes to light as part of one grand mosaic whose pieces are properly adjusted and set in place by extensive research. Israel is seen as being in a symbiotic relationship with its neighbors — borrowing, adapting, transforming, and influencing. Thereby the substantial historicity and reliability of the biblical records have been for a greater part corroborated by archaeological finds. Nevertheless, as stated above, archaeology's purpose is not "to prove" the Bible, but to discover, illustrate, explain, inform, supplement, illuminate, and, at times, even to correct. By affording the ability to study the Bible against its contemporary background, it becomes an indispensable tool to the understanding of the life of our ancestors and to the broadening of the knowledge of our past.

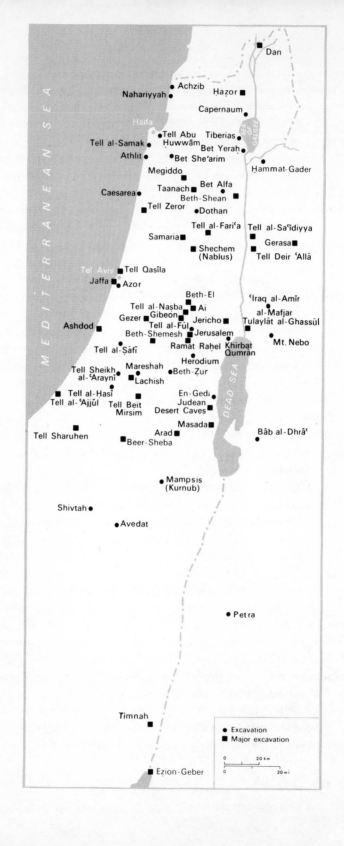

MEDITERRANEAN SEA

DEAD SEA

SEA OF GALILEE

Dan

Achzib
Nahariyyah   Hazor
                    Capernaum
Haifa
        Tell Abu   Tiberias
Tell al-Samak Huwwām
               Bet Yerah
Athlit   Bet She'arim
        Megiddo   Hammat-Gader
                    Bet Alfa
            Taanach Beth-Shean
Caesarea Tell Zeror
                    Dothan
                Tell al-Fari'a Tell al-Sa'idiyya
        Samaria   Gerasa
                Shechem   Tell Deir 'Allā
                (Nablus)

Tel Aviv Tell Qasīla
Jaffa   Azor

            Beth-El   'Iraq al-Amīr
        Tell al-Nasba Ai   al-Mafjar
        Gibeon   Tulaylāt al-Ghassūl
    Gezer Tell al-Fūl Jericho
Ashdod   Jerusalem
    Beth-Shemesh   Mt. Nebo
                Ramat Rahel Khirbat
Tell al-Safi   Qumrān
                Herodium
Tell Sheikh Mareshah Beth-Zur
al-'Arayni Lachish
                    En-Gedi
Tell al-Hasi   Judean
Tell al-'Ajjūl Tell Beit Desert Caves
            Mirsim   Masada
                            Bāb al-Dhrā'
Tell Sharuhen   Arad
            Beer-Sheba

                Mampsis
                (Kurnub)

Shivtah
    Avedat

                Petra

Timnah

● Excavation
■ Major excavation

0   20 km
0   20 mi

Ezion-Geber

CHRONOLOGICAL TABLE

DATE	ARCHAEOLOGICAL PERIOD	HISTORICAL PERIOD	
12,000–7500 B.C.E.	Mesolithic	Pre-History	Natufian Culture
7500–4000 B.C.E.	Neolithic	Pre-History	Yarmukian Culture
4000–3150 B.C.E.	Chalcolithic	Pre-History	Ghassulian Culture
3150–2850 B.C.E.	Early Bronze I		Bet Yerah Culture
2850–2650 B.C.E.	Early Bronze II		
2650–2350 B.C.E.	Early Bronze III	Early Canaanite	
2350–2200 B.C.E.	Early Bronze IV (III A)		
2200–2000 B.C.E.	Middle Bronze I		
2000–1750 B.C.E.	Middle Bronze II A	Middle Canaanite	
1750–1550 B.C.E.	Middle Bronze II B		Hyksos Period
1550–1400 B.C.E.	Late Bronze I		Egyptian Rule
1400–1300 B.C.E.	Late Bronze II A	Late Canaanite	El Amarna Period
1300–1200 B.C.E.	Late Bronze II B		
1200–1150 B.C.E.	Iron Age I A		Israelite Invasion
1150–1000 B.C.E.	Iron Age I B	Israelite I	Philistine Invasion
1000– 900 B.C.E.	Iron Age II A	Israelite II	
900– 800 B.C.E.	Iron Age II B		
800– 586 B.C.E.	Iron Age II C	Israelite III	
586– 332 B.C.E.	Persian		
332– 152 B.C.E.	Hellenistic I		
152– 37 B.C.E.	Hellenistic (Hasmonean) II		
37 B.C.E.–70 C.E.	Roman (Herodian) I		
70– 324 C.E.	Roman II, III		
324– 640 C.E.	Byzantine		
640–1099 C.E.	Early Arab		
1099–1291 C.E.	Crusader		
1291–1516 C.E.	Mamluk		

Note: B.C.E. (Before the Common Era) is the equivalent of B.C.
 C.E. (Common Era) is the equivalent of A.D.

Map: Archaeological sites in Erez Israel

Part One
ARCHITECTURE

1
CITIES

Knowledge of architecture in the biblical period has been limited both by the lack of information on architectural details in the ancient records and by the infrequent survival of the buildings themselves as the passage of the centuries and the activities of succeeding generations of builders contributed to their eventual destruction. Of those buildings which have been found among the ruined cities of Canaan and early Israel, we are fortunate if one or two layers of masonry remain above the foundation level.

Throughout most of the biblical period, men built their own homes, and their towns, too, were the creation of their own unskilled, communal efforts. Thus, the vast majority of structures that have survived, including town walls, gates, and temples, are "homemade" in character. Only in periods of exceptional prosperity or political expansion do we find, both in the northern kingdom and in Judah, traces of ambitious architectural projects. These were official or religious in nature, and display the handiwork of professional craftsmen and the sophisticated use of foreign styles or materials.

URBANIZATION

The first mention of a city in the Bible appears not long after the Creation narrative. The Bible relates that Cain, the firstborn son of Adam, built a city for his son Enoch (Gen. 4:17). It is interesting to note that later accounts of the Sumerians, whose culture is the most ancient in Mesopotamia, relate that the first city to be divinely created was called Eridu. This name bears a striking resemblance to that of Enoch's son, Irad. The antiquity of Eridu, located some 12 miles south-southwest of ancient Ur, is well documented; it is the oldest site excavated in southern Mesopotamia, its pre-urban levels reaching back to the 6th millennium B.C.E.

The point at which a settlement becomes a "city" is a subject of discussion by students of urban culture. There is, however, a large measure of general agreement that in antiquity a "city" was a settled community having a socially stratified population that practiced a variety of trades and professions and was capable of producing surpluses of food for those of its members who were not engaged in agriculture. The development of a pre-urban settlement into a city is the result of an extremely complex interrelationship of economic, social, and technical factors. However, it is generally assumed that the first criterion of an urban settlement is the appearance of communal building projects, first a temple, then a palace, followed by city fortifications, etc. Such undertakings require an organized labor force for their execution, as well as direction and control, generally exercised by a ruling class which interprets its own needs and those of the entire community. Another distinguishing feature of the ancient city would be the marketplace, the hub of commercial activity.

Figure 1a: Town-planning in the city-state Arad in the Early Bronze II period (c. 2850–2650 B.C.E.). The model, prepared by the Israel Museum, shows one of the living quarters with blocks of houses divided by streets and squares, enclosed with a thick wall

Figure 1b: Clay model in the shape of a house found at Arad

Figure 2: Religious
structure in the Early
Bronze site of Ai

Technical limitations have precluded the archaeological excavation in the
Fertile Crescent of a complete city with all its historical levels retained
intact. Thus we are not in possession of all the data concerning ancient
urban development. It is certain, however, that the process of urbanization
began in Mesopotamia at about the end of the 5th or the beginning of the
4th millennium B.C.E. The first settlement that displayed distinctive urban
features (the existence of a temple) was the city of Uruk, which had been
established on the ancient banks of the Euphrates River. The creators of this
urban culture were most probably the Sumerians.

In Syria and Erez Israel, cities probably began to develop under Mesopotamian influence in the 3rd millennium B.C.E. They were generally established at the junctions of highways and on the plains, in places close to
natural water supplies and easy to defend. Excavations on various sites have
laid bare city walls (Arad (fig. 1a-b), Ai, Megiddo), houses, and religious
structures (Jericho, Megiddo, Arad, Ai (fig. 2)). Jericho is exceptional
among the cities of the Near East in having a thick wall and a tower dating
back to a period which is ancient even by comparison with Mesopotamia.
These structures have been variously identified by scholars as dating to the
7th, 6th, or 5th millennium, i.e., to a period which was pre-agricultural,
pre-pottery, and pre-literary. In this sense, the origin of ancient Jericho
remains an archaeological enigma.

The upheavals in the Near East during the first half of the 2nd millennium B.C.E. accelerated the process of urbanization both politically and

Figure 3:   Tell Megiddo from the north. The major visible structures are:
(1) gate area; (2) water installation pit; (3) south stable complex (Ahab) and
palace (Solomon); (4) silo; (5) Shumacher's shaft; (6) high place; (7) three
temples (Early Bronze); (8) north stable complex; (9) fortifications

Figure 4:   Model of Tell Megiddo from the north. The straight angle gate
and the reconstructed wall are of the Middle Bronze period

materially. This is reflected both in the finds of the main archaeological sites in Erez Israel (Shechem, Megiddo (figs. 3,4), Gezer, Lachish, etc.) and in Egyptian epigraphic sources which list dozens of important cities in the region (Jerusalem, Acre, etc.). All these were large urban settlements protected by fortifications of a type which had been previously unknown. It seems likely that the development and fortification of these cities was the work of both Semitic and non-Semitic ethnic groups.

In the course of the 2nd millennium B.C.E. a type of city known to scholars as the "city-state," or "city-kingdom," gradually emerged throughout Syria and Erez Israel, and remained in existence, though with certain modifications and on a reduced scale, into the 1st millennium B.C.E. (They are not to be confused with the classical city-state, the Greek *polis*, which was quite different in origin, development, and character.) The written records discovered at Alalakh, Ugarit, and Tell el-Amarna, which reflect conditions during most of the second half of the 2nd millennium B.C.E., reveal several typical features which characterized the city-kingdoms throughout that period: the territorial, political, and organizational dependence of the outlying settlements on the mother city; the relatively restricted territory of the city-state; its monarchic-dynastic or oligarchic rule; the existence of a privileged and economically powerful social elite which first emerged as a result of military considerations, but which later assumed a mercantile character; a rigid social and professional hierarchy; and the delineation of specific rights and obligations for the various social classes.

It was "cities" of this type that the semi-nomadic Patriarchs encountered in their wanderings in Canaan. Later, it was these same cities that were attacked by the Israelite tribes struggling to occupy Canaan.

THE PATRIARCHAL PERIOD

It is generally agreed that the Patriarchal period dates to the 18th—16th centuries B.C.E. Thus it coincides for much of its duration with the period of Hyksos invasion and domination of Egypt. In modern scholarly usage, the term "Hyksos" (used first by Manetho in his 3rd century B.C.E. Egyptian history) refers to a people or group of peoples who were actively involved in a complex series of migrations and conquests, and contributed to extensive processes of acculturation throughout the region encompassing Egypt, Canaan, and Syria.

The arrival of Abraham and his family in the vicinity of Shechem marks the end of their wandering from Ur of the Chaldees, by way of Haran, to

Erez Israel (Gen. 11:31–12:6). There they found several rather limited areas suitable for their semi-nomadic, pastoral economy. These were the Jordan rift valley and the Arabah, the hilly region of western Canaan and the northwestern Negev area around Gerar. Here they could pasture their flocks without encroaching on anyone's rights and yet remain within easy access of permanently settled urban centers where they could barter for the domestic necessities that they required.

That the Patriarchs always chose to camp in the neighborhood of a town is known from the biblical account. Thus, Abraham's first encampment in Canaan was "the place of Shechem . . . the terebinth of Moreh" (Gen. 12:6). Then he traveled south "unto the place where his tent had been at the beginning, between Beth-El and Ai" (Gen. 13:3), and later went to Hebron (Gen. 13:18). Other biblical passages mention Gerar (Gen. 20:1) and Beer-Sheba (Gen. 22:19). Isaac lived mainly in the Negev (Gen. 24:62); the Bible relates that during a drought he went to Gerar, and from there to Beer-Sheba; he died in Hebron. It was from Beer-Sheba that Jacob set forth to northern Mesopotamia, in flight from his brother Esau. In the Jacob narrative, the Bible again mentions all the places where his grandfather Abraham had camped: Shechem, Beth-El, Hebron, and Beer-Sheba.

The Bible does not describe these cities at any length; the references to them are for the most part incidental and fragmentary. Embedded here and there in the biblical narrative, however, is a more detailed description of one or another city. For example, the account of the purchase of the Cave of Machpelah (Gen. ch. 23) contains details about the ethnic composition of the Hebronites and about their political organization. Similar details about Shechem are found in the story of Dinah, daughter of Jacob (Gen. ch. 34).

Archaeological excavations in Erez Israel have yielded a wealth of evidence dealing with many aspects of life during this period. From the first half of the 18th century onward there was extensive development in the construction of towns and fortresses. Settlements have been discovered all over the country, with the greatest concentration found along the coast and coastal plain. They were fortified with massive defense walls and ramparts (see Fortifications and fig. 4).

The progress made in the construction techniques of the defensive wall was matched in other architectural elements, such as the development of the city-gate and the increasing sophistication in the building of houses for rulers and nobles. Corollary developments appeared in the preparation and equipment of tombs, in the manufacture of pottery, and in the artistic level of workmanship.

ISRAELITE SETTLEMENT OF CANAAN

The conquest of Canaan is presented by the author of the Book of Joshua as a unified, continuous, complete action carried out under the leadership of Joshua within a rather delimited time. The success of Joshua's campaign determined the fate of the Israelites and their land. After the death of Moses, Joshua led the tribes of Israel across the Jordan, conquered Jericho and Ai, and, after defeating the alliance of the kings of the south, headed by the king of Jerusalem, took the royal cities in the mountains and lowlands of Judah (Josh. 10:31). Finally, he also defeated the alliance of the kings of the north, headed by the king of Hazor, in the battle at the waters of Merom (Josh. ch. 11). The list of the kings of Canaan whom Joshua defeated (ch. 12) includes the names of 31 cities and territories (according to the Greek translation, the Septuagint, only 29), including some which are not mentioned in the descriptions of Joshua's battles.

According to the narrative in the Book of Joshua, "there remains yet very much land to be possessed." The account even includes a list of the districts which had yet to be conquered (Josh. 13:1ff.). Nonetheless, the Bible also holds that most of the Land of Canaan came under Israelite control in the time of Joshua, and that it was he who divided the country among the tribes and delineated the boundaries of their respective territories.

The Book of Judges continues the biblical narrative, relating the deeds of the Israelites after Joshua's death: their struggle with the Canaanites, with the neighboring lands, and with invaders; the wanderings of the tribes in the land; and their tribal quarrels before the kings succeeded in imposing a form of unity upon them. In contrast to the Book of Joshua, the Book of Judges, particularly chapters 1, 4, and 5, implies that the conquest of Canaan was not a unified national action but a composite process of small wars carried on over a long period of time by individual tribes or by unions of tribes.

Thus, modern scholars tend to regard the Book of Joshua as the end result of a long, complicated process of literary creativity, and the expression of the final crystallization of a uniform, national-religious conception of the historiography of the Israelites. Embedded in the book is a wealth of details regarding significant events that occurred during the lengthy period of conquest and settlement, and that left a deep imprint in the collective memory of the people. These incidents had been preserved in various traditions, in fragments of ancient chronicles, epic poems, folk tales, and legends. One comes to the conclusion that many sources, Israelite, tribal, and even

local, were combined and blended into a continuous narrative and attributed to the period of Joshua's leadership.

In an attempt to throw more light on the process of the Israelite conquest of Canaan and the beginnings of their settlement in the land, scholars
have sought corroborative information from directly or indirectly relevant
archaeological discoveries. Archaeological evidence indicates that in the
second half of the 13th century B.C.E. many Canaanite settlements were
destroyed. These would include the royal cities familiar to us from the Tell
el-Amarna and biblical sources. On the ruins of those relatively great cities,
later levels point to the presence of sparsely populated settlements or even
temporary settlements of semi-nomads (see below).

This was the fate of the important urban center of Hazor, which was
destroyed by the Israelites and razed by fire (Josh. ch. 11). Excavations
have revealed that both the king's fortress and the large lower city adjoining
it were destroyed at the close of the Late Bronze Period (end of the 13th
century B.C.E.), and that a settlement of semi-nomads arose on its ruins in
the 12th century.

An archaeological survey in the hills of central Galilee (fig. 5) has dis-
closed many traces of small new settlements similar to the semi-nomad
settlement at Hazor and dating to the 13th—12th century. The new settlers,
distinguished by specific pottery of a different type (fig. 6), cultivated
virgin land in this area of rocky hills and forests. One may conclude that this
was the hub of the early settlement of the tribes assigned to the uninhabited
portion of Canaan. It is either from there that they spread to Canaanite
cities in the north of Galilee, or the cities were first destroyed by them and
then the whole Galilee was settled.

Excavations in other parts of the country, such as the southern part of
the hills of Ephraim, the land of Benjamin, and the Shefelah, have similarly
revealed the establishment of many settlements at this time. Some of these
arose on the ruins of older Canaanite cities after a shorter (e.g. Beth-El) or
longer (e.g. Mizpeh, Ai, Shiloh) period of time. But most of them were
founded at new sites which had not been settled previously (e.g. Gibeath-
Benjamin, Ramah, Bethlehem). These would point to the beginnings of
Israelite colonization of Canaan.

Excavations at al-Jīb (6 miles northwest of Jerusalem) indicate that a
settlement existed there from the Middle and Late Bronze periods, and
reached a peak in the Iron Age (12th century B.C.E.). Scholars tend to
identify the site with Gibeon which, according to the Book of Joshua, was
"a great city, as one of the royal cities" (10:2), and the center of the Hivite

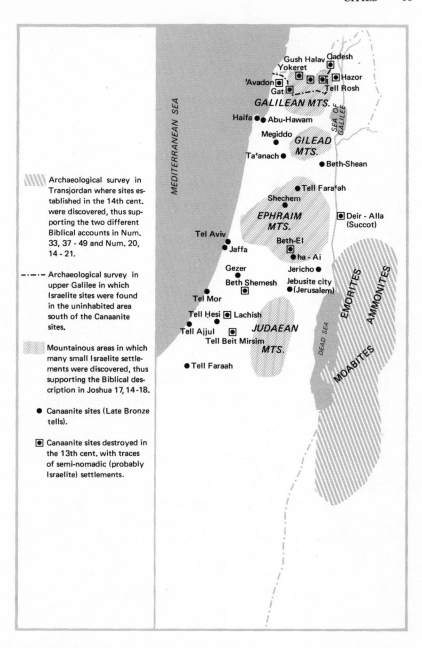

Archaeological survey in Transjordan where sites established in the 14th cent. were discovered, thus supporting the two different Biblical accounts in Num. 33, 37 - 49 and Num. 20, 14 - 21.

Archaeological survey in upper Galilee in which Israelite sites were found in the uninhabited area south of the Canaanite sites.

Mountainous areas in which many small Israelite settlements were discovered, thus supporting the Biblical description in Joshua 17, 14-18.

● Canaanite sites (Late Bronze tells).

◉ Canaanite sites destroyed in the 13th cent. with traces of semi-nomadic (probably Israelite) settlements.

Figure 5: The Israelite settlement of Canaan in the beginning of the 12th cent. B.C.E.

Figure 6:   Typical jars ("collared-rim" jars) of the first Israelite settlement in Canaan

cities which made peace with Joshua and accepted his authority.

A number of tells in the Lowland — particularly Tell Beit Mirsim, and Beth-Shemesh — have also yielded evidence of the destruction of Canaanite cities at the end of the Late Bronze period. Lachish, however, presents difficulties in this respect. On the one hand, it would appear that the Canaanite city was destroyed at the end of the 13th century B.C.E., most probably by the Israelites. On the other hand, a number of finds uncovered at the summit of the mound, and in the cemetery, would indicate that in the days of Pharaoh Ramses III (c. 1195–1164 B.C.E.) Lachish was a fortress manned by a garrison of Sea Peoples. According to archaeological evidence, a possible solution to this seeming contradiction is the positing of a small semi-nomad settlement, probably Israelite, in the brief interval between the reigns of Merneptah (c. 1124–1214 B.C.E.) and Ramses III.

Undoubtedly, archaeological research sometimes raises very complicated questions at the same time that it solves other problems. The excavations at the village of Beitin have revealed that the Canaanite Beth-El which, according to the Book of Judges, was conquered by the Israelites (1:22–26), was indeed destroyed toward the end of the Late Bronze period, most likely in the third quarter of the 13th century B.C.E. However, archaeological finds at Ai and Jericho have not corroborated biblical tradition. On the contrary, excavations at et-Tell, east of Beth-El, which is identified with Ai, indicate that the ancient city was destroyed in approximately the 23rd century B.C.E., and that it remained uninhabited until about 1200 B.C.E., when a small Israelite settlement arose on the site. Similarly, the excavations at Tell al-Sultān, the site of the biblical Jericho (see below, Fortifications), have yielded but few buildings, graves, and implements from the last stage of the Late Bronze period (the period of the Conquest of Canaan), and are completely lacking in any walls from this period.

Various attempts have been made to interpret the archaeological evidence found at Ai and Jericho in the light of the biblical account of the Israelite conquest of these two royal cities. According to one hypothesis, the stories of the conquest of Jericho and Ai belong to the category of etiological legend, which is prevalent in Joshua (ch. 2–10). These were stories which sought to explain unusual local phenomena, such as the crumbling walls of ruined Jericho, the heap of stones in the valley of Achor (Josh. 7:24–26; "a heap for ever" named Ai, which means "the ruin"), the gate of the destroyed city of Ai where a great heap of stones stood "to this day," etc. Other hypotheses explain the absence of a Late Bronze wall at Jericho in terms of its having been exposed to the elements and consequently eroded away over the course of many centuries, or of its not ever having existed, since the Middle Bronze period glacis proved adequate for the defense of the town.

The discrepancy between the finds at Ai and the biblical account of its conquest has been explained in terms of the mound having served as a temporary military outpost for the inhabitants of Beth-El, leading to a confusion between the conquest of the latter and the conquest of Ai. Another possibility is that et-Tell may not be the biblical site of Ai.

THE MONARCHY

Various types of urban settlement appear in the Bible in contexts relating to the period of the monarchy. These clearly reflect the manifold economic, administrative, and military activities of the Israelite kings.

The most obvious way to differentiate between the types of cities is the external distinction between a walled and an unwalled settlement. In the Bible, "camps" are contrasted with "strongholds" (Num. 13:19), and "fortified cities" with "unwalled villages" (I Sam. 6:18). Other biblical expressions include "a town that has gates and bars" (I Sam. 23:7) and "open towns" (Esth. 9:18). However, the presence or absence of a wall is only of

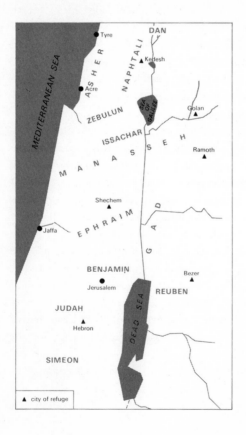

Figure 7:   Cities of Refuge

Figure 8:   A stone horned altar of the late Israelite period from Megiddo. It reminds us of several instances of manslayers seeking refuge by holding "the horns of the altar" reported in the Bible

secondary importance to a city. There are more functional ways in which to differentiate between types of urban settlement.

In its origin, the city was both a military stronghold and an administrative center serving many functions, and the Bible uses functional terminology to describe various cities. The "store city" was the center in which royal supplies and equipment were kept (I Kings 9:19; II Chron. 8:6; 11:11–12; 17:12). Excavations in Ereẓ Israel have not yielded any identifiable storage cities, although many small storage pits for grain have been found.

Still other cities which had specific functions were the 48 levitical cities (Num. 35:1–8; Josh. ch. 21; I Chron. 6:36 ff.), which were set apart for the exclusive residence of the Levites. Some scholars regard the lists of Levite cities as a utopian ideal rather than a reality, but a more likely explanation is that they were ritual and administrative centers in which the Levites were settled during their integration into the national governmental apparatus during the reign of David. In some passages, six "cities of refuge" (fig. 7) are included among the levitical cities (Num. 35:6ff.; Deut. 4:41–43; 19:1–13; Josh. ch. 20; 21:13ff.). The exact nature of these cities of asylum is not clear.

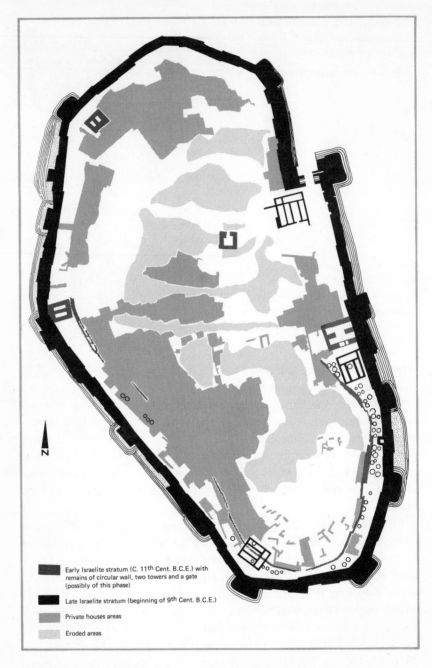

Figure 9: Plan of the Israelite city Mizpeh (Tell al-Naṣba)

Other "cities" mentioned in the Bible include the "city of merchants," a description of Canaan whose inhabitants engaged in mercantile relations (Ezek. 17:4), the "city of priests" (I Sam. 22:19), and a "royal city" (II Sam. 12:26). Expressions such as "city for chariots" and "city for horses" (I Kings 9:19; 10:26; II Chron. 8:6) refer to specific quarters within a city, as has been demonstrated by the excavations of Megiddo (see p.52).

Neither written sources nor archaeological excavations provide a complete understanding of the structure, extent, population, and layout of the ancient city. One can only assume that cities varied considerably, depending on the topographical nature of the site, the city's function, and whether it grew organically in a gradual process or was built at the command of a ruler.

Most probably, cities in Erez Israel were usually planned, and their development was controlled or modified by the nature of the terrain. At Tell al-Nasba (fig. 9) and Tell Beit Mirsim for example, the walls enclosed a city built on a hill, and the houses followed the curve of the walls.

Few cities of the period of the Israelite monarchy have been sufficiently excavated to provide detailed data concerning their domestic and communal

Figure 10:   Rectangular planning in the Israelite citadel at Arad. The model, prepared by the Israel Museum, shows: (1) main gate; (2) central courtyard; (3) waterworks and cistern; (4) temple complex

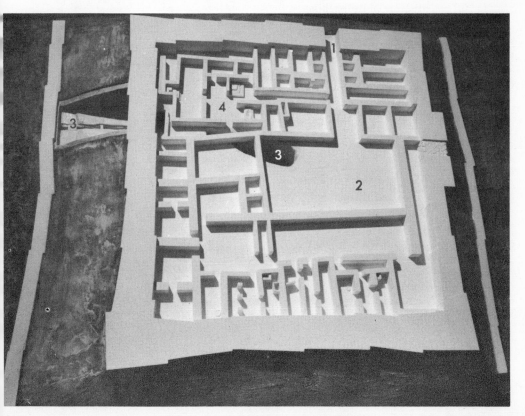

life. It is apparent, however, that cities built on hills were usually crowded, in order to accommodate as many families as possible within their walls. Even today, in villages of the Near East, entrance to one house may be from the roof of that built below it on the hillside. Doubtless, such architectural methods were practical in preceding periods.

In general, the Israelite town was planned as a circle, with a central complex of houses encircled by a street and a wall with attached houses (like Tell Beit Mirsim and Tell al-Naṣba). Other cities, (like Arad – fig. 10; Samaria – fig. 13; Megiddo – fig. 53) were planned carefully according to their functions.

On the basis of measurements of partial excavations and extended calculations, it may be asserted that, in general, the ancient cities occupied a restricted area. A large city might cover an area of about 20 acres and accommodate more than 3,000 inhabitants. Cities of medium size had from several hundred to a thousand inhabitants. A few cities, mainly capitals like Jerusalem and Samaria, has populations of as many as 10,000 or 20,000.

Many cities in Mesopotamia, Syria, and, apparently, Erez Israel were divided into sectors. Sometimes the inhabitants of the various quarters achieved a certain degree of administrative independence within their common urban structure. In most instances, probably, the character of a particular quarter was determined by the professional composition and class structure of its inhabitants.

Towering above the city, at its most easily defensible point, rose the inner fortified area, the acropolis or citadel, which was the center of government and the main military stronghold. The acropolis was a complex of government buildings, and included the palace of the ruler, the temple, the offices of the senior government officials, storehouses, etc. It is uncertain whether a small fortress city such as Tell al-Naṣba had a citadel; excavations have revealed no evidence either for or against any conclusion. Larger cities, however, almost invariably had a citadel. Hazor (fig. 49) is an excellent example, with the great expanse (600 by 1,200 yards) of its city (Khirbet Waqqas) topped by the much higher Tell el-Qedah at its southwest corner.

Around the acropolis were houses, crowded together with narrow streets winding between them. A few open spaces were generally situated near the inner side of the city gates. Known as "the square at the city gate." this open area served as a gathering place for the city dwellers, and for public assemblies (Neh. 8:1; II Chron. 32:6). The city gate itself was a meeting place for the elders and ministers of the city (fig. 11a-b). Here lawsuits were heard and legal sentences were executed (Deut. 21:19; 22:24; Ruth 4:4ff.).

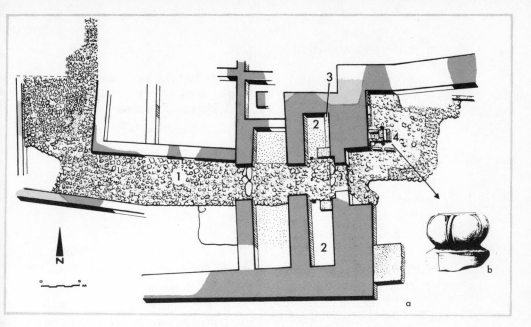

Figure 11a: Plan of the Israelite gate at Dan, showing: (1) paved path leading into the town; (2) guardroom; (3) a bench; (4) four-columned structure, probably a canopy for a statue or for the king, as recorded in II Samuel 19:9: "Then the king arose and sat in the gate"

Figure 11b: Drawing of one of the column bases which probably supported the canopy near the gate

Apparently the city gate was also a center for commercial transactions (Neh. 3:1, 18; 17:39), but the main business of the city seems to have been conducted in markets. These were probably squares that were open during the day and could be locked at night (Eccles. 12:4). A parallel term to "market" is *ḥuẓ* ("outside" or "street"), which was used specifically for international commercial transactions (I Kings 20:34), but was also found in connection with local trade (cf. "the bakers' street *ḥuẓ*," Jer. 37:21).

SOLOMON'S ARCHITECTURAL ACHIEVEMENTS

The construction of the Temple was the most important event in the reign of Solomon, and his most magnificent achievement. But his building activities were not confined to this alone. Both the Bible and archaeological evidence point to the fact that this period must have been the golden age of Israelite architecture. The Book of Kings informs us that Solomon built many cities, some of which were set aside as garrison towns for cavalry and chariots, while others were used for storage. In Jerusalem, Solomon built a great palace for himself which is described at length (I Kings 7:1–13), and also a special palace for one of his most important political assets, the daughter of Pharaoh. It is also stated that he built the walls of Jerusalem and the "Millo."

The nature of this last work is unclear, but it must have been of importance, for it is mentioned in connection with the revolt of Jeroboam against Solomon. Jeroboam had been put in charge of all the labor force of the House of Joseph. "And this was the reason why he lifted up his hand against the king. Solomon built the Millo, and closed up the breach of the city of David his father" (I Kings 11:27). The word "Millo" means "fill' and it is taken to represent the filling in of the depression which separated the City of David to the south from the northern plateau on which the Temple stood. By this means, the city was extended northward. Since the Temple must have been surrounded by a strong defensive wall, by connecting the city to the Temple, Solomon in fact strengthened the one vulnerable approach to the city – its northern side. (For a different explanation of the term "Millo," see Fortifications; fig. 12.)

From the relatively sparse remains of Solomon's great building operations throughout the country, we are made aware of his distinctive use of masonry. Large blocks of hewn stone were fitted exactly one on top of the other. The stones are often dressed, with a border along three sides of the stone facing and a rough boss left in the center. This type of stone dressing was common in other eras as well, but with slight differences (see below, p.33). The famous Herodian masonry also has borders, but the stones are larger and the central boss is flattened and smoothed. Hellenistic masonry, on the other hand, is smaller than the Solomonic stonework and all four corners are dressed, although this feature is also occasionally found among stones of Solomon's time.

One of the cities specifically mentioned as having been built by Solomon is Megiddo. This is one of archaeology's most important sites in Israel and it has been extensively excavated. Apart from the fortifications and the monumental gate found here and attributed to Solomon (which will be dealt with later), several large buildings have been unearthed which undoubtedly belong to the same period. Two of these buildings are so large (650 and 590 sq. yards respectively) that they are both termed palaces. Yigael Yadin has suggested that the smaller ("the Northern Palace," fig. 52) was built for the commander of the district, Baana ben Ahilud. Baana was one of the 12 district governors appointed by Solomon, whose duty it was to provide food

Figure 12: Eastern slope of the Ophel hill (City of David), showing the site of the Jebusite city and the terracing — an example of what could be the "millo" (= filling) referred to in I Kings 9:15 and 24.

for the royal household one month of the year. His was one of the most important districts, stretching from Beth-Shean to Megiddo and including the Valley of Jezreel. A person of such rank would require a palace. The larger palace in Megiddo ("the Southern Palace," fig. 53), according to Yadin, was reserved for special ceremonies and for the king himself when he came to visit the northern town.

OMRI AND AHAB: SAMARIA

A second great period of building activity took place in the northern kingdom of Israel during the reigns of Omri and Ahab. The Bible, though, makes only brief mention of their building achievements.

Omri was the founder of the dynasty of the House of Omri and chose a new capital city. "He bought the hill of Samaria from Shemer for two talents of silver; and he fortified the hill, and called the name of the city which he built, Samaria, after the name of Shemer, the owner of the hill" (I Kings 16:24).

Archaeological excavations at Samaria revealed (fig. 13) an upper city (acropolis) on the summit of the hill, and a lower city on the slope of the hill. The lower city was scarcely excavated, though some architectural remnants show that the city was extended about 800 m.

Figure 13: Plan of the enclosure at Samaria: (1) wall enclosure; (2) palace; (3) tower; (4) storage house ("ostraca house"); (5) palace (the "ivory house"); (6) pool

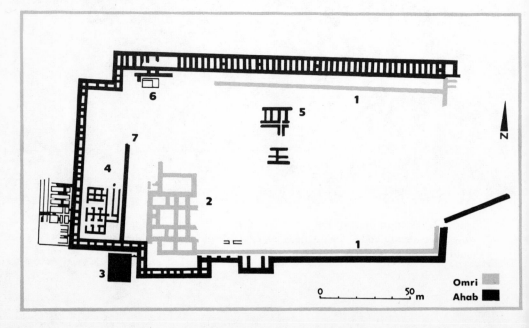

The upper city served as the king's citadel. Excavations distinguished here six strata of the Israelite town, which were preceded by a small Iron Age village. The Israelite town was established by Omri (first period of building) extended by Ahab (second period), and then occupied by Jehu and others (third period) and Jeroboam II (fourth period) until it was destroyed by Sargon II in 722/1 B.C.E.

The first city was established on artificial filling which leveled the mound by forming a podium. It is most likely that Omri (882—871) started to build his palace when he was still in his first capital at Tirza, and then, six years before his death, moved to Samaria. The capital in Samaria was a well-planned town with a royal enclosure, rectangular in shape, which was surrounded by a wall. Inside the wall part of the palace of Omri was uncovered. It was a central courtyard surrounded by rooms, built of nicely dressed stones.

In the second period of building — Ahab's period (871—852 B.C.E.) — the royal enclosure was extended and surrounded by a casemate wall which was strengthened with towers. In the south the enclosure was not extended but only the wall was doubled and thickened. On the eastern side three proto-Aeolian capitals, which probably decorated the approach to the enclosure, were found. In the enclosure the following remains were un-covered: a tower; a storage house with 63 Hebrew ostraca (inscribed potsherds), most of them receipts for tax wine and oil deliveries brought to the king's house; a pool which is believed to be the pool where Ahab's chariot was washed after his body was brought from the hills of Gilead; the palace of Ahab in which a large amount of small ivories, probably inlayed in furniture, was found. This fits the biblical account of "the acts of Ahab . . . and the ivory house which he made" (I Kings 22:39) and the exhortation of Amos: "Woe to them that are at ease in Zion and trust in the mountain of

Figure 14:   One of the small ivory panels found in the "ivory house" of King Ahab at Samaria, depicting the Egyptian god Hah

Figure 15:   Inscribed fragment of an ostracon with Hebrew letters LRMLA (to Rmla?). It was found with more fragments in the so-called "Ostraca House" at Samaria

Samaria, which are named chief of the nations . . . that lie upon beds of ivory, and stretch themselves upon their couches, and eat the lambs out of the flock . . ." (Amos 6:1—4). The discovery of the ivories, together with the biblical sources, indicates the expansion of wealth in the upper classes in the time of Ahab.

Another key strategic town which seems to have been completely reorganized by Omri and Ahab was Hazor (fig. 48). In Solomon's time only the western part of the upper tell (i.e. the mound containing remains of the ancient city from various periods) had been fortified. Under Omri and Ahab the town was laid out anew and extended to the east, to cover the whole of the upper tell. In the center stood a large building with two rows of pillars running down the middle and dividing the space into aisles. These pillars stood some six and a half feet high. The building itself, which was surrounded by paved courts, is thought by Yigael Yadin to have been a storehouse, perhaps accommodating the king's share of the local produce. Standing in the center of the city, it certainly must have been an imposing building.

At the western limit of the mound a great citadel was erected in the 9th century B.C.E. (fig. 30). Its walls were relatively thick, serving as part of the city wall. Toward the conquest of Tiglath-Pileser III in 732, changes were made: the citadel was surrounded with the city wall and a defensive tower was erected outside the wall (fig. 49). It must have been the last point of resistance against the enemy, for it was attacked from the eastern side which faces the town. This part of the fort was completely destroyed, down to the foundations, and the building was set afire. To the east of the citadel two proto-Aeolian capitals, resembling those at Samaria and Megiddo, were found. A lintel discovered nearby obviously fitted over the capitals, forming a decorated entrance to the citadel.

Archaeology not only fully bears out the biblical description of Omri and Ahab as city-founders and builders, but also adds fuller dimensions to the picture. The remains uncovered at the three major sites of Samaria, Megiddo, and Hazor are proof of the superb building ability of these rulers and of the power of the kingdom in their days. Despite the fact that, according to the biblical account, the Arameans under Ben-Hadad managed at one time to penetrate to Samaria itself and lay siege to the city, there can be no doubt as to the greatness of Israel during this period.

THE PERSIAN PERIOD

The period of Persian domination of Erez Israel (587–332 B.C.E.), including the first return to Zion, is as obscure in archaeological finds as it is in historical records. Yet the material culture of the Persian period has clearly distinguishable features and it might be expected that its remains would be identifiable. However, one must keep in mind the fact that Erez Israel was but a tiny part of a vast and complex empire which encompassed many nations and diverse governmental frameworks, and which maintained extensive commercial ties with foreign nations. The wide variety of governmental forms and the tolerance of the central authorities on the one hand, and the lengthy period of relative security and flourishing trade on the other, had two seemingly contradictory results. There was a renewal and burgeoning of local cultural forms in ancient centers that had existed before the empire came into being, particularly in the provinces which had a uniform ethnic population. Simultaneously, the free passage of merchandise from one region to another, particularly in the areas adjacent to the large mercantile centers, encouraged the assimilation of distinctive cultural forms into uniform, shared, cultural expressions. Thus the material remains of the period reflect both Persian and local influences.

Despite the large number of archaeological sites in Erez Israel that have yielded artifacts of the Persian period, there are relatively few architectural remains from that period. The meager number of such finds, compared to those of earlier periods, is surprising in view of the fact that building was highly developed at this time, as is evident from excavations in Iran and Greece. This period saw the application of the Hippodamian principles (named after a Greek architect from Miletus, 5th century B.C.E.), in which city streets were laid out in a grid pattern, meeting at right angles.

Scholars have sought to explain the paucity of archaeological finds from the Persian period as a result of the decline in the number of urban settlements in Ereẓ Israel after the destruction of the Temple. However, rather than reflecting historical reality, the fragmentary nature of the archaeological finds is more probably the result of various other factors, three of which are enumerated below.

1) During the Persian period, many tells were abandoned and were not resettled (Megiddo, Tell Jamma, Tell al-Ḥasī, Jericho, etc.). Thus, the uppermost layer of settlement was that of the Persian period, and this layer was particularly exposed to the ravages of erosion.

2) In those sites which continued to be settled (Samaria, Shechem, Ashdod, Ashkelon, Ramat Raḥel, etc.), the remains of the Persian period were destroyed by intensive Hellenistic-Roman construction above them.

3) In most of the large excavated sites of this period (Hazor, Megiddo, Tell al-Far'ah, Tell Jamma, Lachish, etc.), palace-fortresses or other large public buildings covered much of the ancient tell. It is probable that the dwelling area of the city was then moved to the lower slopes, or to the surrounding plain, and thus remains outside the area of the excavations.

A thorough investigation of the excavations of the Persian period in Ereẓ Israel yields a picture of a varied urban life that differed from region to region. While the destruction of the cities, followed by a gradual resettlement of the land, was true of most of Judah, in the northern part of that region and in Benjamin all the settlements (Tell al-Naṣba, Gibeon, Beth-El, Tell al-Fūl) continued to be populated even after the destruction of the Temple. The area along the coast (and perhaps even in Galilee) appears to have been heavily settled during this period, and a rich urban life undoubtedly existed there. One may recall Herodotus's description of Gaza: "A town, I should say, not much smaller than Sardis" (III, 5). Indeed, examination of building remains in the coastal region provides examples of well-planned settlements.

A certain level of city-planning is evident in the excavations of Tell Abu-Hawam (near Mount Carmel) which date from the Persian period. A building has been uncovered which faces on a main thoroughfare that more or less parallels the longitudinal axis of the city. In Shikmonah (south of Haifa), one section of a dwelling quarter has houses built with great symmetry along two intersecting streets. A similar picture emerges from the excavation at nearby Tell Megadim, which has revealed a built-up area bisected by a wide, straight central road. On either side of the road there are narrow lanes which intersect with it at right angles. The housing complexes between these lanes are further divided into sub-units uniform in their size and shape.

2

BUILDING MATERIALS
AND METHODS

Historically, building depends on the materials provided by nature. In Ereẓ Israel these included limestone of varying quality, a few other types of rock, wood, reeds, and mud. When, in rare cases, we can recognize the work of professionally skilled builders, it is in the fine shaping and carving of these materials, and in the use of exceptionally large structural units, such as large tree trunks which enabled the construction of wider roof spans, or, in later periods, the finely dressed masonry blocks, sometimes of huge size, chosen for esthetic effect or for special strength.

The most common building material was mud, which could be found everywhere, most particularly in the valleys and plains of Ereẓ Israel, and which was easily and quickly fashioned into building material. Mud was used either in its natural state, as mortar for filling in or smoothing out walls made of rubble, or was formed into sun-dried bricks.

The first bricks were molded singly by hand. They were oval or rounded in form and varied in size. Examples of these early bricks have been found in houses in Jericho, Beth-Shean, Gezer, and Teleilat Ghassul. The method of brickmaking was simple. A shallow pit would be dug and filled with water. When the earth and water formed mud, chopped straw would be mixed in and thoroughly kneaded, by trampling, into a thick mixture. It was the labor of having to fetch the straw, added to that of puddling the clay, which seemed so grievous to the Israelite laborers in Egypt (Ex. 5:7). The hand-formed bricks formed from the claylike substance would then be placed in the sun to dry. In the excavations of Tell al-Khalayfa (Ezion Geber?), a brickyard of this nature was found (c. 9th century B.C.E.) with a supply of bricks ready for use.

In the Early Bronze Age, the manufacture of bricks was speeded up by the use of molds of square or rectangular form, shapes that have remained standard ever since (fig. 16).

From the Bible we learn that two types of trees were used in construction — the inexpensive sycamore used for simple houses (Isa. 9:9; I Kings

Figure 16: Brickmaking in the 15th cent. B.C.E. depicted on a fresco in the tomb of Rekh-mi-Re (18th dynasty) at Thebes

10:27), and expensive lumber such as that from the cedar and cypress trees (I Kings 5:24) which were imported from Lebanon, the sandalwood tree (I Kings 10:11–12) brought from Ophir, or the local olive tree (I Kings 6:23, 31,33). These costly woods were used for the construction of public and governmental buildings and the homes of the wealthy (cf. Jer. 22:14–15). Egyptian construction methods point to the use of locally grown palm trunks sawn into planks which were used as rafters over very narrow spaces.

It is difficult to find evidence of the use of reeds in building, but we may assume that people living in the low-lying, marshy areas of the coastal plain, and around the upper reaches of the Jordan River, built their houses at least partly of this most accessible material. Indeed, in the earliest Neolithic strata at Jericho, there are traces of round or apsidal houses in which reeds were combined with hog-backed (plano-convex) bricks to produce a booth-like or possible beehive-shaped dwelling. Chalcolithic burial places on the Plain of Sharon have yielded clay ossuaries of rectangular shape, with ridged roofs. These are interpreted to be models of indigenous houses, in which the roof was formed by reeds drawn together at the top in a gable effect.

The most important building material of the pre-biblical and biblical period was stone. In the central region of Erez Israel limestone was used. This was the main rock formation of the hilly spine of the country. In eastern Galilee, basalt was commonly used, and along the coast the basic building stone was kurkar limestone.

It would appear that until metal tools came into use, stones could not be quarried and dressed, so that until the end of the Chalcolithic period buildings were constructed of piles of stone rubble, pebbles or small pieces of rock which had been broken off from large formations by natural causes.

Until the Late Bronze Age, when hewn stones were occasionally incorporated into late Canaanite buildings, the finest masonry structures lacked squared corners or true plane surfaces. Ashlar (hewn stone) masonry came into general use only in the period of Solomon, or perhaps during David's reign.

3

ARCHITECTURAL ELEMENTS

FOUNDATIONS

Laying the foundation of a city or a temple was an elaborate ceremony in the ancient Near East, and at times it was apparently accompanied by human sacrifice (Josh. 6:26; I Kings 16:34).

While the methods used to lay a foundation varied, in general it would seem that the first step was to dig trenches in the virgin soil or in the layers of rubble left from previous constructions. When the foundations of large buildings or fortifications were to be laid, the builders dug deep trenches and tried to reach bedrock. When buildings were erected on the rubble of previous constructions, an attempt was made to add strength to the building by erecting the walls at least partially on the remains of older walls exposed when the foundation trenches were dug.

Great care was taken to keep the foundations of the walls dry, so that the mud-bricks of which they were made would not crumble in the course of time. Even in the earliest periods of antiquity, when walls were built entirely of brick, they frequently rested on one or two courses of rough stones (as in the Late Chalcolithic strata in Beth-Shean and Megiddo). At a later period, before laying the foundation courses (if they were of brick), the ditches would be covered with a layer of sand, so that the water would penetrate that layer and run off, and not saturate the bricks. This method of construction has been found at Tell al-Ḥasī (14th century B.C.E.), where a 4½ inch layer of fine yellow sand covered the trenches under the foundations of the brick structures. A similar technique appears at Gerar, in strata dating from the period of the Israelite monarchy.

Stone foundation layers were not necessarily laid in a symmetrical fashion, and in some places the stones were set at different depths, according to their size, so that their upper surfaces would provide a more or less level area on which the brick walls could be erected. However, attempts were made to provide a ground plan on the foundation layer and to level

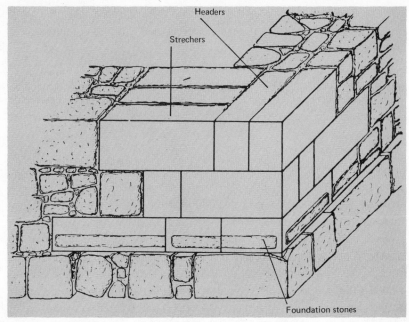

Figure 17: "Headers and stretchers" method. The stones of the low row
are dressed with borders along three sides, leaving a rough boss in the center

those sections where the walls would stand. For this purpose, two rows of
stones would be laid on either side of the outer edges of the foundations,
and the space between the rows would be filled with small stones. An
improved technique may be seen in the foundations of the first palace at
Tell al-'Ajjūl (3200–3000 B.C.E.), where the foundation layers were made
of carefully dressed stones. The lowest course was sunk to half its height in
a trench quarried out of bedrock, with the upper half protruding above the
level of the floor, so that it formed a kind of dado at the bottom of the
walls. The external rows of stone blocks laid along the edges of the foundation layer were set on their narrow side (they measured approximately
9×30×30") and the spaces between them were filled with smaller stones.

During the Israelite period in Samaria (fig. 17) foundation trenches
were dug in bedrock to a depth of 10 ft. When walls were erected on
sloping ground, trenches were not dug, but level terraces were built on
which the foundation layers were set. The first course would be made of
stones set vertically, and the layers above them were generally arranged in a
header-stretcher fashion, with one horizontal and two upright stones. At the
edges of the external walls, the foundations would rest on three stepped

terraces. The header-stretcher technique and the placement of angular hewn stones at the corners of the outer walls strengthened the inner joints against crumbling or sagging.

In both Samaria and Megiddo other evidence attests to the care taken in construction. When cornerstones were laid, a string dipped in ocher was strung between them (cf. Isa. 28:17; II Kings 21:13) to provide a guideline for erecting the walls. In various excavations evidence of ocher paint remains on the stones.

WALLS

Walls are frequently mentioned in the Bible. City walls (see below, Fortifications) and house walls are referred to by the same term (Jos. 2:15; 6:5).

Excavations of mud-brick walls set on a one- or two-layer stone foundation have not yielded sufficient information from which to draw conclusions about the development of construction methods. Neither can we establish the size of the bricks used in various periods, nor the form of the rubble supports erected on either side of the foundation edges or the way in which they joined the face of the walls.

In general, until the Israelite period, the building remains that have been excavated rarely stand higher than the foundation layer, so that it is difficult to ascertain whether the walls were of brick construction. Even where there are stone layers up to 5 ft. in height, it is suggested that these were only high stone pediments, and that the walls above them were probably built of mud-brick.

Figure 18:   Main hall in the temple at Ai, with a row of column bases and wall of thin stone slabs set horizontally

A construction technique typical of the Early Bronze III period (as attested in Ai, Lachish, and other places) is the use of small, thin slabs of stone set horizontally (fig. 18). It has been suggested that this early use of stone copied the technique used in laying mud-bricks.

Other buildings of the Early Bronze period reflect a lack of care in construction: the use of crude stone blocks, the irregular foundation lines, the haphazard placement of pebbles and stone chips to fill spaces between stone blocks. It is frequently difficult to ascertain whether the stones were joined with mud mortar, or whether they merely rested one on the other. In the Middle and Late Bronze period, the layers of stone are more regular, the blocks are partially fitted one to the other and, almost invariably, they are joined by mortar.

A marked improvement in construction methods appears during the time of Solomon. Practically for the first time in the history of building in Erez Israel, beautifully hewn and dressed stones, known as ashlar masonry, appear (see Cities, above). However, rough stone construction continued to be used for private dwellings. Since these techniques of stone-cutting were found in other places, such as in the Phoenician city of Ugarit from a period predating Solomon by at least 200 years, one may assume that these techniques were brought to Erez Israel by the Phoenician craftsmen sent by Hiram of Tyre to David and Solomon, and that they were then adopted by Israelite craftsmen.

A distinctive element of building in the period of the monarchy is the use of hewn stones whose external surface is dressed with narrow (varying in width) borders on two or three (only occasionally on four) sides, while the center of the block protrudes in a roughly rounded fashion. This type of ashlar masonry was probably used only in the foundation courses which were set in the trenches. The courses above ground level usually had smoothed surfaces without borders and protruding centers, layed alternately breadthwise and lengthwise, usually two masonry lengthwise and one breadthwise (the "header-stretcher" method, fig. 17).

Another distinctive feature of construction in Solomon's time is the use of hewn stone pilasters (engaged columns) that stood at the corners of the house and at regular intervals along the walls. The stones in these pilasters were arranged alternately, one row horizontally, the next two rows vertically. The walls between the pilasters were built of roughly chiseled stones, undoubtedly as an economy measure. (The Bible comments on the costliness of hewn stones; cf. I Kings 5:3.) The pilasters were usually crowned by capitals of the proto-Aeolian type (fig. 19).

Figure 19:
Proto-Aeolian
capital on pilasters of a
reconstructed portal at
the Israel Museum

In the period of the divided monarchy, another technique for strength-ening walls appeared (e.g., Tell al-Naṣba), and rough stone walls were found from which crude, horizontally laid stone pilasters emerge. These were set into the layers of stone and served to strengthen and add stability to the walls, particularly in their upper reaches. This is similar to the technique of setting wooden beams horizontally into the walls, either within the masonry courses, or on the external surfaces, where they served to hold the walls in place (cf. the description of Solomon's Temple: "And he built the inner court with three rows of hewn stone, and a row of cedar beams," I Kings 6:36).

CEILINGS

Although, as noted above, no excavations in Ereẓ Israel have yielded a building with a completely preserved and roofed ground floor, partially collapsed ceilings were found at several sites. From such a remnant in Tell Beit Mirsim scholars have estimated that the room beneath it had rafters measuring about 6½ × 10 inches, spaced about 20 inches apart. Across the beams thinner planks of wood were laid, apparently untrimmed branches and young tree limbs. A thick layer of mud plaster was spread on these, to provide a smooth surface for the roof or the upper floor. The surface of the rafters and planks was also plastered on the underside, which became the ceiling of the floor below.

Where the span between the walls of the room was greater than the length of the beams, or where it was feared that the rafters would not bear the weight of the roof or upper story, a row of pillars was erected along the middle of the room to support the rafters, or to serve as a resting place for the edges of two beams whose other edges reached the walls on either side. Pillars of this type were found at Ai and in various temples dating from the Middle and Late Bronze and Early Iron periods. The pillars appear to have been wooden, but stood on stone bases. The charred remains of such a pillar were found on a stone base in the hall of the palace at Ai.

The flat roofs which resulted from this method of construction were smoothed with stone cylinders which were rolled by hand, or with a handle set at either end of the cylinder. Such cylinders have been found in many excavations. The roofs would be replastered each year before the rainy season, to seal the cracks that would develop in their surface during the summer heat.

DOORS

The Bible distinguishes between the term *petaḥ*, which is the entrance to a house (Gen. 43:19) and *delet*, which is a device for closing and opening the entrance. Thus, while *petaḥ* applies to the entrance to a tent (Gen. 18:1) and a house, the term *delet* is used only in connection with a house. The door had two main components: a fixed frame and a moving board or slab. The frame had two doorposts which were its vertical sides; a lintel — its upper horizontal side; and a sill or threshold — its lower horizontal side. Wider doorways occasionally had a third vertical beam on which two door-leaves (Isa. 45:1), one attached to each of the doorposts, converged when shut. The doorway was constructed as part of the wall, but the doorposts, lintel, and threshold were built in after the building was completed. Finally, the door itself was set into this framework.

At the top and bottom of each doorleaf, a projecting hinge of wood, metal or other material was set within sockets or depressions in the lintel and threshold (cf. I Kings 7:50). Doors generally opened inward; they were prevented from swinging outward by ledges at the outer edges of the lintel and the threshold. Sometimes the door was suspended on some pliable material, such as leather or rope, slung between the door and the doorpost at two points, which served as hinges to enable the movement of the doors back and forth. A number of excavations have yielded the remains of metal coverings on hinges and sockets that served to protect them from wear.

The threshold was of stone, either cut to size and laid slightly higher than the floor, or built up from smaller stones. It was built slightly higher than the level of the floor and the street in order to keep out water and dirt. Doorposts were made either of wood or stone. Isaiah 6:4 probably refers to stone doorposts standing at both ends of the threshold. Doorposts made of wood are implied in the law about the Hebrew slave (Ex. 21:6; Deut. 15:17), according to which a Hebrew slave who, when the time of his release arrived, preferred slavery to freedom was to be placed against a doorpost and have his earlobe and the doorpost pierced with an awl as a symbol of his enslavement for life. The lintel might also be made of stone or wood and was placed horizontally across the doorposts.

The size of a doorway was related to the size of the building. Doorways to private dwellings from the Israelite period, preserved in the Negev, were lower than man's height, while the entrances to large buildings, such as palaces and temples, were proportionately higher and wider. Very large doors were erected at the gates of fortified cities (Judg. 16:3). The doors of luxurious buildings were made of costly wood (I Kings 6:31,34) or were overlaid with metal, usually copper, or even gold, like the doors of the Temple. Various cylinder seals and monuments show single or double doors set within a decorative framework.

An integral part of the door was its bar or bolt, a device used to lock the door from the inside or the outside. The bar consisted of a movable horizontal beam which, when slid into a slot in the doorpost, prevented the door from opening. The lock was somewhat more complex and could be locked or unlocked from the outside (II Sam. 13:17,18). Another way to lock the door from inside was to put an iron bar on the inner side in a fitting depression (cf. I Sam. 23:7).

WINDOWS

According to the Book of Joshua, a window played a vital role in the escape of the two spies sent by Joshua to reconnoiter Jericho's military weaknesses (Josh. 2:15). While the soldiers of the city searched for the two men, Rahab let them down by a rope from the window in the city wall. A somewhat similar episode involved Michal, the daughter of Saul, who helped her husband David escape from her father by letting him out through the window (I Sam. 19:12).

Actually, the architectural concept of a window had already been mentioned earlier in the biblical narrative, when Abimelech, king of Gerar, saw Isaac and Rebecca together through a window (Gen. 26:8).

Judging from the above, and from other biblical references (e.g. Jer. 22:13–14), the window was a common architectural feature in ancient times. As early as the Chalcolithic period, builders had sufficient skill to set windows in their houses. They were usually placed in the upper part of the wall, and evidently only in the wall opposite the entrance. This is evident from the excavation of clay ossuaries in which the bones of the dead were stored, and which were modeled after the houses of the living.

A relief from the period of Ramses II, depicting the Egyptian attack on Ashkelon (1293 B.C.E.), shows windows set in the wall over the city gate and in the central tower. The latticed window shown here is typical Egyptian work which has not been found in Ereẓ Israel. In Egypt, such windows were carved out of a single block of stone, and were set within the wall like the window frame of our own time.

Figure 20: Ivory carving with the theme of "the woman at the window," from Nimrud, c. 8th cent. B.C.E.

– Figure 21:   Balustrade of decorated small columns topped by small capitals
of proto-Aeolian type. From the Royal Palace at Ramat Raḥel, c. 1000
B.C.E.

A wall relief from the palace of Sennacherib in Nineveh depicts the
Assyrian siege of the Israelite city of Lachish (fig. 22). Clearly visible are
the windows, high up in the towers of the outer city wall. Although the
events depicted here date from the 7th century B.C.E., scholars are of the
opinion that similar architectural details must have existed in earlier periods
as well, for excavations indicate that ancient towns were always closely
settled, with the dwelling-houses built into the city wall.

More intriguing is the theme of "the woman at the window" (fig. 20)
which has been found in a number of places, appearing, with slight variations, in ivory carving from Samaria, Nimrud, Khorsabad, and other sites.
The carvings show an inset window with a balustrade, above which appears
the head of a woman with long hair falling in tresses over her shoulders. A
somewhat similar carving in bronze was found in Cyprus at Enkomi, but
here the balustrade is not represented by columns with a crossbar, but by
three horizontal bars. The window with its bars recalls the "lattice" through
which Ahaziah fell from his upper chamber (II Kings 1:2).

"The woman at the window" is a theme which occurs twice in the Bible
in literary form. In the Song of Deborah, the prophetess describes Sisera's
mother waiting for him to come back victorious from the wars: "Out of the
window she peered, the mother of Sisera gazed through the lattice" (Judg.
5:28).

A similar scene appears in the biblical description of the death of
Jezebel: "And she painted her eyes, and adorned her head, and looked out
of the window. And as Jehu entered the gate, she said, 'Is it peace, you
Zimri, murderer of your master?' And he lifted up his face to the window,

Figure 22:   The city of Lachish as depicted on a wall relief from the palace
of Sennacherib at Kuyunjik (Nineveh), 704–681 B.C.E. It shows the siege
of the city by the Assyrians and the tower of the city gate with windows

and said, 'Who is on my side? Who? ' Two or three eunuchs looked out at
him. He said, 'Throw her down.' So they threw her down" (II Kings
9:30–33).

    The ivory carvings bring both these scenes vividly to mind. The way the
window is inset gives a definite impression of peering, while the open upper
half might allow a body to be thrown through it. Findings at Ramat Raḥel
(fig. 21) prove that this type of window was not just an artistic expression,
but a representation of an architectural reality.

Figure 23:   Reconstruction of fortress temple at Shechem. After G.E. Wright

UPPER CHAMBERS

Another architectural theme common in the Bible is that of the "upper chamber." It was into such a chamber that Ehud was invited when he killed the Moabite king, Eglon, during their private interview (Judg. 3:20–24). Elijah brought the son of the woman of Zarephath back to life in such a room (I Kings 17:19); and the Shunnamite had a room such as this built for Elisha, in which he later worked a miracle similar to that performed by Elijah (II Kings 4:10). These were the main dwelling and sleeping rooms in the house (cf. II Kings 9:13,17), and there guests would be accommodated (cf. I Kings 17:19; II Kings 4:10,11).

There are definite indications that both public buildings and private dwellings often had more than one story. Thus, the fortress temple at Shechem (c. 1650–1100 B.C.E.) had walls over five yards thick (fig. 23). While such a width undoubtedly served a defensive role, it is also considered an indication that the temple had two, or even three, floors. It is quite possible that the pottery stands found in Late Canaanite temples at Beth-Shean which were used for burning incense are models of such multistory temples with windows.

STAIRWAYS

Once upper rooms were built, stairways had to be constructed as well. In this connection we may note an interesting solution developed by Yigael Yadin to a difficult passage in the Book of Kings. The Bible relates that Hezekiah, king of Judah, fell ill. The prophet Isaiah went to see him and informed him of his imminent death. At this news, Hezekiah turned his face to the wall and prayed. Isaiah then returned to him and told him that his prayer had been heard; God had granted him another fifteen years of life. Hezekiah was evidently suspicious of the new message, for he asked Isaiah for a sign. "And Isaiah said: 'This is the sign to you from the Lord, that the Lord will do the thing that He has promised: shall the shadow go forward ten steps (*ma'alot*), or go back ten steps.' And Hezekiah answered: 'It is an easy thing for the shadow to lengthen ten steps; rather let the shadow go back ten steps.' And He brought the shadow back ten steps, by which the sun had declined on the steps of Ahaz" (II Kings 20:9–11). The word *ma'alot* in the text refers to actual steps, and not, as is often translated, "degrees."

Elsewhere, the Bible refers to altars built on the roof of the "upper chamber" of the house of Ahaz, which were probably connected with sun worship (II Kings 23:12). Yadin hypothesizes that Ahaz built an upper chamber which had two stairways leading up its sides to the roof (fig. 24). These steps, according to Yadin, served as a sundial. The angle of the walls of the chamber threw a shadow onto the steps, a shadow which moved along one stairway as the sun rose in the sky, and moved up the second stairs as the sun sank. The miracle was that the shadow, instead of moving

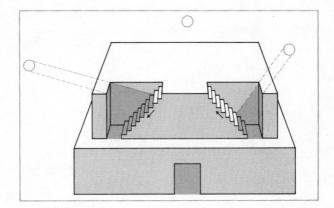

Figure 24: "The steps of Ahaz." After Y. Yadin

up the steps, receded ten steps. Archaeological research indicates that stairs built along the side of a wall, such as the above, were not uncommon in the period.

At Tell al-Naṣba, the first three steps of a stairway were found near one of the typical Israelite houses. In many sites houses of the Israelite period were probably of two stories, but it is not certain whether steps or ladders were in use (fig. 29).

Excavations revealed several buildings containing such narrow rooms that scholars believe they were intended to support a stairway, or at least to support a ladder. Such are the rooms in the fortress temple at Shechem (fig. 23) and Megiddo, and the guardrooms of the gates at many sites.

One may also note the two rows of steps attached to the inner walls of the great round silo found at Megiddo (8th–7th century B.C.E.; see below, fig. 32). One row of steps was used to descend; the other to ascend. These were built of single rough stones, spiraling one above the other in an overlapping fashion, like the threads of a screw.

4

DOMESTIC BUILDINGS

The Hebrew word for "house" (*bayit*) appears some two thousand times in the Bible. It may refer to any dwelling, from the simplest house of a peasant to a palace and the temple. By implication it may also refer to the family living together in one house (e.g. Gen. 7:1; 42:19). It is also applied to the smallest social unit (tribe, family, house; e.g. Josh. 7:14), which is some-times called "father's house" (*beit av*; Num. 1:2); and to the extended family over the course of several generations, as the "house of David" (Isa. 7:2; I Kings 13:2; etc.). Other usages include "house of the Rechabites" (Jer. 35:2), "house of Levi" (Ex. 2:1), and "house of Israel" (Ps. 115:12).

Figure 25: Plan of a dwelling house at Tell Beit Mirsim stratum G (Middle Bronze IIa) showing: (1) main hall (closed courtyard); (2) rooms; (3) staircase (?)

Figure 26: Plan of dwelling house at Tell Beit Mirsim stratum D (Middle Bronze IIb–c), showing: (1) open courtyard with granary and well with two units of rooms (2,3) on its southwest

26

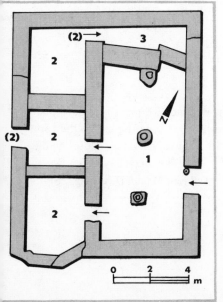
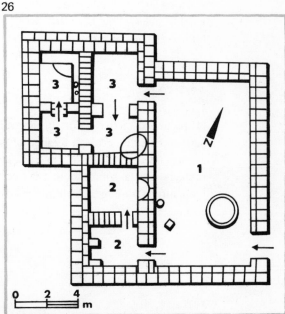

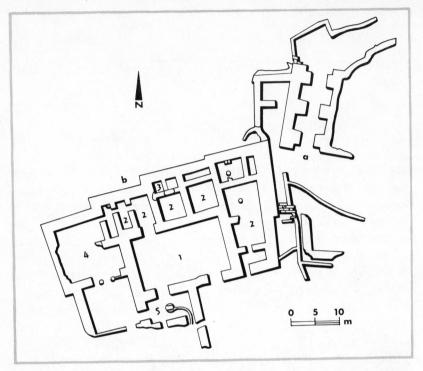

Figure 27:   Plan of the palace (b) and the gate (a) at Megiddo dating to the Late Bronze–Early Iron Age. The palace consists of a large courtyard (1) surrounded by small rooms (2), a hall (4), a bathroom (5). In one of the rooms (3) a treasure of gold and ivory was found

However, the Bible does not provide any description of houses. Fortunately, archaeology has been able to provide a considerable amount of information about the development of housing in the biblical period.

PRE-ISRAELITE

In the period of the Middle Bronze Age, we find two main types of buildings, apparently occupied by men of wealth. One type, typical of the 18th century B.C.E., consists of a main hall with a row of columns supporting the roof and several rooms around it (see fig. 25). The second type, known as the courtyard-house, is well preserved in Tell Beit Mirsim D (see fig. 26). In general, there is a tendency toward transition to the open courtyard surrounded by rooms, a type which dominated the Late Bronze period. Examples of such are the palaces of Megiddo (see fig. 27), Taanach, and Beth-El.

ISRAELITE

The Israelite house appears first as a homogeneous structure in the Early Iron Age (12th–11th centuries B.C.E.). In general it is a house which has an inner open courtyard with a porch and two perpendicular rooms. Such houses were discovered in Tell Qasila (see fig. 28) and Tell Jamma. In the 10th century the so-called "Israelite house" became crystallized. It is usually a quadripartite, sometimes tripartite, house, consisting of wide rooms with long perpendicular rooms (see fig. 29a-b).

The origin of the "Israelite house" is uncertain. It is still unclear whether it is of Phoenician origin, of Late Canaanite tradition brought by the Sea Peoples, or an independent Israelite invention.

Figure 28:   Model of an Early Israelite house, based on the excavations at Tell Qasila near Tel Aviv: (1) central open courtyard; (2) inner porch; (3, 4) living rooms

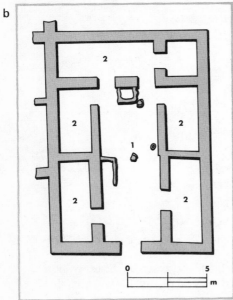

Figure 29a, b: The quadripartite Israelite house. A reconstructed drawing from Shechem (a). A plan from Tell al-Far'ah (b) with an inner courtyard (1) surrounded by rooms (2)

Figure 30: Model of ground floor of the citadel at Hazor in its first phase
(9th cent. B.C.E.), showing: (1) entrance; (2) staircase leading to the first
floor; (3) casemate wall of the 10th cent., filled with earth and joining
(4) quadripartite houses. For the second phase, see fig. 49

5

OUTBUILDINGS

GRAIN PITS, GRANARIES, AND STORAGE ROOMS

The construction of storage facilities for grain has been among the earliest of man's building efforts.

Excavations from various periods have revealed structures which may have served as public storage rooms.

An unusually large granary excavated at Beth-Shean is considered to date from the 13th century B.C.E. Here, a complex of buildings comprised part of the city fortress. One was the inner tower, another may have served as the quarters of the Egyptian garrison. Between these two structures stood a round building constructed of mud-bricks laid one directly above the other (not in an alternating pattern) on a foundation of rough basalt stones. Part of the building was probably sunken into the ground. Its sides are about 10 inches thick, and it is estimated to have been about 11 ft. deep. Its inner diameter is approximately 12 x 13 ft.

Another unique structure was exposed in the palace at Megiddo, within the walls of the city gate (existing, with several changes, from the Middle Bronze IIc until the beginning of the Israelite period). The rooms yielded a treasure of ivory objects and jewelry, and other precious items, suggesting that this was the treasury of the royal palace (fig. 27).

Almost all the excavated settlements of the Iron period, particularly during the time of the Israelite monarchy, have yielded large numbers of granaries or storage rooms (cf. II Chron. 32:27). The most typical were found at Hazor, Beer-Sheba, and Tell Beit Mirsim. These structures were either built as parallel series of rooms (usually four) or a large hall divided by two rows of columns (fig. 31). These were undoubtedly the storehouses mentioned frequently in the Bible from the days of King Solomon on, sometimes as a term by itself, and sometimes in the phrase "store cities" (see Cities, p. 15).

It is clear that parts of private houses were also used for storage purposes.

Figure 31; Aerial view of a large storage house at Hazor with two rows of pillars (3); Solomonic gateway (1); and casemate wall (2).

One may cite, as an example, the complex of rooms and courtyards excavated at Tell Qasila (Early Iron Age). Dozens of containers and clay vessels were found stored, row after row, in one of the rectangular courtyards. A nearby room yielded goblets, jars, cups, and wine jugs. Various vessels and pieces of charred wood were found in the broad courtyard of this complex. This again reflects the probability that the rooms on the ground floor in the typical Israelite house were storerooms.

Still another type of storage structure was common in the Israelite period, both for private and communal use. These were the round grain storage pits or silos dug into virgin soil or into earlier layers of rubble. Sometimes the sides were covered with mud-bricks or rough stones set in

Figure 32: Silo with steps around the inside from Megiddo, stratum III (780–650 B.C.E.). Depth: 23ft. (7m.)

mud mortar; but at times they were merely mud plastered or left untouched.

A large number of such pits were found at Tell Jamma, in various strata dating from the 11th century B.C.E. through the Persian period. Similar pits were also found at many other sites. A silo found in Megiddo (780–650 B.C.E.) (fig. 32) may serve as a typical example. Its base diameter was about 23 ft., its upper diameter was close to 36 ft., and it was about 23 ft. deep. Its floor and walls were covered with rough stones, and two sets of stairs (evidently one for descending, the other for ascending) hugged the wall. Seeds and chaffs found between the stones indicate that the sides of the pits had never been plastered. This was, evidently, a public storehouse, perhaps serving the Assyrian garrison that was stationed in the city.

OVENS

Ever since man discovered how fire could be maintained and exploited, it has been one of his most important assets, providing light and warmth, enabling him to cook, bake (see p. 220), wage war, craft vessels, and send messages. It served his daily, mundane needs, and became part of his religious rituals. It is not surprising, then, that almost every archaeological site which has preserved traces of man's settlement has also yielded signs of the use of fire.

Excavations of the Israelite period have yielded the remains of round ovens which stood in the courtyards of the buildings. They were built of mud-bricks plastered on the outside, and generally had an air hole on one side. When the layer of accumulated ash within the oven had grown too thick, the top part of the oven would be broken off and the sides raised to form a new oven. Remains of ovens with two and sometimes three air holes, one above the other, indicate than an oven was rebuilt more than once.

At Tell Qasila, in Israelite strata, piles of clay weights covered with a thick layer of ash were found near a pottery. B. Mazar suggested that these objects were heat-retainers.

STABLES

Both Solomon and Hezekiah maintained extensive stables. "And Solomon had forty thousand stalls of horses for his chariots, and twelve thousand horsemen" (I Kings 5:6). "And Hezekiah had exceeding much riches and honor; and he provided him . . . stalls for all manner of beasts, and flocks in folds . . . he provided him . . . possession of flocks and herds in abundance" (II Chron. 32:22–29).

Thus far no structure, neither in a private home nor a palace, in any strata preceding the Israelite layers of the Middle Iron period, has been definitely identified as a stable or stall. Nonetheless, it is surmised that some of the outbuildings or the walled courts belonging to earlier structures served this purpose (see above).

Only when we reach the beginning of the Second Iron Age do we find remains that may be identified as stables. The most interesting and extensive are those found at Megiddo, where two sets of buildings, one in the southwest and the other in the northeast of the site, occupied one-fifth of the entire area (fig. 53). They have been assigned to the period of Ahab, despite prior identification with Solomon (on the basis of the biblical verse cited above).

These stables (fig. 33) were built in groups of four, five, or six structures without open spaces between them. Each building was divided into three lengthwise sections by two rows of stone pillars. The pillars stood on deep

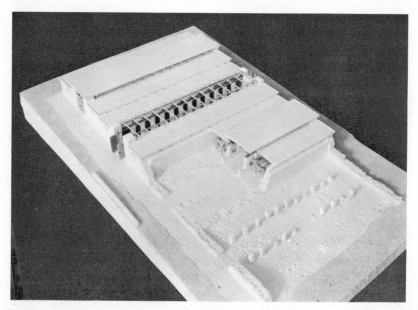

Figure 33:   Reconstructed model of the stables in Megiddo

stone bases and served two purposes: to support the roof and to provide separate stalls for the horses. Between each two pillars there was a stone trough which held fodder for the horses, except for the space between the last pillar and the wall, which was a passageway for entering and leaving the building. The horses stood facing one another and were tethered by ropes which passed through holes in the pillars. The central section of the building was paved with hard plaster, and the chariots may have stood thereupon. The stalls, however, had floors made of small, rough stones. The walls were made of stone in their lower half at least; the roof was probably plastered and rested on crosswise beams, and had three sections: a higher middle section and two lower side sections. In the space between these two roof levels there were undoubtedly two rows of clerestory windows. The two units of stables opened to a broad, paved, walled yard, in the center of which was a water trough. A passageway from the yard led to a subterranean tunnel that in turn led to the wells that provided Megiddo with water in time of siege. Several stone stalls were also found in the area.

The excavations of the stables provide information concerning the number of horses and chariots in them. In the southern complex there were five stables, each housing 150 horses for 50 chariots (three horses for each chariot). In the northern complex there were three units for 450 horses and 150 chariots.

This clarifies a phrase used in the Bible. It concerns Zimri, who became famous in Israel as a traitor who slew his master the king (II Kings 9:31), and who is described as "commander of half his [the king's] chariots" (I Kings 16:9). It would appear that chariot cities such as Megiddo were set up at various strategic places in Israel, each under the command of an officer faithful to the central authority of the king in Samaria.

6

CULTIC STRUCTURES

The cosmogony and thought processes of ancient man incorporated almost complete dependence on the approval of supernatural beings to ensure the continued existence of his settlement, the fruitfulness of its land, the well-being of its flocks and inhabitants. Thus, ever since man began to build permanent settlements, he included within them cultic sites dedicated to the gods, as well as a dwelling place for them, so that they would be near when he needed their help and defense, or wished to pacify them and seek their favor. Even in the most ancient of excavated settlements, one can identify sites dedicated to the gods. Many such places are mentioned in the Bible, and modern archaeological research has added to the list.

In the ancient Near East, the cult was characterized by permanent sites noted for their sacredness. Such sites retained this attribute despite shifts in population and consequent changes in the dominant religion of the area.

The Bible employs specific terms that refer to different types of cult places, although the usage is not always consistent. Three general types of cultic constructions can be identified by specific terminology: the temple (*bet YHWH* or *mikdash*), the high place (*bamah*), and the altar (*mizbe'ah*). The Tabernacle used during the Israelites' wandering in the desert represents a separate type of cultic phenomenon (see below).

ALTARS

The altar originally was the place where sacrificial slaughter was performed. By biblical times, however, animals were no longer slaughtered upon the altar, but nearby. Nor was the altar restricted to animal sacrifices; it also received grain, wine, and incense offerings. The altar also fulfilled non-sacrificial functions, such as testimony (see Josh. 22:26–29) and asylum (see below).

Altars are found everywhere in the ancient Near East, in strata dating back to the very earliest periods of history. It has been suggested that their origin lies in the sacred stone which had magical properties and was considered to be the resting place of the gods; in the earliest times such a stone served both as a monument and an altar. Another hypothesis (mentioned above) holds that the altar was created simultaneously with the beginnings of permanent settlement in the Near East. However, the altar undoubtedly played a role even in semi-nomadic societies, as is evident in the patriarchal narrative.

There are two main types of altars: the popular (or "simple") altar which stood in an open place and the more elaborate altar associated with a temple and standing in its courtyard. Both served the same purpose — the offering of sacrifices — although the temple altar enjoyed an additional measure of holiness. Simple altars were undoubtedly located in or near almost every settlement; sometimes a town had more than one such altar. In contrast, there were but few temples with their elaborate altars.

According to biblical tradition, the Patriarchs erected many altars. Scholars have claimed that these were local cultic sites which the Israelites subsequently adapted for their own use. However, it has been suggested that these are not to be associated with Canaanite cities, and their location beyond the city walls is more typical of the encampments set up by nomads in the vicinity of a settlement. The Book of Genesis relates that Abraham erected altars at the terebinth of Moreh near Shechem (12:6,7), between Beth-El and Ai (12:8; 13:3—4), at the terebinths of Mamre outside Hebron (13:18), and on one of the hills in the land of Moriah (22:9). Isaac erected an altar in Beer-Sheba (26:25), and Jacob sacrificed there (46:1); but in the patriarchal narrative, Beer-Sheba was not a settlement, but merely a well. Jacob erected altars on Mt. Gilead (31:25, 46—54), on the parcel of land which he bought outside of Shechem (33:18—20), and near Beth-El (35:1—7). Thus it is clear that the Israelites had an ancient tradition of erecting altars in open places, which had nothing to do with the cultic sites of the Canaanites or with the establishment of temples in settlements.

THE FORM OF THE ALTAR

Altars were constructed of three kinds of material: stone, earth, and metal. The choice depended on such factors as permanence, cost, and, in Ereẓ Israel, whether the altar stood alone or was attached to a sanctuary.

Altars of earth are explicitly commanded in Exodus 20:24 (cf. II Kings 5:17), but none has been found, since they could not survive the ravages of time. Nor, for that matter, were any of the altars mentioned in the Bible built of earth. These, the simplest and least pretentious of all altars, were exclusively the creation of the common folk. Brick, technically also earth, so common a material in Mesopotamia, was not used in altars constructed in Israel; a Canaanite brick altar, however, has been found in Beth-Shean (fig. 37).

Stone altars are not decomposed by time, and archaeological excavations have unearthed abundant pre-Israelite specimens. Their form ranges from unworked, detached rocks, to slightly hollowed surfaces, to hewn natural stone, and to completely man-made structures. Some undisputed examples are at Gezer, Hazor, Megiddo, Nahariyyah, and Arad. At Arad, the Israelite sanctuary contains an altar three cubits square and five cubits high (the exact dimensions of the Tabernacle altar in Ex. 27:1). It is a simple structure built of earth and unworked stones (in accordance with Ex. 20:22).

The Bible speaks of altars made of natural rock (Judg. 13:19–20; I Sam. 6:14; 14:33–35; I Kings 1:9) or of an artificial heap (Gen. 31:46–54; Josh. 4:2–8, 20ff.; I Kings 18:31–32). All biblical altars, with the exception of those in sanctuaries, seem to have been built of stone.

Manoah, for example, offered a sacrifice "upon the rock unto the Lord" (Judg. 13:19). A large rock in the field near Beth-Shemesh was used by the local people as an altar (I Sam. 10:14–16), and a large rock rolled into place by Saul after he defeated the Philistines also served as an altar (ibid., 14:33–35). It is possible that, in the course of time, these rocks were worked upon in some fashion, to adapt them to their function. In Taanach and Megiddo, rocks which have retained traces of slightly hollowed depressions that were chipped into them have been classified as altars of the Canaanite period. In Zorah (on the northern side of Valley of Sorek) and Petra (Transjordan), altars made of one huge rock have been found, with hewn steps leading up to them. According to the Bible, the Israelite altars did not have steps.

A common form of altar was that made of heaped stones. Thus, Jacob built a heap of stones on Mt. Gilead and called it gal-ed (heap of witness): "And Jacob said unto his brethren: 'Gather stones,' and they took stones and made a heap" (Gen. 31:46–54). The biblical narrative contains several references to altars built of twelve stones, symbolic of the twelve tribes: those built by Joshua at Gilgal (Josh. 4:2–8,20–24) and by Elijah on Mt. Carmel (I Kings 18:31–32). Similarly, Exodus 24:4 relates that Moses erected an altar below Mt. Sinai, with twelve pillars "according to the twelve tribes of Israel."

Yet another type of altar was constructed of layers of stone, but they were simple in the extreme, and generally had only two layers — the base and the upper layer which was the altar itself (cf. Ex. 27:1; 38:1; 29:12; Lev. 4:7,18; etc.).

THE TABERNACLE ALTARS

Although the two altars in the Tabernacle (fig. 34) have not survived the centuries, a combined study of biblical references and archaeological finds can provide an adequate picture of what they were like. The bronze, or burnt-offering, altar stood in the courtyard. It was made of acacia wood plated with bronze, and it had "horns" (*keranot*) (Ex. 27:1–8; 38:1–7) on which the blood of the purification offering was daubed. The horns also provided refuge for those seeking asylum; the fugitive could seize them and

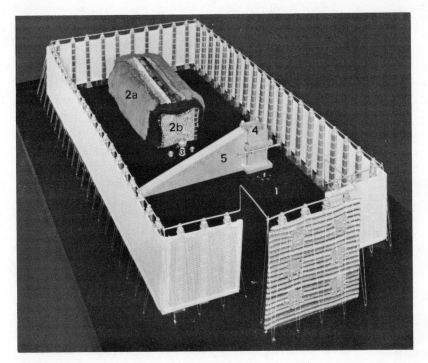

Figure 34:   Model of Tabernacle, showing: (1) court; (2) sanctuary (a. ramskin covering; b. screen); (3) laver; (4) bronze altar (for burnt offering); (5) sloped ramp

claim sanctuary. This sanctuary, however, was not extended to murderers (Ex. 21:14; I Kings 2:28—34).

Beneath the horns was the *karkov* ("rim" or "border") which seems to have been a projecting rim, and is exemplified by many small altars in Erez Israel. The *mikhbar* ("net" or "grating") was a bronze mesh that covered the upper half of the altar beneath the rim; neither its appearance nor its function is understood.

Since the altar was part of a portable sanctuary, it was fitted with four rings and two staves. Moreover, it was hollow and hence not burdensome. At each encampment it would be filled with earth and rocks (in actual conformity with Ex. 20:21ff.). The same system of hollowed altars is known from some Assyrian excavations.

The second altar in the Tabernacle was the gold, or incense, altar (see below) which stood within the Tent of Congregation. It too is described in detail in the Bible (Ex. 30:1—10; 37:25—28). Its dimensions were 1×2×2 cubits and, like the sacrificial altar, it was made of acacia wood and had horns, rings, and staves for carrying. But it was a solid structure and was plated with gold which extended over its top. It stood directly in front of the curtain covering the Ark of the Covenant, flanked by the golden candelabrum (Ex. 25:31ff.) and the golden table (ibid., v. 23ff.). Incense of a prescribed formula was burned upon it daily.

THE ALTARS IN SOLOMON'S TEMPLE

In the account of the building of the First Temple, there is no mention of the sacrificial altar (I Kings ch. 6—7). The Chronicler indeed attributes the building of an altar to Solomon (II Chron. 4:1), but its size (20 × 20 × 10 cubits) most likely corresponds to the Temple altar of his own day. However, there are allusions to the sacrificial altar in the account of the construction of Solomon's Temple (I Kings 9:25) and under the name of "the bronze altar" (I Kings 8:64; II Kings 16:14—15). The silence of I Kings ch. 6—7 is hard to explain.

It has been conjectured that Solomon did not build an altar but utilized the one used or made by King David (II Sam. 24:21) for his tent sanctuary (II Sam. 6:17). Bolstering this hypothesis is the fact that the altar was movable (II Kings 16:14) and that on the first day of its use, it proved undersized (I Kings 8:64). However, the explicit references to its construction (I Kings 9:25) and Solomon's penchant for the new and the expensive, e.g., the bronze laver "sea" (I Kings 7:23–26), would argue against the omission of a sacrificial altar from his temple-building program. The problem is yet unsolved.

More is known about its replacement, the altar constructed by King Ahaz (II Kings 16:10–16). It was a copy of the altar in the main temple of Damascus, probably that of Hadad-Rimmon (II Kings 5:18). It was called the "great altar" (II Kings 16:15) and was therefore larger than Solomon's. One had to ascend to it (*ibid*. v. 12); apparently it was not made of bronze, since that name was reserved for Solomon's altar. This may have been the model for Ezekiel's altar (see below). Ahaz had Solomon's altar moved to the northern part of the courtyard, where it was reserved for Ahaz's private use (*ibid*. 14,15b). That the First Temple had an incense altar inside the sanctuary is known from the reference to the "golden altar" (I Kings 7:48) and from the episode of King Uzziah burning incense upon the altar inside the Temple (II Chron. 26:16b).

EZEKIEL'S ALTAR

Ezekiel's vision of a new temple (Ezek. 40–48) includes a minute description of its sacrificial altar (43:13–17). It consisted of four tiers, each one cubit less per side than the tier below. Since the uppermost tier had a horizontal area of 12 X 12 cubits, the ones underneath were respectively 14 X 14, 16 X 16, and 18 X 18 cubits. The heights of each tier, from top to bottom, are given as $1 + 2 + 4 + 4$, with another cubit for the horns. Thus, the total height of the altar is 12 cubits. Because the long cubit is used (app. 20½ inches), the altar was about 20½ ft. tall, even higher than the altar attributed to Solomon by the Chronicler (II Chron. 4:1). It was ascended by a flight of stairs on its eastern side. The edges of two of its tiers were apparently shaped into troughs, the one at the base called "the *ḥeik* of the earth" and the other, in the middle, called "the *ḥeik* of the ledge" (Ezek. 43:14,17). Their purpose was to collect the blood of the sin-offering which was daubed at these points (43:20).

It has been suggested that Ezekiel's altar corresponded to the one he remembered from the First Temple, in which case it would be an exact description of Ahaz's altar. Supporting this view is the Syrian-Mesopotamian influence evident in certain of its features. It may be recalled that Ahaz copied a Damascene altar. Its storied structure resembles the *ziggurat* temple-tower. The uppermost tier is called *ariel* or *harel*; the latter term means "God's mountain" and may be related to the Akkadian *arallû*,the name for both the netherworld and the world-mountain. Perhaps Isaiah's symbolic name for Jerusalem, *Ariel*, is also derived from this altar (Isa. 29:1–2,7).

Ezekiel also envisions an incense altar inside the Temple which he calls "the table that is before the Lord" (41:22). That it is made of wood may reflect the fact that in 597 B.C.E., Nebuchadnezzar stripped all the Temple cult implements of their gold (II Kings 24:13).

INCENSE ALTARS

All the biblical accounts of the Tabernacle in the wilderness speak not only of the sacrificial altar, but also of an incense altar within the sanctuary (see above). Yet scholars have been nearly unanimous in declaring this to be an anachronistic insertion based upon the practices of the Temple, arguing that the burning of incense was a much later introduction. Their suspicion is strengthened by the placement of its description not in the text containing the rest of the inner sancta (Ex. ch. 26), but after the description of the entire Tabernacle and its paraphernalia (Ex. 30:1–10) – an afterthought, as it were.

The objection is fallacious. The fact that it is not found in its "logical" place is in itself reason to suspect that another kind of logic obtained there. Indeed, it can be shown that the description of the Tabernacle is divided in two parts: Exodus 26:1–27:19 describes the Tabernacle in blueprint; and Exodus 27:20–30:38 describes the Tabernacle in operation. Since the incense altar is described functionally (Ex. 30:7–8), it therefore belongs in the latter section. Furthermore, the use of the candelabrum (27:20–21), the investiture of those qualified to service it (28:1–29:37), the *tamid* offering (29:38ff.), and the incense offering are all part of a single cultic activity to be conducted twice daily by the high priest. Further evidence is that other cultic instruments, i.e., the laver and the anointment oil, are mentioned even later, when their use is described (30:17–21,23–30). Therefore, there is no textual evidence to deny the existence of an incense altar in the Tabernacle. Moreover, archaeological excavations in Ereẓ Israel have yielded many small altars – too small for animal offerings – dating back to the Bronze Age. Some actually approximate the dimensions of the Tabernacle incense altar and are even equipped with horns (Megiddo) (fig. 8). Thus, the incense altar would appear to be standard equipment for Canaanite temples.

Reference to the incense altar of Solomon's Temple is found in the construction account (I Kings 6:20–22; 7:48) and in the incense offering ascribed to King Uzziah (II Chron. 26:16). In his blueprint for the new Temple (Ezek. 41:22), Ezekiel may have been thinking of the incense altar he saw in the Temple (as a priest, he had access to it).

The term *hamman*, generally (but mistakenly) translated as "sun pillars," is mentioned in the context of illegal worship in Israel (Lev. 26:30; Isa. 17:8;19:9; Ezek. 6:4; II Chron. 14:4; 34:4,7). According to II Chronicles 34:4, its place was on the altar and thus it could not be very large. Its connection with incense was verified by the appearance of the word in a number of Nabatean and Palmyrean inscriptions, one of which is engraved on a small altar whose other side contains a bas-relief of two figures burning incense. Excavations at Lachish have produced small elongated objects whose cup-shaped upper portion bears traces of fire; plausibly these, too, may be classified as examples of a *hamman*.

HIGH PLACES

Typologically, a high place is merely a large altar. Once a simple altar standing in an open place reached a certain size and degree of popularity, it became a "high place." Its ritual functions remained limited to those of an altar: sacrificial offerings. For example, at Ramah, where Samuel lived, there was a high place at which the entire town would gather to sacrifice. It may have developed from the altar which Samuel built in his city (I Sam. 7:17).

W.F. Albright, however, suggested that the origin of the high place was a funereal installation which later took on other functions. Indeed, Josiah destroyed a cemetery near the cult place of Beth-El "there in the mountain" (II Kings 23:16–17). Albright's interpretation remains open to question; most of the evidence in support of it comes from Greek and other external contexts.

The Bible mentions high places at Gibeon (I Kings 3:4) and at Gibeah of the land of Benjamin where bands of prophets would prophesy (I Sam. 10:5,10,13). Jeroboam erected "houses of high places" (*bet bamot*, i.e. concentrations of altars) at Beth-El (I Kings 12:31) and in the cities of Samaria (I Kings 13:32). The *bet bamot* is not to be confused with *bet YHWH* or *bet elohim*, which refer to temples. The Moabite Mesha stele uses both terms, *bamah* and *bet bamot*, perhaps interchangeably, when speaking of that king's cultic activities.

A well-preserved pre-Israelite high place dating from the Early Bronze Age stands in the temple precincts at Megiddo (figs. 35, 36). It is a large circular

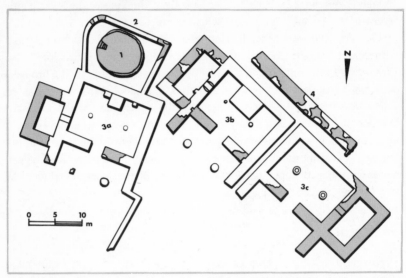

Figure 35:   Plan of sacred area from Early Bronze III at Megiddo: round high place (1); wall (2); three megaron temples (3a,b,c); temenos wall (4)

Figure 36:   Canaanite high place near remains of one of the three temples

platform of stones, with stairs leading up to it. It is likely that the altar stood on top of the high place, since large quantities of bones and potsherds were found in the earth deposits immediately above. Elsewhere the altar may have stood in front of the high place, which was kept for cultic stelae, statuaries, etc.

Biblical descriptions of cultic activity at the high place provide some details of its structure. Thus, Samuel ascended the high place at Ramah to bless the slain offering and subsequently to partake of it (I Sam. 9:13–14,19). When the sacred meal was over, he and those "called" to the celebration descended from the high place and reentered the city (9:25). The descent from the high place is also recorded at Gibeah (I Sam. 10:5,10,13). The text even mentions a special "chamber" where the thirty "bidden" people would eat of the sacrifice; after them all the people would eat thereof (9:12–24). If all of this activity actually occurred at the high place, it must have been a very large and complex installation. In any event, the place of the sacrifice itself was probably an open-air installation not intended to serve as a residence for the deity, as was the case of the temple, but rather as a site that the deity would visit when invoked.

The account of Samuel at Ramah states that the high place was located outside the city. Elsewhere too the Bible speaks of the "high places of the gates" (II Kings 23:8). During the 1969 excavations at Ashdod, a Middle Bronze installation of probable cultic function was unearthed outside the city wall, but it has not yet been fully interpreted. In 1966 the expedition under K. Kenyon in the Ophel area of ancient Jerusalem discovered a cult installation with two stelae (stone monoliths) above which stood an altar. The installation was almost immediately outside the contemporary city

Figure 37:
Canaanite
brick altar, c.
15th cent. B.C.E.,
uncovered at
Beth-Shean, with
two steps leading
up to it

Figure 38:   Two stone incense altars found in the Holy of Holies *(devir)* in the Arad temple

wall. This site dates from the 7th century B.C.E., and was apparently a pagan site, one of those condemned by the writer of the Books of Kings (II Kings 23:4; cf. Jer. 31:39).

Primarily on the basis of the location of the high places outside the city walls, Y. Kaufmann concluded that the Israelites did not adapt preexisting idolatrous cult places for their monotheistic needs, but constructed new installations at sites outside the settlements. Citing evidence pertaining to altars located outside the towns and in the open country, he thus minimized the connection between pre-Israelite and Israelite cultic activity. However, verification of any reconstruction of early Israelite religious practices would require more extensive knowledge about the history of particular sites than we have at present.

Historically, the main problem with respect to the Israelite high place is to determine when and to what extent it was considered a legitimate cult place by strict monotheistic standards. The "great high place" at Gibeon (I Kings 3:4) was certainly legitimate when Solomon offered sacrifices and experienced a theophany there shortly before construction of the Jerusalem Temple, notwithstanding the fact that the Ark had been brought to Jerusalem long before (*ibid*. 3:15). The Books of Kings regard the high places as illegitimate beginning with the time of Solomon, but the references are couched in the language of a later ideology.

It is reasonable to assume that the Israelite high place was differentiated from the avowedly idolatrous one that came into official disrepute late in the monarchic era, at about the time of the Assyrian conquest of the northern kingdom, roughly the last quarter of the 8th century B.C.E. Ahaz came under Assyrian influence in cultic matters (II Kings ch. 16–17), but his successor Hezekiah took measures to eliminate the high place as a legitimate Israelite cult site (*ibid*. ch. 18–19). There can be little doubt that Hezekiah's measures were aimed at bringing northern Israelites to Jerusalem, and at ridding the Israelite cult of foreign influences. Any success he might have achieved, however, was temporary, because of the long period of Assyrian influence under King Manasseh. It was not until Josiah ascended the throne of Judea, and Ashurbanipal king of Assyria died, that the attempt to eliminate the high place which had become a focal point for cultic pollution could be resumed in earnest.

About the year 622 B.C.E. Josiah carried out a reform which has been considered a turning point in Israelite religion. He dismissed the priests who had officiated at these cultic sites, and proceeded to destroy the high places in Jerusalem and its environs and in the cities of Judea. He was especially concerned to destroy the cultic center at Beth-El, which had undoubtedly kept many worshipers from Jerusalem (II Kings ch. 22–23).

It is interesting that Deuteronomy, which gives doctrinal expression to the illegitimacy of worship at local cult places, never uses the term *bamah* ("high place") but rather *makom* ("place") (e.g., Deut. 12:3), a generic term for a cultic installation (cf. Ex. 20:21), known outside the Bible primarily from Phoenician inscriptions.

TEMPLES

The biblical terms used to designate a temple are *bet YHWH* or *bet elohim*. These phrases have their origin in the thought processes of the ancient Middle East, where the temple was considered to be the dwelling (*bet* =

house) of the god. There, one provided for the deity's needs through the intermediary of special servants, the priests. Other biblical terms connoting a temple appear only infrequently and have additional applications, e.g. tent, hall, dwelling place.

Apart from several unspecified references, the term *mikdash* (sanctuary) is applied exclusively to two temples, at Shiloh and Jerusalem (e.g. I Sam. 1:7; I Kings 3:1). (The cult place established by David to house the Ark after it had been brought to Jerusalem was designated as *bet YHWH* (II Sam. 12:20).) The term *mikdash* is also extended to objects that partake of a measure of holiness (see e.g. Num. 18:19). It is also applied to the entire area of the house of the Lord (see Ex. 25:8; Ezek. 43:21; etc.) and is frequently used to designate a specific temple, whether within Erez Israel or outside its borders (Josh. 24:26; Isa. 16:12; etc.). Finally, it is applied to the Temple in Jerusalem (Isa. 53:18; Ezek. 5:11).

Structurally, the temple differs from the altar in its outer appearance, which reflects architecturally the concept of its being the dwelling place or house of God. The Israelite temple was equipped with furnishings and utensils which symbolized the presence of God at that place: an Ark, cherubs, a table for shewbread, a candelabrum, a curtain. Non-Israelite temples might also have a statue of the god in residence.

The cultic activities at the temple extended beyond those associated with the altar; although almost every temple had an altar (generally in its court-yard), the reverse was not true. The altar at the temple had greater status than other altars. The three pilgrim festivals were to be observed by sacrificing at a temple; visiting a local altar did not fulfill this obligation. In addition the firstlings of the animals, thanksgiving offerings, and other specific sacrifices were to be offered at a temple.

In contrast to the large number of altars, the Bible mentions only about a dozen temples (see below). Several temples coexisted with the Temple in Jerusalem, and served specialized functions that were not in direct competition with the latter's unique status. All these temples were founded long before the belief in a single, divine residence became official doctrine in the last period of the Israelite monarchy.

THE TABERNACLE

The main source of information regarding the portable sanctuary constructed by the Israelites in the wilderness at the command of the Lord may be found in two groups of verses: Exodus ch. 25–31 and ch. 35–40. The former chapters take the form of instructions on how to build the Tabernacle. The latter chapters are largely a repetition of the material, using the past tense, i.e. describing the execution of the instructions.

No trace of the Tabernacle has remained, but one may surmise that it resembled other sanctuaries in the ancient Near East in that it realized in architectural form the concept of a dwelling place for the divinity. As it is described in the Book of Exodus, the Tabernacle was partly a tent and partly a flat booth built of wood, animal skins, and woolen curtains. This would reflect the living patterns of the semi-nomadic Semitic tribes among whom the Israelites are included.

The Bible describes the appearance of the Tabernacle in detail. It was formed of ten curtains of violet, purple, and scarlet fabric with woven (embroidered) figures of cherubim. Each curtain measured 28 × 4 cubits (a cubit is about 1½ ft.). They were sewn together to form two sets of five curtains each. Attached to the long edge of each set were 50 loops of violet thread; the other two sides were joined by 50 gold clasps.

The curtains were supported by 20 *kerashim* ("planks") of acacia wood on the north, 20 on the south, and eight on the west (rear) wall. Each *keresh* was ten cubits high and 1½ wide, and was gold-plated. The thickness is not stated, but is variously estimated by the authorities as four fingers (c. three inches), half a cubit, and one cubit. An older view regarded the supports as solid boards, but such an assumption would make the structure unwieldy. Most exegetes now accept the view of A.R.S. Kennedy that *keresh* denotes a light, open frame, consisting of two side arms joined together at the top, the middle, and the foot by cross rungs, with two tenons projecting below. Such frames would have the added advantage of permitting the beautiful curtaining to be seen from the interior. Each frame was fitted, by means of the tenons, into two silver bases. Thus on three sides (north, south, west) the frames formed a continuous framework and the bases provided an unbroken silver foundation. The fourth, or east side, had no frames; it served as the entrance and was closed by a screen. The frames were further strengthened on each side by five bars of acacia wood overlaid with gold, which passed through gold rings; one bar ran across the whole length of the side, and above it were two bars of half this length, matched by two similar bars below it. It also appears (the instruction in Ex. 26:22–25 is obscure) that two frames were fastened to each corner on the west side, to serve as buttresses. In all there were 48 frames and 100 bases.

The curtains were placed lengthwise across the frames, forming a roof over the sanctuary and providing an excess of nine cubits on the north and south sides (9 + 10 + 9 cubits) and completely covering the rear end to the ground (since the shrine is 30 cubits long and the curtaining is 40 cubits). It seems that the extremities of the curtains were fastened at each end by clasps or loops to pegs affixed to the frames.

Over the curtaining was spread a "tent" formed of 11 curtains of goats' hair, each measuring 4 × 11 cubits. These were made into two sets of five and six curtains respectively, fastened together by 50 loops (perhaps of goats' hair) and bronze clasps. On the east side the first curtain was doubled and suspended over the front of the Tabernacle; along the three other sides, this covering reached to the ground. Alternatively there were 12 cubits hanging down, like the train of a dress, on the west side and the overlap in front was tucked under the curtaining. On top of this entire structure were spread, for protection from the weather, two more coverings (Ex. 26:14), one of rams' skins dyed red and the other of skins of tahash (dugong or dolphin; the exact meaning is in doubt). Possibly, in view of Exodus 40:19, there was one covering made of both kinds of skins.

The sanctuary was divided into two unequal parts by means of the *veil* (or veil of the screen), which was a beautiful portière, "skillfully worked," made of the same fabric as the curtains. It hung from golden clasps and was draped over four acacia pillars overlaid with gold and set in silver bases. This partition was placed 20 cubits from the entrance of the Tabernacle, exactly beneath the clasps that joined the two sets of curtains together. The inner room, a perfect cube of 10 cubits, was called the "*Holy of Holies*" or the "*Most Holy Place*," while the outer room, measuring 10 x 20 cubits, was known as the "*Holy Place*." In Solomon's Temple (see below) the two compartments, designated respectively *devir* and *heikhal*, were twice the size of the rooms in the Tabernacle, but retained the same proportion of one to two.

The eastern end of the Tabernacle was closed by "a screen for the door of the tent." It was made of less costly material than the veil, the fabric being embroidered but not with cherubim; it was suspended from golden hooks on five pillars of gold-plated acacia wood set in bronze bases. The fabric and the bases were like those of the screen in the court (see below).

The sanctuary was surrounded by a rectangular enclosure, measuring 100 cubits from east to west, and 50 cubits from north to south (a double square of 50 cubits each); it was called "the court of the Tabernacle" (Ex. 27:9). The area was screened by five white curtains "of fine twined linen" five cubits high, hung on 60 acacia pillars fixed into bases of bronze set five cubits apart. Each pillar had a silver fillet at the top and the linen curtains were attached to the pillars by means of silver hooks. Added rigidity was given to the pillar by cords and bronze pegs. The curtains on the north and south sides were 100 cubits long, that on the west was 50 cubits long, while the east side had two short curtains 15 cubits long, suspended from three pillars, which extended from the corners toward the center. This left an opening of 20 cubits in the middle, which was enclosed by a screen of fine linen embroidered in colors and hanging from four pillars.

The exact position of the Tabernacle within the court is not stated. The generally accepted view is that it was situated in the western square, its entrance being 50 cubits from the door of the court in the east, while on the north and south sides there was a space of 20 cubits between the Tabernacle and the curtains of the court.

ISRAELITE TEMPLES

The Bible provides very little direct testimony regarding early temples. That they existed can be deduced from biblical narratives that relate events generally associated with a temple, e.g. fulfilling a vow, or entering into a covenant with God. Moreover, any activity whose description concludes with the phrase "before the Lord" points to the existence of a temple, since this is a technical term associated with the divine service.

The most important temple in pre-monarchic times was located at Shiloh (Judg. 18:31). One tradition holds that it was the Tabernacle which remained at Shiloh after the conquest of Canaan (Josh. 18:1; 19:51). But another tradition holds that the temple at Shiloh was constructed of stone (I Kings 1:9; 3:3) and had doors (ibid. 3:15). This temple housed the most holy cultic object of the Israelite tribes, the Ark of the Covenant, and was thus the center of the religious union entered into by the tribes. It was apparently destroyed in the war with the Philistines, at the end of the period of the Judges (Jer. 7:12–14; 26:10; Ps. 78:60), in the 11th century B.C.E.

Excavations undertaken at Shiloh by several Danish expeditions have not unearthed the acropolis area of the site, where one would expect the temple to be found. Remains of walls of Iron Age construction indicate that the site had large dimensions, and the Bible alludes to chambers or buildings other than the sanctuary itself (I Sam. 3:2–3).

It is not clear why Shiloh was chosen as the site of this important temple. The selection of Jerusalem and most other important sites follows known patterns, but there is no evidence that the early Israelites were attracted to Shiloh by virtue of its prior religious, demographic, administrative, or strategic significance. The archaeological survey undertaken by the Israel Department of Antiquities in 1967–68 noted what appear to be the remains of small settlements in the area, dating approximately from the period of Israelite habitation. Shiloh is located several kilometers east of the ancient main road to Shechem (Judg. 21:19). It is reasonable to assume that it was selected as a cultic center for the Israelite tribes primarily because of its imposing position, and because it was fairly central in the early area of habitation.

Temples at Beth-El and Dan are also mentioned in narratives dating from the end of the period of the Judges. There are traditions that the Beth-El temple site was associated with Jacob (Gen. 28:22), and that the installation at Dan originated with the settlement of the tribe of Dan (Judg. 18:27–31). Jeroboam son of Nabat erected golden calves in both temples (I Kings 12:28–29), and thereafter each was known as a "royal sanctuary" (cf. Amos 7:13). Jeroboam also expanded the altar in the temple at Beth-El (I Kings 12:32), and built a special "house of high places" there (see above). It seems that the temple at Dan was destroyed when Naphtali was exiled by Tiglath-Pileser III in 732 B.C.E. (II Kings 15:29). The Temple at Beth-El was probably destroyed when the kingdom of Israel fell to Assyria in 721 B.C.E. In the reign of Josiah, who extended his rule over much of the northern kingdom, only the large altar and one cultic *asherah* statue (see p. 271) remained at Beth-El. Josiah burned the *asherah* and destroyed the altar together with the remaining high places in the kingdom (II Kings 23:15–19).

The site of Beth-El was partially excavated by W.F. Albright and further by J.L. Kelso. Massive remains were uncovered. Ancient Beth-El (now Beitin) is situated 3,965 ft. above sea level, about 10½ miles north of Jerusalem, on a site commanding major crossroads. The archaeological remains indicate the preeminence of Beth-El in pre-Israelite times and throughout almost the whole Israelite period. Among the finds was a cylinder seal with the images of a god and goddess and the name of the goddess Ashtoreth written in hieroglyphics, showing that Beth-El was undoubtedly an important Canaanite cultic site that was later appropriated by the Israelites for their own use.

In 1966 excavations were begun under A. Biran at Dan, situated in upper Galilee. Although conclusive evidence of a sanctuary at Dan is still unavailable, there can be little doubt of its existence in ancient times.

There is biblical evidence of a temple at Gilgal, near Jericho, dating from the period of the Judges and thereafter. This was one of the sites where Samuel judged; the others were Beth-El and Mizpeh (I Sam. 7:16). At Gilgal Saul was crowned king before the Lord (*ibid.*, 11:14–15), and there the Israelites gathered to make war against the Philistines (*ibid.* 13:4–15). After the war against Amalek, Saul brought to Gilgal the best of the spoils (I Sam. 15:12–21), and there Samuel hewed Agag in pieces before the Lord (*ibid.* v. 33). In the Books of Amos (4:4; 5:5) and Hosea (4:15; 9:15; 12:12), Gilgal is mentioned alongside Beth-El; but these citations may refer to Gilgal on Mt. Ephraim, near Beth-El.

Not far from Gilgal was Mizpeh, in the territory of Benjamin, where a temple existed in the period of the Judges (Judg. 20:1–3, 8–10). The importance of Mizpeh as a gathering place for the people is evidenced from I Samuel 7:5–12. The site was one of the centers of Samuel's activity, and there Saul was chosen king (I Sam. 10:17–24). At Gilgal Samuel wrote the book of the rules of the kingdom and laid it "before the Lord" (*ibid.*, v. 25). One tradition associates the temple at Mizpeh in Gilead with the covenant entered into by Jacob and Laban (Gen. 31:44–49).

The Bible ascribes the setting of the covenant established by Joshua between the tribes of Israel and the Lord to Shechem; there Joshua laid down statutes and ordinances and wrote them in a book (Josh. 24:1, 25–26). In the days of Abimelech, a temple dedicated to *ba'al berith* stood at Shechem, which was also called *Beth-El Berith* ("the house of the Lord of the covenant"). The temple housed a treasure of silver (Judg. 9:4,27,46), which was common to ancient temples. This temple, evidently Canaanite, is identified with the remains of a large building found in the 1956–63 excavations of Shechem.

The Bible also refers to temples at Nob (I Sam. 21:1–10), Hebron (II Sam. 2:4; 12:3; 15:7), Beth-Lehem (I Sam. 20:10), Ophrah in the territory of Manasseh (Judg. 8:27), and Gibeath Shaul (II Sam. 21:6,9). The Book of Judges (ch. 17–18) tells of a small temple built by Micah on Mt. Ephraim, for which he made a molten image, an *ephod* and teraphim (see p. 264,268), and to which he consecrated one of his sons as priest. All the appurtenances along with the priest were taken by the Danites and transferred to their own temple at Dan.

Excavations undertaken by Y. Aharoni from 1962 to 1967 at Arad (fig. 45), a town in the vicinity of Beer-Sheba, have uncovered the remains of a building that would qualify as a temple by virtue of its structure and contents, and in the light of what is known about the role of Arad during the period of the First Temple. It would appear to belong to the period of the Israelite monarchy; if so, it is the oldest Israelite temple uncovered thus far.

The sanctuary building at Arad measured approximately 50×40 ft., and consisted of two adjoining rooms, one large and one small. The entrances were along the east-west axis. There was a relatively large courtyard, and a row of rooms attached to the temple itself.

The large courtyard was divided into an inner and an outer portion by thin brick walls in which several threshold stones appear to be remnants of a more ancient altar. The smaller, inner courtyard may be compared to the "porch" of the Temple. Flanking the entrance to the large porch or hall (*ulam*) stood two stone slabs, evidently bases for pillars (which Aharoni compared to the Jachin and Boaz pillars (see p. 255) in the Temple of Solomon). The main room (*heikhal*) was a narrow room with entrances on its long side. The "Holy of Holies" (*devir*) was a small square area (5×5 ft.) in the western corner of the structure. It stood on a slightly higher level than the hall, and three steps led up to it. On the steps were two stone altars, 13 and 17 ft. high, respectively, carefully hewn and concave on their upper surface. On them traces of burnt organic material were found. There was also a niche with at least one cultic stele, a sacrificial altar, and other cultic appurtenances.

Figure 39:   Suggested reconstruction of Solomon's Temple. After C. Watzinger

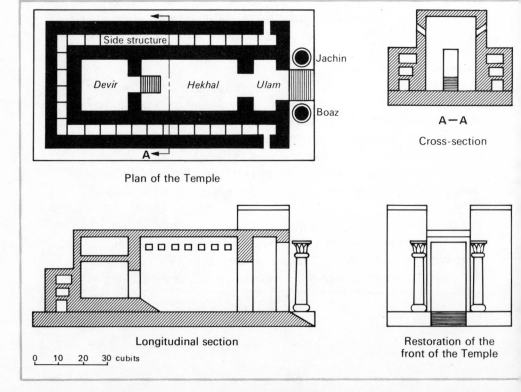

Plan of the Temple

A—A
Cross-section

Longitudinal section

Restoration of the
front of the Temple

0   10   20   30 cubits

It is likely that this building was in cultic use from the 10th down to the late 7th or early 6th century B.C.E. The presence of Levitical personnel at Arad is attested in the personal names which occur on the large numbers of ostraca found on the site. These brief communications and archival records reveal that Arad was in close communication with Jerusalem and leave no doubt that it was a legitimate cult place. Its location indicates, according to Aharoni, that it was a border installation with combined cultic and administrative functions, two institutions which often went together.

The Arad excavations are of primary importance for an understanding of the ancient Israelite cult. The existence of a sanctuary near the southern border of Judah suggests that certain religious duties had to be fulfilled on departure from the land of the God of Israel. Perhaps the accounts of votive activity by the patriarch Jacob while on his flight to Syria (Gen. ch. 28) and on his trek to Egypt (Gen. 46:1) reflect an early feature of Israelite religion, which rendered border sanctuaries necessary.

THE TEMPLE OF SOLOMON

The two principal sources of information regarding the plan of the First Temple erected on Mount Moriah in Jerusalem between the 4th and the 11th years of Solomon's reign are I Kings ch. 6—8 and II Chronicles ch. 2—4. But these accounts differ in several important details. The editor of Chronicles apparently based his information on the Book of Kings and on yet another source (unknown to us) whose description of the Temple plan varied considerable from the former account.

In this respect, one must also note other biblical references to the Temple built by Solomon, some of which complement, while others contradict, these two accounts (e.g. I Kings 10:12; II Kings, ch. 11). One might also seek clarification of the plan of the Temple in the description incorporated in Ezekiel's vision of the future Temple (ch. 40—46) and in the description of the Tabernacle (see above) — if one were able to be certain that Ezekiel's vision was a faithful rendering of what the prophet observed in his youth in Jerusalem; and if one could establish at what period the tradition of the Tabernacle was redacted, and on what it was based.

Josephus includes a detailed description of Solomon's Temple in his *Antiquities*. Evidently he based it on the rabbinic tradition which sought a compromise between the contents of the Books of Kings and Chronicles, and was also influenced by the plan of the Second Temple with which the Rabbis were familiar.

Potentially, the most dependable evidence regarding the plan of the First Temple derives from archaeological finds. Although they are few in number, they are significant in establishing certain principles. Of basic importance is the conclusion that parallels are not to be drawn from finds in contemporary strata of Mesopotamian and Egyptian excavations, since their cultural references differ completely from those of Israel. On the other hand, sites in northern Mesopotamia, Syria, and Phoenicia do provide important parallels to the Solomonic Temple. These sites constitute a

Figure 40:   Suggested reconstruction of Solomon's Temple. After T.A. Busink

unique chapter in the history of ancient religious archaeology.

A basic architectural element common to almost every one of these sites of the first half of the first millennium B.C.E. is what is known as the "king's citadel," a complex of buildings which form a special group of fortifications within a walled city, usually the capital city of a small kingdom. Generally, this complex includes a palace or series of palaces, a temple, and sometimes additional public buildings. Such a king's citadel has been found in excavations dating from the beginning of the Late Canaanite to the end of the Middle Israelite period, in all the countries along the eastern littoral of the Mediterranean.

Typological study of the various temples in this period points to three sources having architectural elements which are also attributed to the Temple of Solomon. The first is the Neo-Hittite kingdoms in northern Syria, especially Zenjirli, Tell Tainat, Alalakh (figs. 41, 42), and Hamath. In this area the temples had an outer courtyard.

They had an outer courtyard leading to an inner court, a "porch" sometimes flanked by free-standing or protruding pillars, a large hall, and a small Holy of Holies, built one after the other on the long axis of the building.

Other important elements are a sidewise casement structure and the fact that they were all part of the "king's citadel." The second source is the Canaanite Temple; there we find the tripartite division with a longer *heikhal* (as in Solomon's Temple) and we can track the development of the *devir* (Holy of Holies). These elements appear in the Canaanite temples at Lachish, Shechem (fig. 43), and Megiddo, Beth-Shean, Hazor (fig. 44), and finally the Israelite temple at Arad, which was erected in Solomon's period (fig. 45). The third source is the Phoenician area which as yet has not yielded any archaeological evidence. Biblical sources, however (I Kings 5:18), mention the fact that Phoenician builders helped construct Solomon's Temple, and it stands to reason that they have followed their own architectural design.

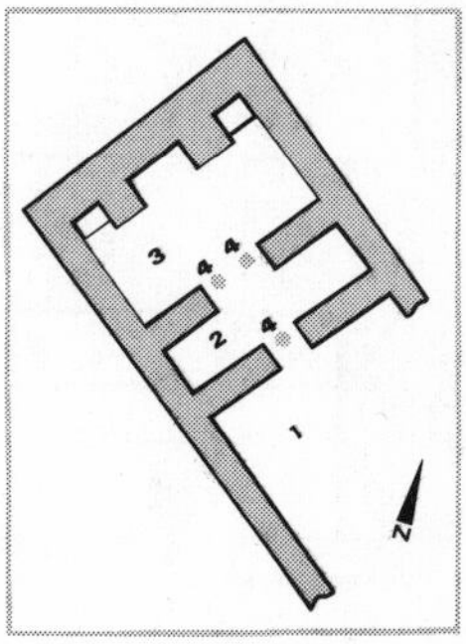

Figure 41:   Plan of temple 1a at Alalakh

(1) entrance hall; (2) main hall; (3) Holy of Holies; (4) column bases

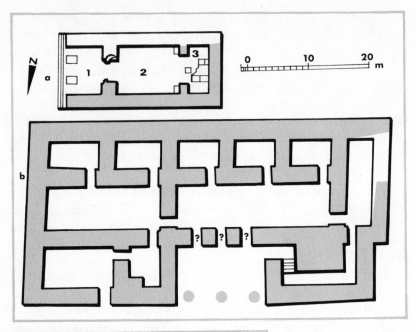

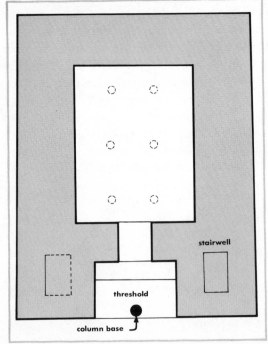

Figure 42: Plan of the temple at Tell Tainat (a) and the king's citadel (b) attached to it. The temple is divided into three sections: (1) entrance hall with two non-functional pillars; (2) long main hall; (3) Holy of Holies *(devir)*

Figure 43: Plan of Late Canaanite fortress-temple at Shechem

Figure 44: Model of Canaanite temple at Hazor, area H (14th cent. B.C.E.): (1) entrance hall *(ulam)*; (2) main hall *(heikhal)*; (3) Holy of Holies *(devir)*

As a result of this cumulative data, we may come to the conclusion that Solomon built a "king's citadel" to the north of the City of David (the Jebusite Jerusalem), on an area between the Ophel Hill and the Temple Mount, and upon the Mount itself. In this complex there was an outer court (I Kings 7:12) with a magnificent porch (*ibid.*, v. 6). In the courtyard stood two splendid structures: the House of the Forest of Lebanon and the Porch of the Chair (e.g. the porch of justice). The House of the Forest of Lebanon was so named because of its many cedar pillars, for which wood was imported from Mt. Lebanon.

Two inner courts opened from this "great court." One was the court of the king's palace; the other, the court of the Temple. According to the Bible, the palace was built south of the Temple, in the western area of the citadel complex. Thus, it would appear that the House of the Forest of Lebanon and the Porch of Justice were located in the east of the great outer court. The eastern section of this court was extended northward, and from this area a westward facing entrance led to the inner court of the Temple which was situated on the Temple Mount.

Figure 45: Reconstructed model of the temple at Arad: (1) courtyard;
(2) altar; (3) entrance hall *(ulam)*; (4) main hall *(heikhal)*; (5) Holy of
Holies *(devir)* with two small incense altars

THE DETAILED PLAN OF SOLOMON'S TEMPLE (figs. 39, 40)

The Temple was 100 cubits (about 165 ft.) long and 50 cubits wide (without the platform on which it was built; Ezek. 41:13—14). Adding together
the dimensions of the rooms of the Temple, the inner and outer wall, the
width of the storehouse — a three-story side structure divided into cells and
chambers which surrounded the Temple on three sides — and its walls, the
total equals almost exactly the dimensions mentioned by Ezekiel. The 2:1
proportion between the length and width of the outer measurements of the
Temple was also followed in the interior: the porch measured 20 cubits in
width and ten cubits in length (1:2); the main hall, 40 cubits in length and
20 cubits in width (2:1); while the Holy of Holies was a square (1:1). The
20 cubits width of the Temple was almost the maximum width which could
be roofed without supporting pillars. Thus the dimensions are not arbitrary
but were arrived at through precise planning.

The function of the porch was to separate the sacred precinct from the
profane. The Septuagint version of Ezekiel 40:49 cites the number of steps
which led to the Temple: "and they ascended it by ten *(eser)* steps" instead

of the original text "and it was by steps that (*asher*) it was ascended." The width of the porch was 20 cubits, and its depth was 10 cubits. The height of the porch is not certain. The only source which mentions its height — 120 cubits — is II Chronicles 3:4 and the text is apparently corrupt. One proposal corrects this to 20 cubits on the basis of the Syriac translation and largely on conjecture, but this is not accepted by all scholars. Some suggest that the porch rose above the main hall, like a tower, following the description in II Chronicles (this interpretation was followed by the builders of the Second Temple). Others lower the porch, and still others conclude from the silence on this point in the main source in the Book of Kings that the height of the porch was the same as the general height of the building (30 cubits). On both sides of the entrance stood supporting pillars, Jachin and Boaz, see p. 225, each 3 cubits wide and 5 cubits thick; the width of the entrance gate was 14 cubits (23 ft.).

The main room (*heikhal*) was entered from the porch through a gate, 10 cubits wide, in which two doors of cypress wood were set. The doorposts, made of olive wood, were apparently composed of four frames set one within the other, like those found in the temple of Tell Tainat. The thickness of the walls between the porch and the main room was 6 cubits. The latter was the largest chamber of the Temple, measuring 40 X 20 cubits (approximately 66 X 33 ft.) X 30 cubits in height. These dimensions were considerable in comparison with those of other Near Eastern temples. The main room served as the principal chamber for divine service.

The word *heikhal* is borrowed from the Akkadian. W.F. Albright maintains that the ancient Canaanite temples initially consisted of one large hall only, called *heikhal*, and that when porches were eventually added on both ends, the name *heikhal* came to denote the principal middle chamber.

The windows of the main room were set in its upper part, since the flanking structure mentioned above rose to about half its height. In the Bible they are called "windows with recessed frames" (I Kings 6:4), a term which is not entirely clear and which has been variously interpreted. By analogy with ivory reliefs found at Samaria, Arslan-Tash, and Nimrud, it may be assumed that these windows were of the type common in that period in Syria and Palestine, i.e., wide on the outside and narrowing toward the inside, an effect achieved by the use of window frames set one within the other (see above, p. 37).

The Holy of Holies, the rear part of the Temple, was designed to serve as a tabernacle for the Ark of the Covenant and the cherubim (see p. 249). Its interior measurements were 20 X 20 X 20 cubits. The 10 cubits difference in height between the Holy of Holies and the main hall has been explained in various ways. Busink suggests that the Holy of Holies was laid as an independent unit — the tabernacle — under the main roof of the Temple. According to K. Galling, the floor level of the Holy of Holies was raised 10 cubits. But the most reasonable solution is perhaps the combination of a slight elevation of the floor, as was common in Canaanite temples, and a lowering of the roof level. It may be assumed that the raised floor of the Holy of Holies served as a sort of platform on which the ark and the cherubim stood (a hint of this may be found in Isa. 6:1).

The jambs of the *devir* gate, in which olive wood doors were set, were constructed like the main room gate and the Temple windows, that is, of five frames set one within the other (I Kings 6:31). There were no windows in the Holy of Holies.

R. de Vaux maintains that the wall between the main hall and the Holy of Holies was merely a thin partition of cedarwood, since the Bible treats the main room and the Holy of Holies as one unit and gives their combined length in one figure — 60 cubits, with that of the main room 40 cubits, and that of the Holy of Holies 20 cubits. Had a dividing wall separated them, their combined length would have exceeded 60 cubits by the addition of the thickness of that wall. De Vaux accordingly emends the text of I Kings 6:16 to read: "He built twenty cubits on the rear of the house with boards of cedar from the floor to the rafters, and *they were a separation* [instead of "he built them for himself"] within the *devir*, as the most holy place." However, a gate made of five frames would necessitate an extremely thick wall, rather than a partition, and evidence of such a substantial wall is provided by the Canaanite and Greek temples and by that of Tell Tainat.

The adjacent building (*yaẓi'a*), whose walls ran parallel to those of the Temple and surrounded it on all sides except the front, was of three stories of varying widths. The inner width of the rooms of the lowest story was 5 cubits and to lay the beams of the roof which formed the floor of the second story, the thickness of the walls was reduced so that the width of the rooms of the second story was 6 cubits and of the third story, 7 cubits. Each story was divided into about 30 chambers. The entrance to this side structure was, according to I Kings 6:8, on the south side, while, according to Ezekiel 41:5—6, it was entered on both sides. The upper stories were reached by *lulim*, i.e., apertures in the shapes of holes. In this building the numerous Temple vessels, utensils, and treasures were stored. The building was a little over 15 cubits high, with each story 5 cubits (about 8.2 ft.) high. A later date for this building has been proposed by some scholars.

THE TEMPLE OF ZERUBBABEL

The Jerusalem Temple is a major focus of attention in post-Exilic biblical books. Deutero-Isaiah foretells that Cyrus shall be divinely charged with the task of restoring the Temple (Isa. 44:28). The Chronicler ends his account (II Chron. 36:22–23) and the Book of Ezra begins its account with the fulfillment of this prophecy (Ezra 1:1ff.), referring to the earlier word of Jeremiah (cf. Jer. 29:10). Issued in 538 B.C.E., after his conquest of Babylon, Cyrus' declaration relates the return to Zion exclusively to the reconstruction of the Temple. The repatriates were to be aided by the Jews remaining behind, and by their gentile neighbors. Temple vessels taken as booty by Nebuchadnezzar were delivered by the treasurer Mithridates to the Davidic prince Sheshbazzar for return to Jerusalem (Ezra 1:7ff.).

Although one source credits Sheshbazzar, giving him the title of governor, with having indeed laid the foundations for the Temple (Ezra 5:14ff.), another gives his nephew (?) Zerubbabel and the priest Jeshua this honor. Despite intimidation from their neighbors, they established an altar in the seventh month (year ?), reinstituted the sacrificial cult, and offered up the special sacrifices required for the festival of Tabernacles. All was performed "as written in the Torah of Moses the man of God" (Ezra 3:1ff.).

Masons and carpenters were engaged for the construction, and cedars from Lebanon were ordered from the Sidonians and Tyrians, to be shipped to Jaffa. Expenses were to be borne by the royal treasury and a memorandum of a royal decree to this effect was recorded in the archives in Ecbatana in Media. It included the dimensions of the Temple and the architectural specification that it was to be built with three courses of stone and one of timber (Ezra 3:7; 6:1ff.). A similar feature was recorded in connection with the courtyard of Solomon's Temple (I Kings 6:36; 7:12).

There is no detailed description of the Second Temple dating from the pre-Maccabean period, but scattered references provide a partial picture of its plan and furnishings. Like its predecessor, the Second Temple had two courtyards (Zech. 3:7; Neh. 13:7; cf. Isa. 62:9; I Macc. 4:38,48). Hecataeus of Abdera, a Greek historian of the 4th century B.C.E., described the inner court as being five pilasters, the equivalent of 500 Greek cubits, in length, and 100 cubits in width (Jos., *Contra Ap.* 1,22), although he may have known these measurements only by hearsay. Alcimus began to destroy the wall of this courtyard (which the author of the Book of Maccabees calls "the work of the prophets"), but died before he could complete the task (I Macc. 9:54–55; cf. *Mishnah Middot* 2,3).

Contrary to Ezekiel's account, the inner court was not limited to the priests alone (cf. Neh. 8:16), and in post-Herodian days the women's court and the Israelite court were situated here, as is evident from the fact that King Alexander Yannai (Janneus) erected a wooden fence to separate the priestly enclosure from the other areas of the court (*Ant.* 13:13,5).

Both the inner and the outer courtyards had several gates (cf. I Macc. 4:57; II Macc. 1:8). Those specified by Nehemiah included the Water Gate (3:26; 8:1,3,16; 12:37). The broad place before the Water Gate (8:1) is to be identified with the broad place before the House of the Lord (Ez. 10:9); the gate is not to be confused with the Water Gate in Herod's Temple (*Mishnah Middot* 1,4). Other gates named by Nehemiah are the Gate of the Guard (12:39), the Gate of Ha-Mifkad (3:31), and the East Gate (3:29). These four gates evidently were in the wall of the outer court. According to Hecataeus there were two gates in the wall of the inner court (*Contra Ap.* 1,22), but more gates were evidently added in the course of time.

Both courts contained chambers (Ez. 8:29; I Macc. 4,38; *Ant.* 11:4,7). Most of them were located in the outer court, and served as storage rooms for the heave offerings and tithes, supplies for the meal offerings, incense, and silver and gold vessels (Neh. 10:38–40; 12:44; 13:5,9). Some were used by the high priests or by the princes. Four such private chambers are known: the chamber of Jehohanan son of Eliashib (Ez. 10:6), the chamber of Eliashib the priest (Neh. 13:4); the large chamber assigned by Eliashib to his relative, Tobiah, from which the latter was evicted by Nehemiah (Neh. 13:5–9); and the chamber of Meshullam son of Berachiah (Neh. 3:30).

The altar in the Second Temple was erected on the site of the first altar (Ez. 3:3). After it had been desecrated by the decree of Antiochus, the Maccabees dismantled it, stored its stones in a special place on the Temple Mount, and built a new altar. The rebuilt altar was constructed of great blocks of stones fit together (*Contra Ap.* 1,22). The Herodian altar had much larger dimensions than its predecessor, and a sloping access ramp was built on its southern side (*ibid.*, 3, 1–3). It is not known whether the pre-Maccabean altar had such a ramp.

As was the case in the construction of the First Temple, the sanctity of the building precluded the use of hewn rocks on which metal, the tool of warfare, had been used. The great stone walls of the Temple were strengthened with wood (Ez. 5:8; 6:4). The measurements of the Second Temple, as recorded in the archives (Ez. 6:3), were 60 cubits in height and 60 cubits in width. However, the width would appear to be exaggerated; it is suggested that the width should be 20 cubits. All the measurements would then conform to the inner dimensions of the Herodian Temple, in which the hall was 40 cubits in length, the Holy of Holies 20 cubits, the partition between them measuring 1 cubit, with the width of the hall equal to the length of the Holy of Holies. The inner height of the hall in the Herodian Temple was 40 cubits, but a second story of 40 cubits stood above it. With the addition of ceilings, plaster, eaves and rainspouts, the total height came to 100 cubits (*Mishnah Middot* 4,6).

7

FORTIFICATIONS

The historical portions of the Bible, from the period of the conquest of Canaan through the period of the monarchy, provide considerable information about contemporary military constructions — fortifications, citadels, garrison cities, etc. Much of this information has been verified or expanded through archaeological research which has shed new light on the fortification and razing of cities during this period of social and political ferment.

In general, one may say that the Canaanite culture of the Middle Bronze II B–C, with its massive fortifications, played a role in the fortifications of the Late Bronze period. Archaeological research found the Middle Bronze period distinguished mainly by its excellent fortifications, whereas the Late Bronze appears to be a period of highly developed cultural life with uninteresting remains of fortifications or none at all. Thus scholars suggest that the fortifications of the Middle Bronze (fig. 46a-b), which were so massively and strongly built, were at least partially reused in the Late Bronze period as well. A good example is Jericho (fig. 47a-b).

JERICHO

Interestingly, the archaeological excavations at Jericho, the site of one of the most dramatic of biblical battles during the Israelite conquest of Canaan, have not been able to clarify the questions which biblical scholars have raised about this event (see above, p. 5).

The biblical narrative relates how, for seven days, Joshua and all the Israelites made a daily circuit around the city walls, and how, on the seventh day, they made seven circuits, after which the people raised a great shout and the wall surrounding the city fell. The fortifications of the Middle Bronze period at Jericho revealed typical elements of Middle Bronze fortifications: a plastered glacis of beaten earth with a brick wall on top of it. In the course of time, two more glacis were added on top of the first one; the last of them was a stone glacis. The glacis was built c. 1750 and destroyed c. 1550 B.C.E.

In the Late Canaanite period the place was resettled, but no evidences of the walls conquered by Joshua were uncovered. The destruction of the Late Canaanite city is dated to the middle 13th century B.C.E. Thus it is possible

Figure 46:   Schematic drawing of the typical elements in Middle Bronze fortifications
46a: (1) fosse (moat); (2) glacis; (3) layers of beaten earth; (4) layers of stones (usually of MB IIc); (5) natural slope of mound; (6) retaining wall; (7) city wall
46b: Cross section of a rampart

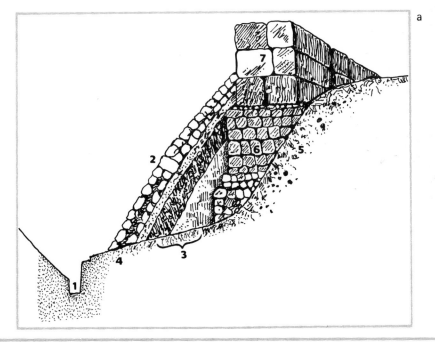

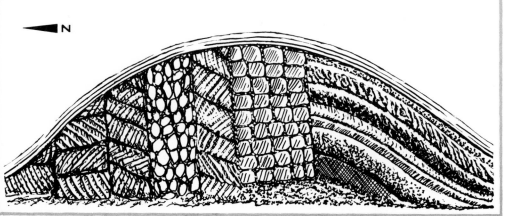

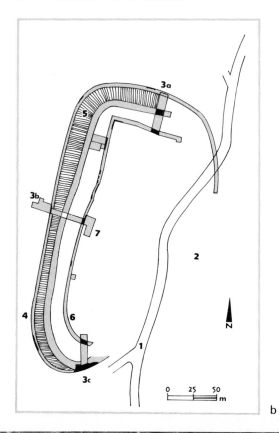

Figure 47:   Aerial view
(47a) and plan (47b) of
Tel al-Sultan.
(1) modern road;
(2) Elisha fountain;
(3a–c) Kenyon's shaft;
(4) retaining wall;
(5) glacis of the Middle
Bronze II period;
(6) Early Bronze wall;
(7) Neolithic tower

that either the Late Bronze wall was eroded, or that the Middle Bronze fortifications proved adequate in the Late Bronze period.

HAZOR

Hazor was one of the greatest of the city states in Canaan at the time of the Israelite conquest. Hazor, situated in Upper Galilee, headed the northern coalition which opposed Joshua and the invading Israelites. According to

Figure 48:   Aerial view of Hazor, showing: (1) the upper tell; (2) the lower tell; (3) rampart; (4) glacis (for details of the areas see pp. 88, 89)

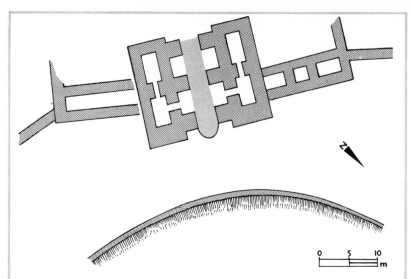

AREA C

AREA B

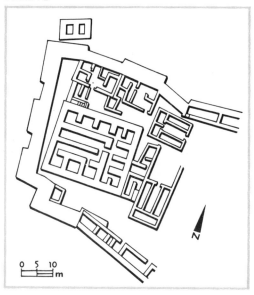

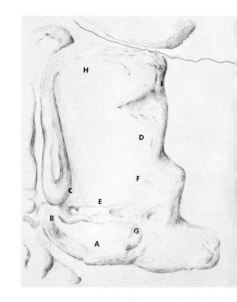

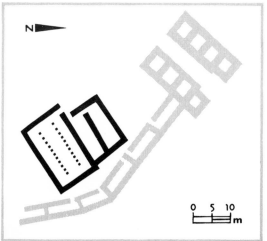

AREA A

AREA C

the Bible it was, apart from Jericho, the only city which was completely burnt by Joshua (Josh. 11:10–13).

At the time of its conquest the city consisted of two major parts (figs. 48, 49): the upper tell covering some 30 acres and rising to a height of about 40 m, and a large lower city spread over a plateau of about 175 acres. The upper tell was fortified in the Middle Bronze period by a heavy wall with towers and a deep, narrow fosse (moat). In the Late Bronze period no fortifications were uncovered, though traces of occupation in this period were found. The lower tell was fortified by defense structures, which is a hallmark of the Middle Bronze period: in the east the natural barrier was strengthened by retaining walls and glacis. On the north and west sides, where the topography did not form a natural barrier, the lower city was enclosed by a mighty rampart of beaten earth. At the bottom of the western rampart, a deep and wide fosse had been dug, the earth from which had been used to build the rampart. On the northeast side of the lower city a series of gates from the Middle Bronze and Late Bronze periods were uncovered. They were all, except the first one, constructed according to a similar principle: a massive gate which had a threefold entrance formed by three pairs of pilasters (pillars adjoining the wall) that jutted out into the entrance passage one after the other on the long axis. Such a gateway is typical of the late Middle Bronze Age period. In Hazor, the approach to the city gate was by a sloping ramp which was supported by a high retaining wall made up of large boulders. The ramp rose parallel to the wall, so that the entry into the gate was at right angles to it.

These massive fortifications dating from the Middle Bronze period continued in use in the Late Bronze Age, the only difference being that the gateway was rebuilt with huge and well-dressed stone blocks and the wall of the city adjoining the gate, which had been of the casemate type (see p. 94 below), was at one stage replaced by a single solid wall of brick about 12 ft. wide. These defenses were most formidable, but Joshua seems to have taken the town without any great effort, for the king of Hazor and its army had been defeated previously at the battle of Merom (Josh. 11:1–9). Jericho and Hazor were the two most important conquests made by Joshua. Other cities such as Megiddo and Beth-Shean remained in Canaanite hands until a later period.

Figure 49:   Drawing of the excavated areas at Hazor with details concerning fortifications: (A) Solomon's gate and casemate wall; (B) Ahab's citadel and offset-inset wall; (G) Middle Bronze fortifications with round tower shaped like a glacis and a moat; (I) Late Bronze gate and casemate wall above the glacis. (In areas H, D, F, E, and C no fortification elements were discovered)

LAISH

Another case where the massive Middle Bronze defenses evidently remained in use until the conquest by the Israelites is in the far north of Israel, at the city of Laish, which after the conquest was renamed Dan. A great rampart, estimated to have been over 30 ft. high, surrounded the town. Its central core was a high wall over 20 ft. wide, built of medium-sized unhewn stones. On both sides of this wall, earth was piled in layers until the high rampart was formed (fig. 46b). The site outside the wall was then covered by a final hardened layer of earth to form a "glacis" (a sloping bank or defensive wall). The final slope to the top of the rampart was at an angle of about 40°. These fortifications were evidently built at the end of the 18th century B.C.E. and were repaired several times during the following centuries prior to the capture of the town by the Danites. It is not surprising that the inhabitants of Laish felt "secure" within such fortifications: "And [the Danites] came into Laish, unto a people quiet and secure, and smote them with the edge of the sword; and they burnt the city with fire ... And they built the city, and dwelt therein. And they called the name of the city Dan ... ; howbeit the name of the city was Laish at the first" (Judg. 18:27–29).

The destruction of this Canaanite town is evidenced by a layer of ash which marks the end of the Late Bronze Age city. The Danites rebuilt and used the same fortifications until the town was again destroyed in the middle of the 11th century B.C.E.

SHECHEM

Many of the wars described in the Book of Judges were fought in the open field. The outstanding exception, apart from Laish-Dan, is the capture and devastation of Shechem by Abimelech, the son of Gideon (Judg., ch. 9). Abimelech, in contrast to his father, who refused the kingship, had himself crowned by the elders of Shechem after murdering his 70 brothers. But his rule did not last long; after three years the Shechemites had evidently had enough of Abimelech and rebelled.

Although the account of the following battle is not quite clear, the sequence of events seems to have been as follows: Abimelech was informed of the insurrection by Zebul, who was in charge of the city on his behalf, and who summoned him to come and reassert his authority. Abimelech thereupon advanced upon the city at dawn, and Gaal, the leader of the insurgents, went out to meet him in battle. Gaal was defeated, and Abimelech pursued him as far as the city-gate but evidently did not succeed in entering the city. Gaal was, however, driven out of the city by Zebul.

The following day Abimelech set an ambush, and as the townsfolk went out to work their fields, he fell upon them and then managed to force an entry to the city. By nightfall Abimelech had captured the town, which he promptly razed and sowed with salt. A last resistance to Abimelech was made by the "men of the tower of Shechem" who entered the *zeriaḥ* (perhaps the hold) of the house of El-berith (El of the Covenant). This building was then set afire, and some thousand men and women died in the inferno (Judg. 9:22–49).

The salient points in the story are that Abimelech succeeded in forcing the gateway when the townsfolk were evidently not expecting further hostilities, and that there was a temple-citadel to which the survivors fled and which Abimelech set on fire.

Figure 50:   Plan of Tell Shechem and drawing of cyclopean wall near the North Gate

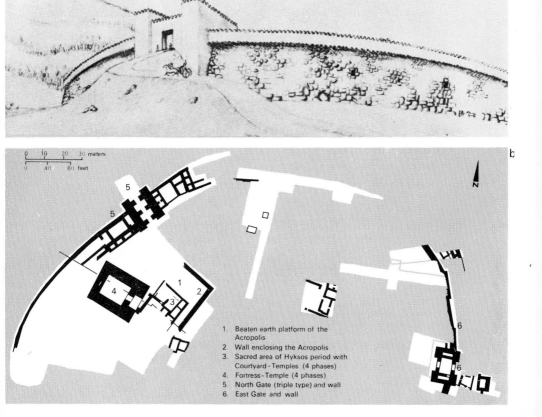

1. Beaten earth platform of the Acropolis
2. Wall enclosing the Acropolis
3. Sacred area of Hyksos period with Courtyard-Temples (4 phases)
4. Fortress-Temple (4 phases)
5. North Gate (triple type) and wall
6. East Gate and wall

According to G.E. Wright this fits the archaeological finds excavated at Tell Balatah, the site of ancient Shechem (fig. 50b). The town was surrounded by a heavy wall (known as a cyclopean wall) (fig. 50a) which was made up of large boulders, some of which were 6½ ft. in width. These were fit roughly on top of each other and the intervening spaces were filled in with smaller stones. This wall, which dates from the late Middle Bronze period, had been strengthened by heavy buttressing and formed the outer defense. A sloping glacis extended upwards from the wall and this was again topped by a casemate wall. This is a construction consisting of two parallel walls, a heavy outer one and a lighter inner one, connected by crosswalls which form chambers or "casemates" between the two walls. In Shechem the complete casemate wall, including the space between the two walls, was over 20 ft. wide. The foundations were built of stone, while the superstructure was built of brick. With such strong defenses it is no wonder that Abimelech did not attempt to breach the walls.

The gateway (Wright's "East Gate") (fig. 50b, 6) was defended by two towers and had a double entrance whose doors were protected by two sets of protruding blocks. Immediately behind the entrance lay the guardrooms. The approach road lay parallel to the wall from the south, so that any attackers advancing toward the gate came under fire long before they reached it. According to the biblical text, Abimelech took a special force under his personal command to capture the gateway after it had been opened and the townsmen had gone out to the fields.

Inside the city, across the town, remains of a four-phase fortress temple (fig. 43) of the late Middle Bronze Age and the Late Bronze Age were found. This was a rectangular room with a podium at one end, somewhat similar to a Canaanite temple in Megiddo. In front of the temple were two sacred pillars (*Mazzevot*) and the base of a nonfunctional column. The walls of the Late Bronze Age temple, while not as wide as the earlier fortress temple, were still some 6½–7½ ft. thick and must have belonged to a structure of great strength. Wright maintains that this building is to be identified with the temple of El-berith mentioned in the Abimelech episode; the citadel which served as the site of the town's final resistance, and which was burnt by Abimelech (see above, p. 91).

Thus, archaeological excavations at Shechem have confirmed the topographical and architectural details of the war of Abimelech: the town defenses, the gateway that was forced, and the temple that served as a citadel after the fall of the city.

GIBEATH-SHAUL

In the time of Saul, first king of Israel, the Philistines were the main enemy of the Israelites, and most of Saul's reign was taken up with wars against them. Excavations carried out just north of Jerusalem, at Tell al-Fūl, have been identified with Gibeath-Shaul, which was Saul's royal residence and the capital from which he ruled his kingdom (I Sam. 11:4; 15:34; 22:6; 23:19).

The excavations revealed the remains of a rectangular fortress tower, dating from the Iron Age. Casemate walls extending from the sides of the tower indicate that it was part of a more extensive fortress. The tower showed clear signs of having been rebuilt. The earlier section was constructed of large rough stones, while the later part was more carefully built of more finely cut stones. The later section also had small apertures which must have allowed air and light to filter into the cellar rooms. The earlier tower had been destroyed by fire, and a layer of ash was found, which may be the remains of the woodwork used inside the fortress. Both fortresses belong to roughly the same period, and are dated to the 11th century B.C.E.

Scholars are agreed that one of the fortresses must represent the efforts made by Saul to fortify his royal capital. Some scholars maintain that the earlier fortress was built by the Philistines and that it was captured and burnt by Saul, who later rebuilt it. More probable is the theory that the fortress was originally built by Saul, destroyed by the Philistines after the battle of Gilboa, and rebuilt later by David. The fortress, though strongly built, does not display the finesse of later fortifications. It does, however, provide an early example of the Israelite use of the casemate wall (though not all scholars agree that the fortress walls were actually casemates).

CITY OF DAVID

The fortress at Gibeah is the only system of fortifications to date which scholars definitely associate with Saul. Remains of fortifications, which can be ascribed to Israel's next king, David, are even less verifiable. The Bible establishes that it was David who made the historic decision to establish Jerusalem as his capital, and it has remained the sanctified center of the Jewish people ever since. Until its capture Jerusalem had been a Canaanite-Jebusite city which evidently contained a citadel called the Fortress of Zion.

David took possession of this citadel and called it the City of David (II Sam. 5:7–9). David further "built round about from Millo and inward" (II Sam. 5:9), but nowhere is it specifically stated that David fortified Jerusalem. It was not until the excavations of Kathleen Kenyon that the question of the walls of the Davidic city was finally settled.

South of today's Old City of Jerusalem is a low elongated hill on which stood the Jebusite town. It was bounded on the east side by the steep Gihon valley, and on the west (originally) by the Tyropoean valley which is now filled in and hardly noticeable. These two valleys met at the southern extremity of the hill. To the north there was a depression (saddle) which separated the hill from the plateau which afterward formed the Temple Mount. It was on the steep eastern slope of the Jebusite hill that Kathleen Kenyon found the remains of a large, heavy wall dating to the Middle Bronze Age (fig. 51). This wall was fairly low down the side of the hill. Immediately above it was another wall which was found to date to the 7th century B.C.E., about the time of King Hezekiah. There were no fortifications which could be dated between these two constructions.

The conclusion reached by Kathleen Kenyon and accepted by other scholars was that David reused the ancient Middle Bronze wall to fortify his city, and that this wall remained in use until about the time of Hezekiah — a period of about 1,000 years. This would fit the biblical account, which does not mention any fortification built by David in Jerusalem. The Millo, referred to above, is explained by Kenyon to mean the fill used for terracing the steep eastern side of the hill. This had to be periodically renewed owing to the constant erosion of the soil on such a steep slope (cf. II Chron. 32:5, where Sennacherib strengthened the Millo).

CASEMATE WALLS

It was during the Solomonic period that the building of fortifications throughout Israel entered a new phase. This period is marked in many of the major archaeological sites by the frequent appearance of the casemate wall, and of a new type of fortified gate, somewhat similar to that of the late Middle Bronze period.

The origin of the casemate wall is ascribed to Asia Minor, where it is associated with the Hittites, and where it is found at various sites of the Late Bronze period. From Asia Minor it is supposed to have reached Israel via Syria. Yadin found a perfect example of a casemate wall in use in Israel

Figure 51:   Excavations in the south hill at Jerusalem (Ophel) which
revealed (1) Jebusite city wall, (2) Israelite city wall

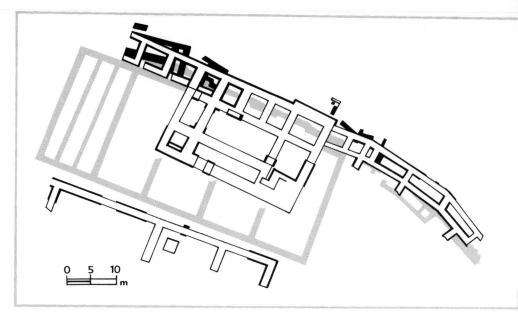

Figure 52: Excavated area near the gate showing Solomonic casemate wall and palace at Hazor. In Ahab's time the casemates were filled and an offset-inset wall took its place, while stables took the place of the palace.

as early as the Middle Bronze Age in the 17th—16th centuries B.C.E. at Hazor (figs. 31, 52, 56) which is the earliest known example in the country. The advantage of this type of wall lies in its great strength on the one hand and the saving of labor and material on the other. The outer wall was usually about 5½ ft. wide, while the inner was just under 4 ft. wide. The space between the two walls forming the casemates was frequently filled in with stones or earth in the lower levels, so that the actual thickness of the wall was doubled or trebled. At the upper levels (and sometimes at unassailable points on the lower levels) the space between the walls could be used for guardhouses, storerooms, armories, or even living quarters. The construction of two thinner walls had a clear economic advantage, even if the casemates were filled in, over the laborious process of building a solid stone or brick wall some 13 ft. in width.

The casemate wall has become a hallmark of Solomon's defensive systems. Remains of a casemate wall were found just north of the Ophel in Jerusalem. This probably represents the joining of David's city with the Temple Mount, which Solomon incorporated into the city when he built the Temple. The finding of a broken proto-Aeolian capital (fig. 19) at this spot strengthens this supposition, according to Kathleen Kenyon, as such capitals were used for major buildings and Solomon's palace could not have been far distant.

But it is at the three sites of Gezer (fig. 76), Hazor, and Megiddo that Solomon's casemates are most clearly identified. Here they are associated with the "Solomonic gate," a new type of fortified entrance which has become a hallmark of his construction.

THE SOLOMONIC GATE

The Solomonic gate bears a remarkable resemblance to the east gate of the Temple as described by Ezekiel (40:5—17). The excavated gates consist of two square towers and three pairs of buttresses. These narrow the passage-way and form six chambers which most probably served as guardrooms or armories. The entrance through the gate was in a straight line, but the approach to the gate was, at any rate in the case of Megiddo and Gezer, at an angle and first passed through an outer gate. The straight entrance through the gate, rather than a turning in the gateway itself, seems to imply the use of chariots, for it would be impossible for chariots to turn inside the narrow gateway. The approach therefore was generally alongside the wall, and a space was cleared in front of the gate which allowed the chariots to turn there. In this way the enemy would be exposing his flank when he attacked the gate, which was always the vulnerable spot in the city's

Figure 53: Plan of the main structures uncovered in Megiddo from the time of Solomon and Ahab

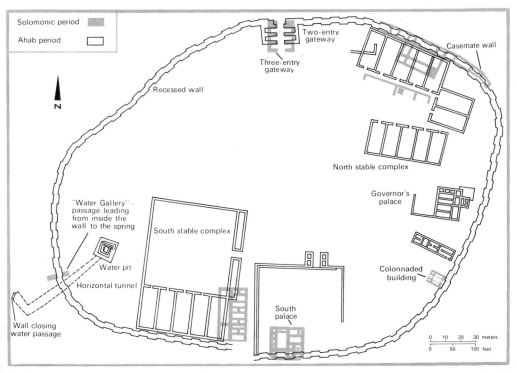

defenses. Although there had previously been some argument as to the date of the Megiddo gate, the discovery of an identical gate at Hazor proved them both to be Solomonic.

Figure 54:   Iron Age gates in Megiddo (for the previous gate, see fig. 4)

Figure 54a: (1) stratum VIa: one-entry pre-Solomonic gateway (11th cent. Philistine?); (2) stratum Va—IVb: three-entry Solomonic gateway with casemate wall (950—924); (3) stratum IVa1: reused Solomonic gateway on raised level with offset-inset wall

Figure 54b: Post-Solomonic gates: (1) stratum IVA: two-entry gateway (c. 875—850, Omri period); (2) stratum III: one-entry gateway of the Assyrian period (c. 733/2—630)

Figure 54c: Half of the three-entry gateway at present. It shows: (1) the original Solomonic phase; (2) the second phase of this gate when its level was raised (one of the entries is still closed); (3) part of the post-Solomonic two-entry gateway

a

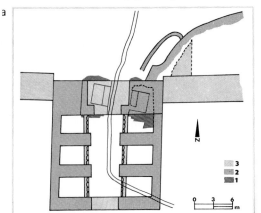
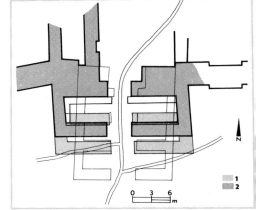

c

From his knowledge of the gate at Megiddo (fig. 54a) and Hazor (figs. 31, 49) Yadin had guessed that the gate at Gezer (which had previously been described as a "Maccabean castle") would be identical. He based this guess on the biblical text which mentions the three cities together as having been built by Solomon. "And this is the account of the levy which King Solomon raised; to build the house of the Lord, and his own house and Millo and the wall of Jerusalem, and Hazor, and Megiddo, and Gezer" (I Kings 9:15). This was verified in the 1967–71 excavations at Gezer. It was therefore clear that the casemates as well as this type of gateway were Solomonic.

Megiddo (fig. 53), however, presented a problem which Yadin termed "the fly in the ointment" preventing a perfect analogy of the three cities. As the Bible specifically mentioned Solomon's chariot cities — though not necessarily identifying Megiddo as such — scholars had attributed the stables discovered at Megiddo to Solomon. The excavators of Megiddo found that the stables were in the same stratum as a solid "offset and inset" wall, and since this wall was attributed to Solomon, the stables were also attributed to him. However, a palace in the southern tell, undoubtedly belonging to the Solomonic period (10th century) was found underneath the offset and inset wall. Yadin determined to find the explanation for this discrepancy, and in a further excavation at Megiddo uncovered a casemate wall which ran underneath the offset and inset wall. This, then, was the Solomonic wall associated with the great gateway of the palace mentioned above and with a large palatial structure near the gate (see above, p. 20). The solid wall and the stables were now attributed to Ahab, who is known to have possessed a huge force of chariots (see below).

Archaeology had again substantiated biblical information and found the remains of Solomon's fortifications at Jerusalem, Gezer, Hazor, and Megiddo. As Yadin put it, "Hardly ever in the history of archaeological diggings has such a short verse in the Bible helped so much in identifying and dating actual remains found by the spade."

DAN

The great Solomonic gate was built only during the reign of Solomon. Immediately afterward a modified version came into being. An outstanding example has been found in the far north of Israel, at Tell Dan.

Dan had a long tradition as a cult center (see above, p. 70). When the Danites settled in the town they brought with them the graven image made by Micah (Judg. ch. 17–18), and Dan remained a center of worship "until the day of the captivity of the land" (Judg. 18:30). When the northern tribes revolted against Solomon's son, Rehoboam, and elected Jeroboam as head of the new kingdom of Israel, the latter immediately created two cultic centers in order to attract the people and discourage their pilgrimage to the Temple in Jerusalem. He set up two golden calves, one in Beth-El and the other in Dan.

Under Jeroboam's rule, Dan was not only a center of worship meant to rival Jerusalem, but also a northern bastion against the rising power of Aram. Although the Bible does not mention any fortifications erected by Jeroboam, the gate excavated at Dan is clear evidence of his efforts to turn Dan into a major stronghold. The monumental dimensions of the gate (58 × 97 ft.) (figs. 11, 55) exceed even those of the Solomonic gates, but the plan is different. Instead of three pairs of buttresses following the towers there are now only two, forming four guardrooms instead of six. According to Yadin, this new type of gate was more solid and compact and could better withstand enemy battering. Despite its great strength, however, the gateway at Dan stood for only a short while; its ruins were found covered with a layer of ashes some 3 ft. thick.

Figure 55:   Tentative reconstruction of the Israelite gateway at Dan (for the plan see fig. 11)

The gate was dated to the period of Jeroboam, the period of its destruction matches the biblical account of the later wars between Baasa, king of Israel, on the one hand, and Asa of Judah and Ben Hadad of Aram on the other. "And Ben-Hadad hearkened unto king Asa, and sent the captains of his armies against the cities of Israel, and smote Ijon, and Dan . . ." (I Kings 15:20).

The Solomonic gate at Megiddo was also replaced by a gate similar to that at Dan. The gateway was shortened and the structure widened. As at Dan, there were only four guardrooms, but the gateway became more compact, and therefore more readily defensible.

THE OFFSET-INSET WALL

After the Solomonic period, there was a change in the construction of the defensive wall, resulting in a sturdier structure. A solid wall, made of stone, or having a stone foundation with a brick superstructure, took the place of the casemates. This was the "offset and inset" wall (figs. 49, 53); that is, a wall with slight salients and recesses. A stretch of the wall would be built slightly forward, and the next stretch would be recessed by about half a yard, to be followed by another stretch of wall jutting forward. The salients and recesses are usually found on both the outside and the inside of the wall, but occasionally they are found on the outside only.

The purpose of these salients and recesses was to give a more extensive area of fire power to the defenders on the wall. The salients acted as towers and were crowned with superstructures which protruded over the wall. This enabled the defenders to cover the recessed stretch of wall with fire from three sides — from the front, and also from the two flanks. The protruding superstructure also enabled the defenders to shoot straight down at an enemy attacking the offset.

One of the best examples of the change from the old to the new type of defenses is to be seen at Megiddo (fig. 52). Here the casemate wall was superseded by an offset and inset wall, 11 ft. thick and evidently built of brick on a stone foundation. According to Yadin it was connected to the Solomonic gate which had been repaired and redesigned. The date of this radical change from casemate wall to "offset and inset" probably coincides with the expedition of Shishak, king of Egypt, in the fifth year of Rehoboam, king of Judah (c. 918/7 B.C.E.). Shishak's campaign against Judah is described in the Bible (II Chron. 12:2–12). The new kingdom of Israel, ruled by Shishak's erstwhile guest, Jeroboam, was also invaded and the capture of Megiddo is recorded in a relief at Karnak. It therefore seems likely that it was Jeroboam who rebuilt the city wall in the new style, immediately after the invasion.

According to Yadin it was the use of a more powerful battering ram, especially as employed by the newly resurgent power of Assyria, that gave rise to the new defensive type of wall. Defense and attack interact on each other. Defenses always stand in relation to the new devices used by the attacking forces, just as new forms of attack are the result of the problems set by the defense.

Similarly associated with Ahab's reign is a change from casemates to offset-inset walls at Hazor. Here the city was previously confined to the western half of the upper tell. Now the casemates were filled in to make them solid, and were incorporated in the new offset-inset wall which extended the fortifications to include the eastern part of the upper tell as well. A lower step at the eastern end of the tell was nevertheless fortified with towers and a double wall, though this was not a true casemate. There were no entrances to the intervening space between the walls. A massive citadel built by Ahab in the 9th century B.C.E. at the far western end of the tell has been described earlier (see p. 24).

The casemate wall did not, however, vanish completely. It remained especially as an inner defensive wall. Ahab himself built casemates in his captial at Samaria (fig. 13). There, the second building phase, which is attributed to Ahab, shows a wide casemate wall. The outer wall is about 6½ ft. wide and the inner is just over 3 ft., while the space between the walls measures almost 24 ft. along the northern stretch of the wall. The fortification was therefore nearly 34 ft. in depth. It surrounded the royal enclosure at the summit and was built outside the older enclosure wall from the time of Omri. The area of the summit platform was thereby extended, and the whole complex turned into an inner citadel. Remarkably enough, on the southeast side of the enclosure the older "inner wall" (see p. 23) was retained, but its thickness trebled, so that at this stretch there was a solid wall 16 ft. wide.

The building of both the old casement type and the new offset and inset type of defenses is therefore attributed to the same period and even to the same person (Ahab). The explanation given by Yigael Yadin for this development stems from the difference in the area fortified. While at Megiddo and Hazor the offset and inset walls were city fortifications, at Samaria the wall defended an inner citadel.

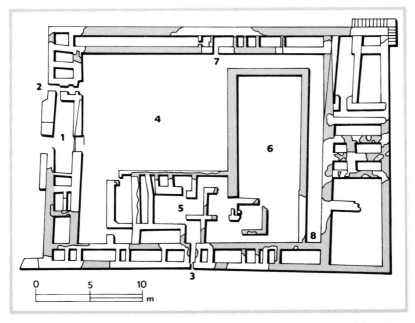

Figure 56:   Plan of the Israelite citadel at Ramat Raḥel, showing: (1) main gateway; (2) wicket; (3) secret wicket; (4) courtyard; (5) living quarter; (6) royal palace; (7) casemate wall of ashlar construction; (8) the place where the balustrade (fig. 21b) was found

Yet another example of the use of both the offset-inset wall and the casemates at one and the same time dates to the eve of the destruction of the kingdom of Judah, and is found at the citadel built by Jehoiakim son of Josiah at Ramat Raḥel, a site not far from Jerusalem. The citadel was constructed around what appears to have been a royal palace (fig. 56). According to archaeological data, these remains are to be assigned to the period shortly preceding the end of the kingdom of Judah, during the reign of Jehoiakim (609–597 B.C.E.), the son of Josiah, who was placed on the throne by Nebuchadnezzar and later rebelled against him. Concerning Jehoiakim's wrongdoings Jeremiah prophesied: "Woe to him who builds his house by unrighteousness, and his upper rooms by injustice; who makes his neighbor service him for nothing, and does not give him his wages; who says, 'I will build myself a great house with spacious upper rooms,' and cuts out windows for it, panelling it with cedar, and painting it with vermilion" (Jer. 22:13–14).

This passage, usually understood as a general denouncement of Jehoia-kim, has been strikingly connected by Aharoni with the specific findings of the palace-citadel in Ramat Raḥel. The excavations which Aharoni carried out there have revealed a solid offset and inset wall, some 10—12 ft. thick, which formed the outer citadel defenses. Within was an open space, flat-tened by a deep fill, which probably served for the army and chariots. The inner palace complex was again surrounded by a wall, this time of the casemate type, with a gate centrally placed at the eastern end. The paving was of huge blocks of limestone which were found cracked and blackened as the result of an intense fire. According to Aharoni, this was no doubt the result of Nebuchadnezzar's conquest. The casemate wall was constructed of well-smoothed ashlar masonry laid by the "header-stretcher" method, which closely resembles the construction in Samaria. In places, however, the stones were laid breadthwise only, mainly in the upper courses of the wall.

Within the walls was a large courtyard with two adjoining buildings. One was the palace itself, and the other was a complex of what probably were storerooms and sleeping quarters. On the floor of the courtyard three proto-Aeolian capitals were found, similar to the ones from Samaria and Jerusalem and belonging to the late Israelite type (fig. 19).

One of the most interesting finds at Ramat Raḥel was a series of frag-ments of small columns decorated with a drooping petal motif and topped by small capitals of a proto-Aeolian type (fig. 21). These columns are remarkable in that they are a replica of the ivory carvings of the "woman at the window" (see p. 38). The conclusion is that these decorated columns must have been a balustrade of a window in the palace building. On top of the capitals were holes which must have been meant for wooden beams. There were also traces of red paint left on the columns and capitals. This, Aharoni maintains, perfectly fits Jeremiah's description, especially of the windows, "panelling it with cedar and painting it with vermilion."

The palace at Ramat Raḥel may have been the construction built by Jehoiakim which so aroused the ire of Jeremiah. This assumption was based on an inscribed seal found in the citadel and attributed to the officer of King Jehoiachin. It symbolized the attitude of the king of Judah who used his power and position for self-indulgence, at the expense of justice for the common man.

Until the reign of Jehoshaphat, the kingdom of Judah was constantly at war with the kingdom of Israel. Of the three kings who preceded Jehosha-phat, two are specifically mentioned as having fortified the cities of Judah. Rehoboam continued his father Solomon's activities and built a whole chain of fortified cities (II Chron. 11:5—12). Those mentioned by name are mostly in the south and west of Judah, but the tribal area of Benjamin which lies north of Judah was also fortified. Asa, the third king of Judah after Solomon and the immediate predecessor of Jehoshaphat, continued Rehoboam's work. "And he [Asa] built fortified cities in Judah . . . For he said unto Judah: 'Let us build these cities and make about them walls, and towers, gates and bars . . ." (II Chron. 14:5—6).

The fortifications of this period seem to differ somewhat from those described above. The wall of salients and recesses was introduced in Judah as well, but in addition to the actual wall there is a glacis at the lower part of the wall. This takes the form of a sloping mass of stones built against the wall which strengthens the lowest part of the wall and makes the approach to it more difficult and formidable. It also serves as a further defensive device against the battering ram.

LACHISH

Lachish was one of the largest cities of the kingdom of Judah. It was situated in the western lowland district of the kingdom and guarded the approaches from the south to the central hill country. In size it exceeded

Figure 57: Reconstructed drawing of the double-walled city of Lachish in the Israelite period

even Megiddo by almost a third, and it seems that there was a special quarter for the king's officials in the city. Lachish occupied a key position in the defenses of Judah, and the fortifications excavated at the site bear out what we know of its importance. The first fortifications of the city date to the 18th century B.C.E. The city was then defended by a plastered beaten earth glacis and a fosse. In the Iron Age, the summit of the excavated mound was surrounded by two walls: the inner one was a solid brick wall on a single stone layer foundation. This wall was of the offset-inset type and was some 20 ft. wide.

The outer wall was further down the slope. It was built in the lower part of sloping stone foundation (probably on the remnants of the Middle Bronze glacis), while the upper part was built of plastered bricks with salients and recesses and was strengthened with towers.

Both walls were strengthened by glacis. A large amount of charcoal was found at the base of the wall, which may be the remains of a superstructure of wood, or may reflect the fact that a quantity of brush was piled against

Figure 58:   Relief from the palace at Khorsabad of the Assyrian king Sargon (721–705 B.C.E.), with a schematic representation of an assault on a city. A simultaneous frontal and flank attack is being mounted against the wall of the city by two battering-ram units

the wall in order to burn it. There also appears to have been a large free-standing bastion protecting the outside of the gate. Later it was incorporated into the outer defenses.

Lachish is not mentioned in the Bible from Joshua's conquest until Rehoboam. However, it appears in the list of cities fortified by Rehoboam (II Chron. 11:5–12). Thus, archaeological excavations revealed no architectural evidence from the period between the 12th and 10th centuries B.C.E. Scholars tend to date the fortifications to King Asa, who is also mentioned as fortifying the cities of Judah.

The fortifications of Lachish strongly resemble the wall relief worked in stone, which was discovered in the palace of Sennacherib at Nimrud and portrays the siege and capture of Lachish (fig. 22). This relief clearly shows the defenses of the two town walls and a tower. However, excavations revealed two phases of Israelite cities which were destroyed and burned. According to finds, some scholars attribute both of them to Nebuchadnezzar (his first campaign in 597 and his second in 587). Others claim that the first city was destroyed by Sennacherib in 701, and that the second destruction was the Babylonian destruction by Nebuchadnezzar.

The fall of Lachish to Sennacherib is not actually mentioned in the Bible, but is referred to indirectly: "And after this did Sennacherib king of Assyria send his servants to Jerusalem — now he was before Lachish and all his power with him. . ." (II Chron. 32:9). "So Rab-shakeh returned, and found the king of Assyria warring against Libnah; for he had heard that he was departed from Lachish" (II Kings 19:8).

A crest of a helmet, found during excavations at Lachish, is a replica of the ones worn by the Assyrians, as depicted in the relief at Nimrud.

MIZPEH

Another site whose fortifications are attributed to King Asa is Tell al-Naṣba, identified as biblical Mizpeh. The Bible recounts how Baasa, king of Israel, made war on Asa of Judah and built Ramah in order to contain Asa and close the border. Asa called on Ben-Hadad of Aram for help, and under the pressure of the latter's attack Asa was able to destroy Ramah. "Then King Asa made a proclamation unto all Judah, none was exempted; and they carried away the stones of Ramah, and the timber thereof, wherewith Baasa had builded; and king Asa built therewith Geba of Benjamin and Mizpeh" (I Kings 15:22).

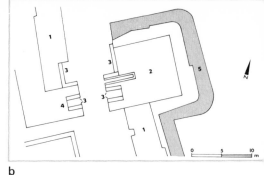

a   b

Figure 59a: The gate at Tell al-Naṣba, from the time of Asa (beginning of 19th cent. B.C.E.)

Figure 59b: Plan of the gate, showing: (1) city wall; (2) eastern tower; (3) benches; (4) western tower; (5) glacis

Excavations at Tell al-Naṣba revealed that the city was surrounded by a plastered offset-inset wall built of very roughly shaped stones with a stone glacis laid against it and a moat. The wall itself is 40–45 ft. high and 13 ft. wide. It was further strengthened by 10 towers and apparently had a dry moat in front of it (fig. 9).

The gateway here was built according to a new plan (fig 59a-b), It was formed by an overlap in the wall, and was further strengthened in that the overlapping wall ended in a massive tower (a modification of the free-standing bastion of Lachish). Thus the enemy must have found the approach to the gate most difficult. Inside the gate two pairs of buttresses narrowed the entrance and, in contrast to the four-chamber gate, formed only one pair of chambers, one on either side. The entrance to the gate was, however, deepened by the protruding tower.

The excavations at Tell al-Naṣba also revealed that the wall was not of uniform quality, nor was it interlinked everywhere, but rather showed signs of having been built in sections by different builders. The reason for this may stem from the circumstances described in the Bible; the wall was hastily built after a general call-up of all available manpower, "none was exempted."

POST-SOLOMONIC FORTIFICATIONS

The post-Solomonic period, then, marks a departure from previous modes of fortifications both in the northern kingdom of Israel as well as in the kingdom of Judah. It is a period of change and experimentation. It is also a time of intensive activity for several of the major kings mentioned in the Bible: Jeroboam, Omri, Ahab, Rehoboam, and Asa. A certain similarity in trends existed in the two kingdoms, as for instance the introduction of the solid offset-inset wall, but this is not the only example. At Tell al-Khalayfa, possibly biblical Elath, a fortified gate has been excavated which closely resembles those at Dan and the post-Solomonic gate at Megiddo (IVA1). Here, too, weak points in the defenses were protected by nearby towers which stand completely outside the wall.

In the northern kingdom, at Samaria, remains were uncovered of what seems to have been a rectangular tower outside the casemate wall (fig. 13), which archaeologists believe helped defend a nearby gate. This is reminiscent of the free-standing bastion at Lachish, and the tower in the overlapping wall at Tell al-Nasba.

The clearest example of a tower outside the wall, which served as an additional element to strengthen the fortifications, is found at Hazor (fig. 49). At one stage the citadel of Ahab was not thought to be strong enough. A wide and solid offset-inset wall was therefore built around the western extremes of the tell. In addition to this a tower was erected at the northern corner, outside the wall, to protect this point. It was probably connected to the city defenses by a bridge. The city was nevertheless captured and burned. "In the days of Pekah, king of Israel, came Tiglath-Pileser king of Assyria, and took Ijon and Abel-Beth-Maachah and Janoah, and Kedesh, and Hazor. . ." (II Kings 15:29).

There had been a previous Assyrian invasion some twenty years earlier (c. 750 B.C.E.) during the reign of Menahem, and the latter had paid 1,000 talents of silver in order to buy off the Assyrian monarch. According to Yadin it was Menahem who put up the additional defenses at Hazor in view of the ever-growing threat from Assyria.

In Judah the kings who succeeded Asa continued to fortify the cities. Of Jehoshaphat the Bible relates: "And he placed forces in all the fortified cities of Judah and set garrisons in the land of Judah and in the cities of Ephraim which Asa his father had taken. . . and he built in Judah castles and cities of store. . ." (II Chron. 17:2,12). So also Uzziah: "And he built towers in the wilderness . . ." (II Chron. 26:10). There is, however, in this period and up to the time of the destruction of the Temple, a return to the casemate wall, at least in the kingdom of Judah.

At one of the outlying posts, at the oasis of Ain Khudeirat in the east of the Sinai desert, identified with the biblical Kadesh-Barnea, stand the remains of a fortress. It was rectangular in shape with casemate walls and towers at each corner. Additional towers guarded in the middle of each side. The walls were built of rough stone, but hewn stone was used for the construction of the towers. The upper part of the fort was built of brick. Against the lower part a glacis was built whose top layer was made of smooth stone. There is some difference of opinion regarding the date of the fortress, with some scholars attributing it to Jehoshaphat, while others hold that it was built later, in the time of Uzziah.

Another fortress, also with casemate walls and a heavy glacis, was found at Gibeah, on the site of Saul's fortifications. This fort commanded the highway to Jerusalem and protected the northern border of the kingdom of Judah. A peculiar feature of the casemate wall here was the fact that the outer wall was the thinner one. The casemates were filled in with earth. Albright had originally identified this fort with the one Asa rebuilt together with Mizpeh. He based this identification on the pottery found at the site, as well as the similarity in the style of the glacis. He also pointed out that some of the stones used for building the glacis had been taken from some other site. These stones had been squared on certain sides and left rough on the others. Albright found that the hewn side had been placed facing inward, which proved that the stones did not originally belong to the fortress at Gibeath-Shaul. There were also traces of burnt wood in the ruins. All this seemed to corroborate the evidence that Asa had built this fortress, for the Bible relates that he took stones and timber from Ramah in order to build Gibeah and Mizpeh. Later excavations and an improved knowledge of pottery led to a revision of Albright's views, and the fortress is now dated to the 7th–6th century B.C.E. According to Sinclair, the fortress could have been built by Hezekiah at the end of the 8th century, to defend the approaches to Jerusalem against the Assyrian king, Sennacherib.

BEERSHEBA AND ARAD

The correlation of archaeological data concerning fortifications with historic events in the Judean kingdom remains extremely difficult. The reversion to casemate walls is evident, not only in the two fortress examples given (there are others) but also in town defenses. Beer-Sheba was a city at the southern extremity of the kingdom of Judah and is mentioned briefly as such three times: "And he [Jehoshaphat] went out again among the people from Beer-Sheba to the hill country of Ephraim. . ." (II Chron. 19:4), "So they [Hezekiah and the congregation of Jerusalem] established a decree to make proclamation throughout all Israel, from Beer-Sheba even to Dan, that they should come to keep the Passover unto the Lord, at Jerusalem. . ." (II Chron. 30:5), ". . . and he [Josiah] brought all the priests out of the cities of Judah, and defiled the high places where the priests had made offerings, from Geba to Beer-Sheba" (II Kings 23:8).

At recent excavations in Beer-Sheba, Aharoni has found three defensive walls of three different periods. The first is a solid brick wall of the offset-inset type, built on a stone foundation, some 13—16 ft. thick and with a glacis. This wall seems to be similar to others of the post-Solomonic period, and Aharoni dates it as belonging to the 10th—9th century. This wall was, however, followed by casemates with very thin walls which are dated to the 9th century. The third and last wall is a much stronger casemate wall dated to the 8th century. This wall also had a glacis before it, plastered over and strengthened at its foot with a revetment wall of stone.

Another site excavated by Aharoni, displaying a somewhat similar development in fortifications, is Arad. Arad is not mentioned at all in the Bible in the period of the monarchy, but it is in the same area as Beer-Sheba and must have been subject to the same influences. At Arad (fig. 10), Aharoni found an offset-inset wall which was dated to the first half of the 9th century. This citadel was destroyed, probably by the Edomites in 734 B.C.E., as recorded: "Then Rezin king of Syria and Pekah son of Remaliah King of Israel came up to Jerusalem to war . . . At that time Rezin king of Syria recovered Elath to Syria" (II Kings 16:5—6). This in turn was replaced by a casemate wall with protruding towers, dated to the end of the 8th century. Aharoni would like to attribute this last wall to Hezekiah, who carried out religious reforms, because it crosses over a temple (see p. 71), indicating that the wall was built only after the temple had previously been destroyed.

KING UZZIAH'S INVENTION

Uzziah, king of Judah, not only built fortresses in the desert but also strengthened the defenses of Jerusalem with towers at strategic points (II Chron. 26:9). Moreover, the towers and walls were prepared for a possible siege: "And he made in Jerusalem engines invented by skillful men *(hish-vonot maḥashevet ḥoshev)* to be on the towers and upon the corners, to shoot arrows and great stones" (II Chron. 26:15).

The meaning of this sentence has been unclear; it is not known exactly what engines Uzziah had made. The phrase generally translated as "engines invented by skillful men" has been taken to refer to catapults, but there is no archaeological evidence for the use of catapults on the walls. Yigael Yadin has therefore proposed a different meaning for the phrase. The word *hishvonot* is elsewhere translated as "inventions" (Eccles. 7:29), which is nearer the meaning of the word, as the root is *hashav* ("thought"). Basing himself on the stone relief at Nimrud, depicting the siege of Lachish, Yadin suggests that *hishvonot* were a new type of battlement structure. In addition to the serrated stone or brickwork of the battlements, a protective wooden framework was erected on which shields were hung. This shielded framework enabled the defenders on the parapets to stand at their full height, instead of crouching, and shoot down or throw heavy boulders at the advancing foe.

HEZEKIAH'S AND NEHEMIAH'S WALLS

Another king of Judah who fortified Jerusalem was Hezekiah. When the threat of invasion and conquest by Sennacherib of Assyria became acute, Hezekiah "built up all the wall that was broken down, and raised it up to the towers, and another wall without, and repaired Millo in the city of David. . ." (II Chron. 32:5).

Kathleen Kenyon, in her excavations of the Ophel, David's City, found above the Jebusite wall which had been reused by David, another wall which she dated to around the year 700 B.C.E. This wall had been repaired and rebuilt several times. The period of its origin, however, fits the time of Hezekiah or Manasseh who, according to the Bible, rebuilt the walls of Jerusalem (II Chron. 32:5; 33:14).

The wall on the southern spur of Jerusalem is not the only one that may be attributed to Hezekiah. Prof. Avigad, in his excavations in the Jewish Quarter of the Old City (fig. 60), discovered the foundation of a massive wall 20–23 ft. wide. This wall rests on bedrock and is built of roughly squared blocks and coarse stones and boulders. The size and the thickness of the wall show that it must have been the city's defense wall. It is dated to the end of the 8th century or the beginning of the 7th century B.C.E., since it was built on a house of the 8th century. Thus the area west of the Temple Mount (the "West Hill"), on which the wall was built, was in the 8th century an open part of the city, which was afterwards included in the city walls. Avigad therefore attributes it to Hezekiah; as recorded in II Chronicles 32:5: ". . . Also he strengthened himself and built up all the wall that was

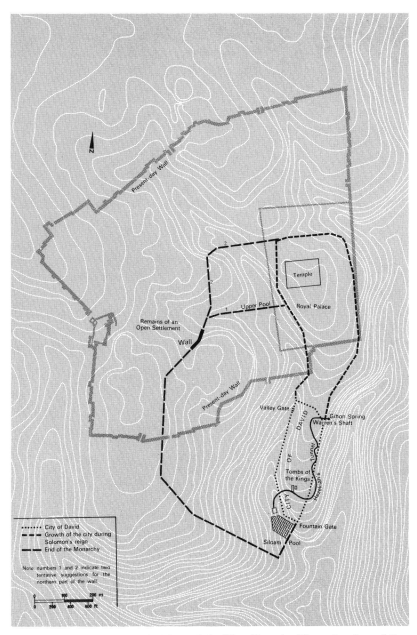

Figure 60:   Jerusalem at the time of the First Temple. The extension of the city at the end of the Monarchy is the suggestion of N. Avigad, after the discovery of the city's defense wall

broken, and raised it up to the towers, and another wall without." The importance of the wall lies in the fact that it proves that the area west of the Temple Mount (the "West Hill") was already integrated in a fortified Jerusalem at the time of the First Temple.

The last time we hear of the fortification of Jerusalem in the Bible is in the Book of Nehemiah. Nehemiah had been shocked at the state of affairs in the new settlement of the returned exiles. He realized his immediate task to be the refortification of Jerusalem. To this end he made a lone night survey around the city, viewing the remains of the walls and gates. The next day he called on the people to rebuild the walls, and this task was completed after 52 days (Neh. 6:15). The wall built by Nehemiah is today identified with a 9-ft.-wide wall at the summit of the east side of the Ophel hill.

According to Kathleen Kenyon the ruins of the preceding walls and the hill revetments were so complete that it was impossible to reuse or rebuild them at this point. So great was the destruction that "there was no place for the beast that was under me to pass" (Neh. 2:14). Nehemiah therefore built his wall on the summit of the hill. This wall had earlier been identified by Macalister and Duncan as David's wall. Kenyon, however, has conclusively proved that the wall dates originally from the 5th–4th century and must therefore have been the wall Nehemiah built when he reconstructed the city's defenses.

8
TOMBS

Regular burial of the dead in tombs dates back to prehistoric times. Indeed, respectful treatment of the dead person was one of the early manifestations of religious ritual, both among nomads and among settled peoples. In the Neolithic period, deceased tribal heads were evidently regarded as religious symbols or totems. This, in any event, would appear to be the significance of several clay skulls, with human features, found under dwelling floors at Jericho (fig. 61).

Archaeological excavations have established that in the Chalcolithic period it was customary to bury the bones of the dead in ossuaries (containers), after the flesh on the skeleton had disintegrated. "Cemeteries" of

Figure 61: Skull of the Pre-Pottery Neolithic period (c. 8000–5000 B.C.E.) found under a dwelling floor at Jericho. The eyes are set with shells and the skull is plastered with clay to preserve the features of the face

115

Figure 62: Pottery ossuary of
the Chalcolithic period, shaped
like a house on four legs, from
Azor

pottery ossuaries have been found at Hadera, Bene-Brak, and Azor (fig. 62),
along the coastal strip of Israel. Some of the containers are shaped like a
house standing on four legs, having a vaulted roof, a door with a bolt, and a
window. Some have painted decorations and human features engraved on
the front.

THE FAMILY TOMB

Excavations at Jericho have revealed communal graves dating from the
Middle Bronze period, in caves outside the city walls. Dozens of skeletons
occupied one cave, reflecting use, perhaps, by one family over several generations. Utensils and gifts for the use of the dead in the next world were
placed in the burial cave. In the Jericho tombs were objects of alabaster and
bronze, scarabs and jewelry, wooden objects and, most rare in Israel
(because of the difficulty of preservation), reed mats and baskets (fig. 63).

Since death was viewed as a transition to a different world where life was
continued, and since the spirits of the dead were considered to have great
capacity for harm or for good, it was also customary to place offerings of

Figure 63: Communal grave of the Middle Bronze I (c. 2200–2000 B.C.E.) from Jericho, reconstructed in Rockefeller Museum, Jerusalem. Each of the bodies was equipped with pottery (for food supply); some of them were also equipped with weapons and some with beads

food and drink in special vessels which were buried in the tomb. For example, a platter with the skeleton of a lamb's head on it was found in a tomb at Afula.

The practice of communal burial was similarly prevalent among the Israelites (cf. II Kings 23:6; Jer. 26:23), and gave rise to the Hebrew expressions "to sleep with one's fathers" (I Kings 11:23), and "to be gathered to one's kin" (Gen. 25:8). Burial in a communal tomb undoubtedly was an expression of the individual's desire to maintain some contact with the community even after death. Thus, Jacob, who died in Egypt, requested that he be buried with his fathers (Gen. 49:29), and the Israelites honored his request, taking his coffin with them when they left Egypt (cf. also II Sam. 19:38).

Archaeology reveals no distinctively Israelite burial practices during almost the entire biblical period. The Israelites followed the mode of burial employed by their neighbors, and shared a common attitude of respectful care for the dead. Biblical biographies ordinarily end with the statement that a man died, and then give an account of his burial (cf. Gen. 25:8–9;

Josh. 24:30; Judg. 2:9). This is more than a literary convention; it reflects the value assigned by biblical society to proper burial.

This concern may also be measured by the frequency with which the Bible refers to the fear of being left unburied. Thus, one of the curses for a breach of the covenant is: "Thy carcasses shall be found unto all the fowl of the air and unto the beasts of the earth" (Deut. 28:26; cf. Jer. 22:19). Surrounding cultures shared this attitude. An Assyro-Babylonian malediction reads: "May he not be buried in the earth, and may his spirit never be reunited with his loved ones."

It was this motivation, to be buried with one's family, that impelled Abraham to purchase a family tomb (Gen. 23:4), but this act had further significance, in that it introduced a new element into the nomadic existence of Abraham and his family, a sense of permanent identification with a particular place. Jacob's request to be buried there, and Nehemiah's request of King Artaxerxes of Persia, to return to Judah, "the place of my fathers' sepulchres" (Neh. 2:3), underscore the important role played by the patriarchal tomb in establishing a sense of rootedness in Canaan.

CAVE OF MACHPELAH

The cave purchased by Abraham from Ephron the Hittite (Gen. ch. 23) was undoubtedly similar to the burial caves noted above. The Bible locates it in "the field of Machpelah before Mamre, the same is Hebron, in the land of Canaan." The site is currently identified with Kharam el-Khalīl, in modern Hebron.

The "Tombs of the Patriarchs" standing today are, of course, not the original structures. They stand in a compound surrounded by a 39 ft. wall distinguished by its hewn stones, which are up to 23 ft. in length. The foundations of the wall are Herodian. Josephus described the tombs of the patriarchs as "of really fine marble and exquisite workmanship" (Wars 4:532), but does not mention the existence of a surrounding wall.

The earliest source on the arrangement of the graves is the Book of Jubilees (36:21), which states that "Leah is buried to the left of Sarah." If one enters the Machpelah compound from the southwest, the tombs of Abraham and Sarah are in the center, the tombs of Jacob and Leah are to their left, and of Isaac and Rebecca to their right (fig. 64).

The original cave lies beneath these structures, and is not accessible to visitors. Thus scholars have not been able to study it, and its appearance can

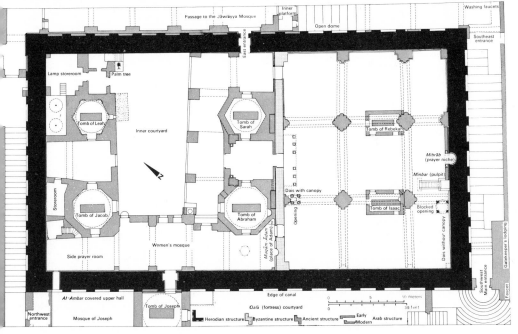

Figure 64: Plan of the mosque built on the site of the Cave of the Machpelah in Hebron

only be inferred from the accounts of travelers in centuries past. It is generally believed that the original tomb consists of at least two caves joined by a passage, and possibly of a third inner chamber.

RACHEL'S TOMB

Another tomb associated with the patriarchal period is the mausoleum in which Jacob buried Rachel "on the road to Ephrath, which is Beth-Lehem" (Gen. 35:20). This tomb, which is traditionally located in Bethlehem (an identification which is still under scholarly dispute, however), is mentioned by Eusebius, one of the first Christians. The most ancient Jewish non-biblical reference to it is in a 10th century C.E. *Guide to Jerusalem*, which was found in the Cairo Genizah.

The existing structure is an 1841 renovation of a late 18th century building. However, travelers' descriptions from the 12th to the 18th centuries indicate that the tomb then consisted of 11 stones (allegedly laid on the grave by Jacob's 11 sons — Benjamin was but a newborn baby and did not participate), covered with a large stone (allegedly laid by Jacob), all roofed over with a dome supported by four pillars, built to mark the holy site.

TOMB-SITES

Other areas in Israel have been traditionally associated with the burial place of various biblical figures, but in no case can a positive identification be made. The tomb of the prophet Samuel has traditionally been located at Nabi-Samwil, the highest mountain overlooking Jerusalem (the Bible locates his tomb in Ramah; I Sam. 25:1). During the Middle Ages Jews would gather from all over the world on the alleged date of his death (28 Iyyar), but this practice has fallen into disuse owing to the doubtfulness of the site's authenticity.

The Tomb of Absalom in the Kidron Valley (fig. 65), southeast of Jerusalem, is popularly held to be the resting place of King David's son. The Bible relates that Absalom built a monument to himself in his lifetime, "for he said, I have no son to keep my name in remembrance" (II Sam. 18:18). This phrase is reminiscent of Akkadian texts which include among the unfortunate beings in the next world, "the man who has no one to recall his name." This mausoleum, however, has been dated to the period of the Second Temple, and is an excellent example of the Jewish art of that time, which was based mainly on Greek decorative elements.

Figure 65: Nobleman's tomb of the first cent. C.E., popularly known as the "tomb of Absalom." It consists of a small tomb-chamber with a round memorial above it

Nearby, at the foot of the Mount of Olives, are other tombs of the period of the Second Temple — the so-called Tomb of Zechariah and the Tomb of the Sons of Hezir. Because of the existence of an old Jewish tradition which holds that at the end of days the Messiah will ascend the Mount of Olives, and it will be there that Ezekiel will blow the trumpet for the resurrection of the dead, the slopes of the Mount of Olives have become, in the course of time, a burial place for the Jews of Jerusalem. According to the Bible, King David was buried in the "city of David" (I Kings 2:10), presumably southeast of the present village of Silwan. Traditionally, the later kings of the Davidic dynasty were also buried there, and the Bible refers to the "sepulchres of the sons of David" (II Chron. 32:33), whose site was still known in the time of Nehemiah (Neh. 3:16). However, the tomb of David was probably destroyed by the Romans after the Bar Kokhba revolt (135 C.E.), and the exact location of the site was subsequently forgotten. Over the years folk tradition has suggested various sites for David's tomb; the most generally accepted location has been Mount Zion.

THE TOMBS OF THE KINGS OF JUDAH

The authenticated site of the royal tombs of the House of David remains one of the enticing puzzles of archaeological research.

The many references to the royal burying-place in the Bible point to an area in the Ophel, in the south of the City of David. Despite searches over the years, however, no great tombs have been found in that area. This may be due to the fact that the southern end of the hill was used in Roman times for stone-quarrying, so that any constructions which survived the destruction of the Second Temple after the Bar Kokhba revolt would have been destroyed by the Roman stone-cutting operations.

Nevertheless, archaeologists have continued the search for the royal cemetery of the Davidic kings. Excavations carried out by Raymond Weill in 1913–14 and 1923–24 uncovered a number of tombs cut in the rock at the south end of the Ophel hill.

Weill identified these tombs on the Ophel with the royal Davidic necropolis. In favor of this identification is the fact that they are evidently not family tombs, but were built only for one or two burials. There are also similarities between the construction of these tunnel tombs and the tunnel of Hezekiah. Thus, for some time, Weill's identification was generally accepted, although there was no actual proof either for or against his thesis.

However, tombs from the First Temple period were found across the Kidron Valley, in and around the Arab village of Silwan. A survey carried out by D. Ussishkin found that these tombs can be divided into three types. One type has a main chamber which is rectangular in shape with a gabled roof. A small chamber or "trough" was hewn out of the rock on one side of the chamber, with a rock ledge at one end, into which had been carved a hollowed headrest. Here the dead person was laid to rest. A ledge running round the side of the trough shows that it was covered by a stone slab. At times a larger trough, with two headrests, had been carved out. This must have been intended for a husband and wife. The places had obviously been prepared in the lifetime of the owners, for whereas there is little difference in other measurements of the various troughs, there is a clear difference in their length. In other words the resting place was made "to measure," to fit the body.

A second type of tomb studied by Ussishkin consisted of two or three connected burial chambers, one behind the other, with straight ceilings and often a right-angled cornice cut between the ceiling and the wall. The dead were laid on rock benches or in simple troughs. There was no ledge, however, to support a covering lid.

The third type of tomb found in the Kidron Valley was of a monolithic construction, in which both the burial chambers and the outer shape of the tomb were hewn out of the living rock, giving the tomb the appearance of a stone building. Thus far three such tombs have been found. The first of these is popularly known as "the Tomb of the Daughter of Pharaoh" (fig. 66), and is dated to the period of the First Temple. It is almost square and is free-standing on three sides, attached to the rock only at the back. Its roof was originally crowned by a masonry pyramid, but the stones have been removed, probably by the Romans. A small entrance followed by a short passage lead to a rectangular burial chamber with a gabled roof. A rock shelf on which the dead body was laid runs along one side of the chamber. Above the entrance a recessed panel had originally been cut with an incised inscription. This had been destroyed when the entrance was widened in a later period so that only the last letter and half of the preceding one remained. Thus there is no possibility today of ascertaining the identity of the owner of the tomb, although N. Avigad points to the Egyptian influence apparent in the architectural construction.

Two other monolithic tombs were found in the village of Silwan. One could not be explored as it was being used as a water cistern. The tomb next to it originally contained two chambers, according to Ussishkin. The first of

Figure 66:   Nobleman's tomb of the First Temple period, popularly known as the "Tomb of the Daughter of Pharaoh," hewn out of the rock in the village of Silwan

these probably had a double resting place. The second chamber branched off to the right, the only such example found so far in the whole Kidron Valley necropolis. (In other tombs additional chambers were always placed behind the first.) According to Ussishkin the side chamber was an addition prepared for a relative of the first couple. The ceiling was similar to the other double-chambered tombs in being flat with a cornice. This monolithic tomb is interesting in that it had two inscriptions. The first of these was incised in a recessed panel over the entrance; the second was to the right, in line with the side chamber to the right of the main chamber.

The identity of the owner of this tomb is unkown. The inscription above the entrance (fig. 67) was partially destroyed and only the last letters of the name still remain. Although the inscription was found in the last century, when it was cut out of the rock and sent to the British Museum by Clermont-Ganneau, it was only in recent years that it was deciphered by Prof. Nahman Avigad. It reads "This is [the sepulchre of . . .]yahu who is over the house. There is no silver or gold here but [his bones] and the bones of his slave wife with him. Cursed be the man who will open this!"

As tombs were constantly broken into by grave robbers looking for valuables, the latter part of the description is understandable. Concerning

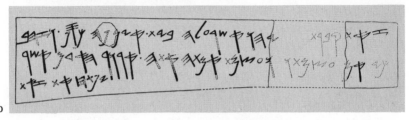

Figure 67:   Inscribed lintel stone (a) and facsimile (b) of one of the First
Temple period tombs hewn into the cliff of the Silwan village. It is
dedicated to the "royal steward" (in Hebrew: *"asher al ha-bayit,"* meaning
"who is over the house") who was one of the highest officials of the
Judean royal court

the first part, the description "over the house" is a title familiar from the
Bible and means "Steward of the House" or "Governor of the Palace." The
tomb itself appears to belong to a wealthy person; it is possible that it was
crowned by a pyramid, like the Tomb of the Daughter of Pharaoh. It was
also very prominently placed, being located directly opposite the City of
David, and was thus clearly visible from the city.

Avigad connects the tomb with a passage from Isaiah: "Thus saith the
Lord God of hosts; go, get thee unto this steward, even unto Shebna, who is
over the house [and say] What hast thou here and whom hast thou here
that thou hast hewed thee out here a sepulchre, as he that heweth him out a
sepulchre on high, and that graveth a habitation for himself in a rock" (Isa.
22:15–16).

The passage echoes the anger of the prophet not only at Shebna but also
at the exaggerated richness of the tomb. Isaiah's question, "What hast thou
here and whom hast thou here?" seems to imply that Shebna, who lived in
the reign of Hezekiah, was bringing foreign influences into Jerusalem.
Shebna has long been thought to have been a foreigner. Avigad has pointed
out that the term used by Isaiah, *sochen* ("steward"), is a common Phoenician synonym for "governor." Ussishkin, too, finds the architecture of the

Silwan necropolis, especially the gabled roof, to be Phoenician in character. Avigad has therefore suggested that this tomb belonged to Shebna (Shebnāyahū), a minister of Hezekiah.

The important point made by Ussishkin is that the Silwan necropolis is undoubtedly the most magnificent belonging to the First Temple period found so far. Architecturally it surpasses those tombs found by Weill on the Ophel, especially the three monolithic ones. Since it is highly unlikely that the tombs of officials or nobles would be more extravagant than those of the kings of the Davidic line, Weill's tombs cannot represent the royal necropolis. The tombs of the kings of Judah — if they exist — still await their discoverer.

THE TOMB OF UZZIAH

The site of Uzziah's tomb is unknown, but an interesting archaeological find spans the centuries between his death and our own time.

The Bible relates how Uzziah, who reigned over Judah for 52 years, led successful armies, strengthened his kingdom, and developed its economy. But then, in an excess of pride, Uzziah attempted to burn incense on the altar of the Temple in person, instead of through the intermediary of the priest. At this, leprosy broke out on his forehead and he was hustled out of the Temple. Uzziah remained a leper until his death, and when he died he was not buried in the tombs of the kings, but in "the field of the burial of the kings" (II Chron. 26:23). This was the best that could be done for a leper.

This was not, however, to be Uzziah's permanent resting place. His bones must have received a subsequent reburial, for a limestone plaque, 14 by 13 inches, was discovered by E.L. Sukenik in 1931, in a monastery on the Mount of Olives (fig. 68). On the plaque, which has been dated to the Second Temple period, was an Aramaic inscription which read:

> Hither were brought
> the bones of Uzziah
> king of Judah.
> Not to be opened!

The ossuary containing the bones has been lost. We do not know where the bones of Uzziah rest today, nor who it was who defied that last appeal.

Figure 68: Epitaph of the secondary burial of King Uzziah made in the late
Second Temple period. It is recorded in II Chron. 26:23 that Uzziah was
not buried in the royal necropolis when he died because he was a leper

9
WATERWORKS

For the land whither you go in to possess it, is not as the land of Egypt from whence you have come out, where you did sow your seed and did water it with your foot, as a garden of herbs; but the land whither you go over to possess it is a land of hills and valleys, and drinks water as the rain of heaven comes down (Deut. 11:10–11).

In Israel during the summer months there is no rain. Nor is the country blessed with many rivers. The supply of water is therefore an acute problem, and in ancient times it was certainly a major consideration when choosing the site for a settlement. A town had to be situated near wells providing a constant water supply, or near a perennial spring whose waters could be used for drinking, washing and irrigation. Later – it is not quite certain when exactly, but probably in the Middle Bronze Age – a way was found of lining cisterns with lime-mortar, which made them waterproof, so that water could be stored for lengthy periods. The winter rains and flash floods could thus be utilized. Spring water nevertheless remained the easiest and surest water supply. Jericho, the world's most ancient city, was situated at the site of an oasis. Dan (Laish) was founded near the headwaters of the Jordan River. But not all the great cities had such abundant sources of water.

Even given a plentiful water supply there remained the problem of assuring this supply in times of war, when the town was liable to face a protracted siege. A city was usually built on an existing tell or a hill, with the fortifications high up the slope in order to make the approach of an enemy as difficult as possible. Spring water, however, is mostly to be found at the foot of the hill, in the valley. The town was therefore faced with a double task: the water had to be made accessible to the townsfolk, while at the same time it had to be withheld from the besiegers. This critical problem was solved with architectural ingenuity that commands admiration to this day.

GIHON AND WARREN'S SHAFT

From the very beginning of its long history, Jerusalem has been plagued by the problem of water-supply. But through the ages, increasingly sophisticated methods were devised to supply Jerusalem's population with water.

The existence of a nearby spring, the Gihon, in the Kidron Valley, must have been a major factor in ancient times in choosing the Ophel, just above it, as the site for the City of David, rather than the slightly higher plateau to the north (fig. 69). In order to ensure access to the spring in times of siege, a

Figure 69:   View of the Ophel hill from the south with Temple Mount at the top, and the place of Gihon spring at the bottom

tunnel about 130 ft. long (fig. 71a) was cut through the rock. It followed a rather circuitous route and had a sharp angle at one point. this route was probably chosen in order to reduce the steepness of the passage, part of which had steps. The tunnel terminated in a shaft some 42 ft. deep, and a horizontal channel connected the spring with the shaft and allowed the water to flow into the heart of the mountain and reach the end of the shaft. In times of siege the townsfolk could safely enter the tunnel from inside the city walls and draw their water up the shaft as from a well. There had been a previous attempt to hew a shaft straight down from the tunnel entrance to the level of the water but a seam of extremely hard rock had been struck, which the tools of those days could not penetrate. The attempt was therefore abandoned and the tunnel and shaft were made instead.

The underground approach to the spring was first discovered by Warren in 1867 and was therefore called "Warren's shaft." Vincent, who examined it, proposed that this provided the solution to the capture of the Jebusite city by David. The Jebusites had defied David to capture the city and had taunted him: "Except thou take away the blind and the lame thou shalt not come in hither" (II Sam. 5:6). Whereupon David called on his warriors: "Whosoever smiteth the Jebusites and getteth up to the gutter. . ." (II Sam. 5:18).

This passage had long remained problematic. Vincent proposed that the "gutter" was none other than the shaft leading down to the spring waters. Joab and David's warriors made their way up the shaft and found themselves inside the city, which thus fell without siege or assault. Almost 3,000 years later, the Parker expedition (1909–11) sent a member up the shaft with the assistance of a Welsh miner, to prove that Joab and his men could have made the ascent. This explanation by Vincent naturally presupposes that the entrance to the shaft was inside the city walls. Joab and his men would thus have found themsleves inside the city defenses, to the rear of the unsuspecting Jebusites, who were taken unawares. However, the city walls, identified originally by Macalister and Duncan, apparently stood at the crest of the hill, well above the entrance to the shaft.

The question was resolved by Kathleen Kenyon when she proved that Macalister's wall could not be dated earlier than Nehemiah, and that the Jebusite wall was further down the slope, well below the entrance to the shaft. The shaft thus provided access to the spring from inside the walls, and was utilized by David to capture the city.

The section of the wall excavated by Kenyon showed a sharp corner

Figure 70:   View inside Hezekiah's tunnel towards its southern exit

which could not have been an inset. Rather it formed the corner of a tower. Kathleen Kenyon believes that this was the northern tower of what must have been the watergate, through which the people descended to the spring in times of peace. It is probable that this was the gate through which Solomon passed when he was anointed king: "And the King [David] said unto them: 'Take with you the servants of your lord, and cause Solomon my son to ride upon mine own mule, and bring him down to Gihon" (I Kings 1:33).

THE WATERS OF SHILOAH

The question of the water supply of Jerusalem appears again in the Book of Isaiah, which mentions "the waters of Shiloah that go softly" (Isa. 8:6). Similarly, Nehemiah, when listing the landmarks of the new wall he had built around Jerusalem, cites "the wall of the pool of Shelah by the king's garden" (Neh. 3:15). Archaeologists believe that both these verses refer to a channel which they discovered hewn out of the rock leading from the spring of Gihon down the valley of Kidron to the southern apex of the Ophel. Here the water was dammed and formed a pool. In the side of the channel were openings which allowed the water to overflow and irrigate the valley on either side. This, it was suggested, was the site of the "king's garden." The gradual gradient of the channel would allow the water to flow only slowly and would fit Isaiah's description of "the waters of Shiloah that go softly." This irrigation system utilizing the water of the Gihon spring is dated to about the time of Solomon.

HEZEKIAH'S TUNNEL

A far more magnificent water system utilizing the Gihon spring is the famous tunnel of Hezekiah (end of the 8th century B.C.E.), which was conceived on a far grander scale than the earlier constructions (fig. 71b).

As the threat of the Assyrian conquests drew ever closer to the kingdom of Judah, Hezekiah set about preparing Jerusalem for an eventual siege. The ancient water shaft (Warren's shaft) must have fallen into disuse long before, and the water of the Gihon flowed down the Kidron Valley in the rock-cut channels along the "king's garden." This constituted a point of potential danger, for the water would be unavailable to the Jerusalemites in the face

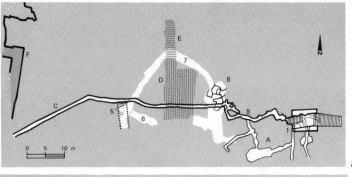

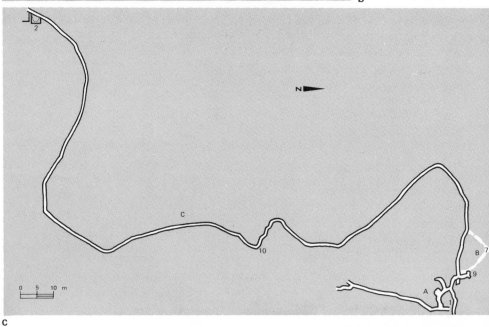

Legend:

A — Earlier tunnels
B — Warren's shaft
C — Hezekiah's tunnel
D — Jebusite wall
E — Israelite wall
F — Hasmonean wall

1 — Gihon Spring
2 — Pool of Shiloah
3 — Ground level of Oph hill
4 — Rock surface
5 — Entrance from inside city
6 — Previous abandoned shaft
7 — Circuitous tunnel and shaft
8 — Horizontal channel allowing water to fl from the spring to end of the shaft
9 — Entrance to Hezekia tunnel
10 — Meeting point of the borers

Figure 71: Cross section of the waterworks in Jerusalem (b); longitudinal sections of Warren's Shaft (a) and Hezekiah's tunnel (c).

of a determined siege, when the source could be blocked or the water polluted by the enemy. Therefore Hezekiah blocked access to the spring from the outside, and dug a tunnel which would bring the water from the spring into the city itself. This great engineering feat is referred to several times in the Bible, as well as in later sources: "And the rest of the story of Hezekiah, and all his mighty deeds, and that he made the pool and the canal and brought the water into the city. . ." (II Kings 20:20); "This same Hezekiah stopped the source of the waters of the upper Gihon and brought them to the west side of the city of David" (II Chron. 32:30).

That this diversion of the spring was connected with the Assyrian invasion of Jerusalem is clear from another passage: "And when Hezekiah saw that Sennacherib was come, and that he was purposed to fight against Jerusalem, he took counsel with his princes and his mighty men to stop the waters of the fountains which were without the city, and they concurred. So many people gathered together, and they stopped all the fountains and the brook that flowed through the midst of the land, saying, 'Why should the kings of Assyria come and find much water?' " (II Chron. 32:2–4).

The event is mentioned also by Ben Sira (early 2nd century B.C.E.): "Hezekiah fortified his city and brought the water to its midst; he pierced the rock with iron and enclosed the pool with mountains" (Ecclus. 48:17). Centuries later, the Rabbis still referred to the blocking of "the upper waters of the Gihon," and included this achievement as one of the three things which Hezekiah did against the wishes of the Sages (Pesaḥim 4:9).

The tunnel was dug simultaneously – like the one in Megiddo – from both ends. Despite the fact that the tunnel meanders, instead of following a straight line, the amount of error at the meeting point of the two ends was minimal. There was a difference of only about 12 inches in elevation! The northern end, however, deviates from left to right several times near the point where the workmen broke through. It seems that the parties could hear the blows of each other's pickaxes when they were about 100 ft. apart, and the work continued from then on in feverish haste.

The length of the tunnel was over 500 yards, and it led to a pool at the southwestern spur of the City of David. The height of the tunnel fluctuates between 4 and 10 ft., with the differences in height probably due to the variable hardness of the rock. The tunnel carries water to this day, and it is still possible to wade through it, though in some places the low ceiling forces one to stoop slightly. Throughout the tunnel, there is a total drop of just over 6½ ft., but there is no gradual decline. Corrections in depth had to be made at several points, and at some places the tunnel actually inclines in the wrong direction.

Had the tunnel been hewn in a straight line, it would have saved over 200 yards of tunneling. Several suggestions have been made as to why this was not done. It is possible that the tunnel had to avoid the tombs of the kings of Judah which, it is alleged, were in this area. (Archaeologists have not yet been able to find traces of the royal tombs.) A more likely explanation is that the tunnel followed an existing crevice in the rock, through which the water seeped, and that the crevice was then widened into a tunnel. This would also explain the use of the term "upper Gihon," as the emergence of the water at the southern apex of the hill would then be known as the lower Gihon.

Some schoolboys bathing in the tunnel in 1880 discovered an inscription commemorating the digging of the tunnel and the meeting of the two excavating parties. It had been incised on a panel on the tunnel wall, not far from its end. The inscription (fig. 72), surprisingly enough, represents only the second half of the text. It reads:

...the tunnel. And this is the story of the tunnel whilst [the miners lifted the] pick each toward his fellow and whilst three cubits [yet remained] to be bored [there was heard] the voice of a man calling his fellow, for there was a split in the rock on the right hand and on [the left hand]. And on the day of the boring through the miners struck, each in direction of his fellow, pick against pick. And the water started flowing from the source to the pool, twelve hundred cubits. A hundred cubits was [the height of] the rock above the head of the miners. (The inscription is now in the Istanbul Museum.)

There are three other panels farther inside the tunnel, but they do not bear any inscription. The explanation of why only the second half of the text was inscribed stems from the method used. The complete inscription was probably first chalked on the rock. The workman, however, would start the inscription from the end, in order not to obliterate the initial markings as he worked.

It has been conjectured that the tunnel was hewn before the danger of a siege by Sennacherib became imminent, and that the workman was interrupted in his task by the arrival of the enemy forces. He was never able to complete his work. The location of the panel at the end of the tunnel, rather than at the point where the digging parties met, was to make it more accessible to the workman.

The tunnel of Hezekiah had one serious drawback; it deprived the Kidron

Figure 72:   Inscription found in the rock wall of Hezekiah's tunnel, late 8th cent. B.C.E. It describes the last moments in the hewing of the conduit, when the two groups of borers were about to meet each other in the middle of the tunnel

Valley of its irrigation water. This was corrected a short time after the excavation of the tunnel, when a channel was hewn which diverted part of the waters of the pool back into the southern end of the Kidron Valley. Part of this channel is still visible today, running under a rock overhang near the pool.

(Another water system thought to have been begun by Hezekiah in the face of the Assyrian onslaught — but never finished — is a huge shaft, more than 65 ft. deep and some 82 ft. wide, discovered at Lachish. That city, unlike Jerusalem, fell before the powerful northern enemy.)

THE POOL OF GIBEON

Some 8 miles north of Jerusalem is the Arab village of el-Jīb. An ancient site next to the village has been identified as the biblical city of Gibeon, an identification which has been borne out by the finding there of jar handles inscribed with the word "Gibeon." In the Bible the city is frequently mentioned, and generally in connection with water. We are informed that Joshua made the Gibeonites serve as hewers of wood and drawers of water (Josh. 9:3—27). There is also mention in the Book of Samuel of a "pool of Gibeon" and in Jeremiah of the "many waters" of Gibeon. After the death of Saul, when David contended with Ish-Bosheth for the throne, Joab and Abner, the generals commanding the two opposing forces, met at "the pool of Gibeon" where a great battle took place (II Sam. 2:12–17). Some 400 years later, Ishmael the son of Nethaniah assassinated Gedaliah, the Jewish viceroy over Judah, who had been appointed by Nebuchadnezzar after the destruction of the Temple. Johanan, the son of Kareah, went to avenge Gedaliah's death and came upon Ishmael by "the many waters of Gibeon" (Jer. 41:12). These various phrases have been puzzling, because there is no river or pool, or "many waters" near Gibeon today.

The answer to this riddle has been supplied by archaeology. In the excavations carried out at Gibeon by J.P. Pritchard, not one but two great waterworks were discovered (fig 73a-c). The first, which later proved to be the more recent in construction, was similar to the Jebusite project at the Ophel. It consisted of a long tunnel with 93 steps, which led down into an underground cistern. The cistern received its water by a twisting feeder-tunnel from a spring. The roundabout route of the feeder-tunnel probably followed an existing crevice in the rock, which was widened to allow a free flow of water. There was also a short passage which led from the cistern chamber directly outside, through an entrance low in the hillside. In the walls near the entry of this passage were vertical grooves with adjoining grooves in the floor. According to Pritchard these grooves were intended to accommodate great stone slabs which could 'close the passage in time of siege. The entrance would then be camouflaged from the outside, while the besieged would have access to the water through the tunnel inside the city. At Gibeon, in contrast to the Ophel, it seems that the tunnel was also used in peacetime, for the steps were found to be worn, and the sides of the tunnel at waist to shoulder height were smooth from the passage of the water-carriers, who steadied themselves against the walls as they made their way up the slippery steps of the tunnel. Niches to hold lamps were found at intervals on both sides of the passage. The outer entrance, at the bottom of the hill, must have been opened for those working in the fields outside the town, so that they would not have to climb up to the town and down again through the tunnel when they were in need of water.

A second water system at Gibeon, far more elaborate, but less adequate, was found quite by accident, immediately next to the tunnel. It was the earlier of the two systems, and probably dates from the 12th century. It consists of a gigantic cylindrical pit which measures 37 ft. across and 35 ft. deep. Leading down along the inside of its wall is a spiral stairway of 40 steps, carved out of the rock (except for the third three). The steps are 5 ft.

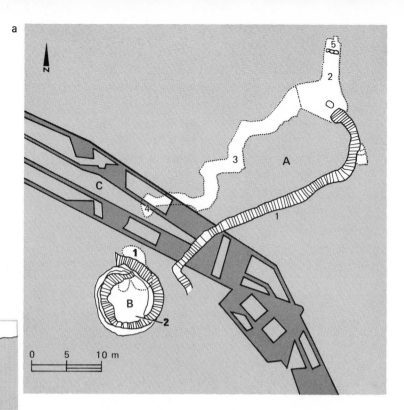

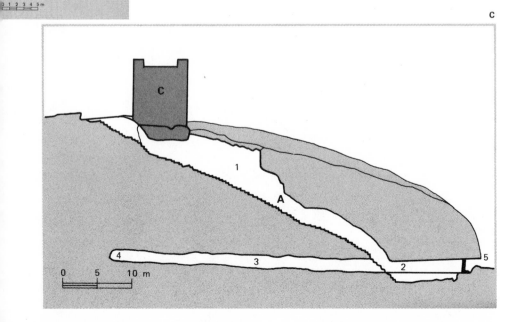

Figure 73: Plan of the two waterworks at Gibeon (a) and cross sections (b, c). The first waterwork (B) is a pool within the city wall (C) with spiral stairs (1) leading to water level (2). The second waterwork (A) consists of a tunnel (1) leading from inside the city to a cistern (2) which is supplied by water from the spring (4) through a sloping tunnel (3). Another entrance (5) led from outside the city.

wide and are protected by a rock balustrade to prevent people from falling into the pit. At the bottom of the spiral stairway, an additional 39 steps lead down through a tunnel, to a kidney-shaped water room which lies at a depth of 80 ft. below the town. This storage-room is not connected with the spring, but lies at the level of the natural water table. It was designed so that the underground water seeped into the room.

Evidently, however, this was not enough to supply the needs of the town, so the second system was prepared. It was clear to the excavators that the stepped tunnel leading to the cistern was dug later than the cylindrical pit, for at one point it veers off at an angle designed to avoid the pit. Pritchard believes that the cylindrical pit was originally meant to reach water level itself, but that the process of excavating proved too ambitious or expensive, so that the project was continued by the tunnel which led to the water room. The great pit was quite a remarkable architectural achievement for its time, and must have been famed in the area. Thus it is very likely that this is the pool of Gibeon. The original pit and water room, together with the second water system of tunnel and cistern, would certainly justify the description of "many waters" used in the Bible.

THE WATERWORKS OF MEGIDDO

A water system attributed to Solomon was found at Megiddo (fig. 74). Far down the slope of the mound of Megiddo was a cave which led to a spring. A passage, some 3 to 4 ft. wide, with stone-faced walls, led from the city to the cave. The passage must have been covered so that it was invisible from the outside. In this way the people of Megiddo could make their way unobserved down to the cave, which was also camouflaged. Inside the cave was found the burned skeleton of a guard who seems to have died at his

Figure 74: Waterworks at Megiddo, showing the gallery (A) and the shaft (B)

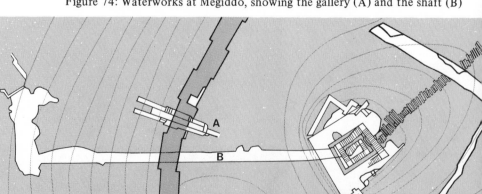

post when the cave was suddenly discovered and attacked. He had never been buried, but had been left where he fell and burned in the conflagration which took place immediately afterward.

The hewn stones which lined the passage at the point where it passed outside the city were similar in type to those of the Solomonic palace and gate of Megiddo, and Yadin has shown that stratigraphically this water system belongs with the other Solomonic remains in the city. Clearly, when Solomon rebuilt Megiddo, with its large palaces, casemate walls, and massive gate, he also made sure of the town's water supply in times of danger. Thus the terse biblical statement that Solomon built Megiddo has been greatly amplified by archaeological excavations which have shown his activities to have covered the three essential features of the ancient city: the buildings, the fortifications, and the water supply.

Solomon's water system at Megiddo was discovered by enemy forces, probably at the time when Shishak of Egypt invaded Israel and captured the city. The passage was therefore blocked during the next stage of the town's development, and a far more ambitious water system was evolved. A great vertical shaft was cut through the debris of earlier settlements and into the rock. Until solid rock was reached, the top part of the shaft was lined with a masonry retaining wall. The vertical shaft became a steep passage which, 115 ft. down, culminated in a tunnel over 200 ft. long, with an arched (rather than square or rounded) ceiling. A close examination of the tunnel showed that it had been hewn simultaneously from both ends. The amount of error in elevation and direction at the point where the two excavations met was remarkably small and one cannot but admire the skill of those early engineers. The tunnel ended at the spring in the cave. Thus the inhabitants of Megiddo could make their way unobserved, down the stairway along the side of the shaft, through the tunnel, to the water cave. The outside entry was blocked, so that the water could be reached only from inside the city.

At a still later stage, the tunnel was deepened to allow the water to flow to the end of the shaft, which was then used as a well. It would seem, however, that this method did not prove too successful, so that new steps were built along the shaft, to allow the people to descend to the water once more. As the shaft and tunnel postdate the Solomonic water passage, they are attributed to Jeroboam or Ahab.

Megiddo had at least one other source of water during the period of the divided kingdom. Leading down from the city gate were steps which had previously been thought to constitute a pedestrian approach to the town. However, when Yadin excavated the foot of the steps he discovered that they turned at a right angle and led to a plastered water cistern. This then provided a second source of water for the inhabitants of the city, although how the cistern was filled is not quite clear yet. In all probability the steps belonged to a covered passageway which would not have constituted a source of danger to the city as it ended outside the fortified gateway.

There exists the possibility that Megiddo had a third method of water supply, through a shaft and channel connected to a spring lying to the north of the city. This possibility has not yet been thoroughly explored. In any event, Megiddo seems to have been endowed with a plentiful supply of water, so that it could withstand a prolonged siege.

THE WATERWORKS AT HAZOR

Similar to the shaft and tunnel of Megiddo, and dating from the same period, is a shaft and tunnel discovered by Yadin at Hazor (fig. 75a-c). The shaft at Hazor, however, is twice as large as that at Megiddo, and is reached by two descending flights of steps which lead to a monumental gate built of hewn stone, in the typical Israelite style of the period.

The top part of the shaft is lined with a rough stone retaining wall, while the lower part is hewn out of the soft rock. Around the side were hewn steps 10 ft. wide. According to Yadin, the exaggerated width of the stairs suggested that pack animals were used to bring up the water. The shaft led to a tunnel which continued the descent to the water table. As at Megiddo, the tunnel's ceiling was vault-shaped. The total depth was almost 150 ft., the shaft being about 100 ft. deep and the tunnel descending some 50 ft. further. It is possible that the tunnel ended in a square quarried pool from which the water was drawn, but this is not yet clear.

Surprisingly, the tunnel was not dug in the direction of a spring which lay to the south of Hazor, but to the west, to reach the water table. According to Yadin this system had the advantage of lying completely within the precincts of the city. It certainly proves that the architects had a thorough knowledge of the geological formation of the rock strata. Such knowledge has already been demonstrated by the other water systems recounted above, but it is particularly striking at Hazor.

Actually the shaft and tunnel at Hazor bear greater resemblance to the great pit and passage at Gibeon than to the system at Megiddo, but the connection with Gibeon — the possibility of the one influencing the other — is, of course, unknown.

a

b

c

Figure 75: Waterworks at Hazor,
in use in the 9th–8th cent. B.C.E.:
(a) top part of the shaft; (b) lower
part of the shaft with steps leading
to the pool; (c) the pool

THE WATER SYSTEM AT GEZER

Another example of a shaft-and-tunnel water system was found at Gezer
(fig. 76). It consists of a rectangular shaft with steps cut out of the rock.
(Only the top two steps have remained.) The shaft is about 27 ft. deep and
leads into a tunnel which slants downward from one side of the shaft. The
entrance to the tunnel is through an imposing archway which is almost as
high as the shaft is deep. The tunnel itself has steps carved out of the rock
all the way down, and is about 132 ft. in length. There are small niches
along the sides which Macalister suggested may have been dug out to help
people grip the walls on their way up. Unlike Hazor and Megiddo, the
ceiling of the tunnel was rounded. The tunnel led to a large cave which was
filled by spring water, at a depth of about 100 ft. underground. Macalister
was unable to measure or gauge the depth of the pool, but the level of the
water in it remained constant even after he had drawn off about 200
gallons.

Macalister and others after him thought that the water had been found
accidentally, and that the purpose of the tunnel was originally to serve
either as a secret way out of the city, or as a means of reaching the spring

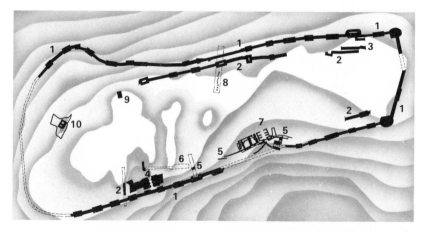

1. Outer wall of the Late Bronze Age.
2. Inner wall of the Middle Bronze Age.
3. Part of the inner wall.
4. Gate of the inner wall, three entry way.
5. Part of the casemate wall.
6. Water tunnel of the Late Bronze Age.
7. Four entry way gate of the Solomonic
   period.
8. High place of the Middle Bronze Age.
9. Wêli (a hole to obtain water).
10. Part of the inner wall (excavation
    of 1934).

Figure 76: Plan of Tell Gezer

outside the walls. However, careful study of Gibeon and Hazor have shown that the geological strata was clearly understood, and that the engineers of these waterworks knew that in order to find water, only the water table had to be reached, and not necessarily the spring itself.

When Macalister discovered the water system of Gezer at the beginning of the century, he dated it at about 2000 B.C.E. Ruth Amiran, in turn, suggested dating it in the Late Bronze period. The discovery of the water system at Hazor and the new dating of the system at Megiddo, both of which evidently belong to the 9th century B.C.E., have aroused renewed interest in the Gezer tunnel. Whereas W.G. Dever, presently excavating at Gezer, still prefers an early date in the Late Bronze Age, Yadin has suggested that the Gezer shaft and tunnel might possibly be from the same period as the waterworks at Megiddo and Hazor. In summation, we may say that archaeological research underscores the vital role of water supply in the development of the ancient city. Moreover, the safeguarding of that supply played an essential part in the planning of the city's fortifications system.

In Israel, the development of water systems dates back to Canaanite times, but it reached a peak in the period of the monarchy. The waterworks discovered and explored by archaeologists add new dimensions to our understanding of the building projects of the kings of Judah and Israel.

Part Two

ASPECTS OF ECONOMIC LIFE

10

AGRICULTURE

FROM THE BEGINNING OF THE BRONZE AGE TO THE CONQUEST

The earliest literary evidence of local agricultural activity is provided by an inscription on the grave of the Egyptian officer Uni, who conducted a military expedition in Palestine during the reign of King Pepi I (beginning of the 24th century B.C.E.). "The army returned in peace after smiting the country of the sand dwellers [the inhabitants of the coastal plain]... after he had cut down its figs and vines." At that time the highway running along the coastal plain and through the Jezreel and Jordan valleys became increasingly important, and many settlements were established along its route. Settlements were also founded in the south of the Judean mountains, for example at Tell Beit Mirsim, usually identified as the biblical Debir.

The Sinuhe scroll (20th century B.C.E.) describes travels of an Egyptian officer in Palestine, and indicates that, in the southern regions of the country, there were settlements which supported themselves by farming and cattle raising. Evidence of many settlements during the 19th century B.C.E. is furnished by the Egyptian "Execration Texts."

Permanent settlements were not established by the Patriarchs, who were nomads. On occasion, however, they would occupy marginal grassland areas and sow crops there. Thus Isaac planted in the Nahal Gerar region "in that year" and as a result of plentiful rainfall, reaped a "hundredfold" harvest (Gen. 26:12).

Other scriptural references suggest that the land of Canaan was closely settled and highly valued at this time. Abraham's and Lot's shepherds quarreled with each other while the "Canaanite and Perizzite dwelt then in the land" (Gen. 13:7). When Abraham sought to purchase a burial plot, he had to pay Ephron, the Hittite, "the full price" (Gen. ch. 23), and Jacob similarly had to pay a large sum for the section of the field in Shechem where he pitched his tents (Gen. 33:19).

Figure 77:   The "Karnak Botanical Garden," the relief in the Temple of Amon at Karnak depicting the plants brought back to Egypt from Palestine by Thutmose III

The depiction at the Temple of Amon of Thutmose's expeditions in Palestine (c. 1478 B.C.E.) and his victory at Megiddo includes reliefs of the plants he brought from Palestine (fig. 77). (This is known as the Karnak "Botanical Garden.") An inscription states that "the amount of harvest brought . . . from the Maket [plain of Jezreel] was 280,000 heqt of corn [150,000 bushels] beside what was reaped and taken by the king's soldiers."

EARLY ISRAELITE AGRICULTURE

In contrast to scriptural references, external evidence on the state of local agriculture just before and after the Israelite conquest is rather meager. Archaeological discoveries indicate that the areas sown and planted in biblical times coincide with the regions watered by rain or irrigation today. An intensively farmed, settled area existed in the irrigated regions of the Jordan Valley, and another along the Mediterranean coast (where the annual precipitation exceeds 12 in.).

There were no stable agricultural settlements in the northern Negev. The land there was cultivated but once in several years, when plentiful rainfall would yield abundant harvests. The southern Negev and Arabah were wastelands, except for desert oases and irrigation projects where waters flowing down from the mountains were collected behind dams. Such projects, however, were limited to the Israelite kingdom.

Forests and woods spread over the hills, in rocky regions which were difficult to cultivate, and in areas where the lack of security made cultivation of the soil and investment in agricultural installations too hazardous. Broad forests also extended along the north and northeast boundaries – in Gilead, Bashan, and the Lebanon. There, in the vegetation along the Jordan and in the deserts, wild beasts lurked (Jer. 49:19; 50:44). During the intervals when the land lay desolate, animals would invade the ruins where forests had begun to grow. Several times the Bible issues a warning against the danger of a too rapid military conquest: "Thou mayest not consume them too quickly, lest the beasts of the field increase upon thee" (Deut. 7:22; Ex. 23:29; Num. 26:12).

During the early period of settlement in Canaan, it would seem that the Israelites were primarily engaged in tending flocks, as in patriarchal days. The Song of Deborah yields no trace of extensive occupation with agriculture, even though the soil was tilled. The tribe of Reuben is described as living "among the sheepfolds, to hear the pipings of the flocks" (Judg. 5:16). Scripture also testifies to the existence of broad grazing lands in Gilead and Bashan in Transjordan, the areas settled by the tribes of Reuben and Gad and half the tribe of Manasseh, all of whom owned much livestock (Num. 32; Deut. 3:19; Josh. 1:14). Although the Bible does portray the land of Canaan as "flowing with milk and honey" (date syrup), no conclusions can be drawn from this expression as to the relative importance of grazing land ("milk") as opposed to soil cultivation ("honey"). Livestock was raised to a limited extent in the border grassland regions and deserts, or was fed on the stubble of the grain fields and the stalks of the vegetable gardens. During the period of the conquest, sheep and cattle were also grazed in the forests which had covered the farm lands.

The Bible states that the Israelites would enter a land highly developed in farming and in established agricultural installations (Deut. 6:11). Special reference is made to hill cultivation where terraced fields were planted with vines and fruit trees and contained water cisterns, oil and wine presses, and tanks. Since the Canaanites had not yet been ousted from the fertile valleys, the wheat fields were not available to the Israelites (Judg. 1:19, 27–36), who settled initially in the hilly regions.

Hill cultivation is intensive by nature; land holdings are small and specialized knowledge and experience are needed for such farming to yield a livelihood. These conditions apparently explain why Ephraim and half the tribe of Manasseh complained to Joshua that the mountain of Ephraim was too small to maintain them. Joshua advised them to go to the forests of

Gilead and Bashan, fell the trees, and settle there. There is an implicit assumption that in securing the dominating heights, they would succeed in dislodging the Canaanites from the valleys (Josh. 17:14—18). Clearing the forests was by no means easy, and was not yet completed in the reign of David, for this region included the "Forest of Ephraim" where the armies of David and Absalom fought each other (II Sam. 18:6—8).

Either through hard-won experience, or by observing the agricultural practices of the indigenous population, the Israelites gradually succeeded not only in mastering agricultural skills but also in organizing permanent town and village settlements. The nomads, enemies of the Israelites from the desert period, now envied the successful Israelite colonization. Together with their flocks, they raided Israelite territory and plundered the fields. Between each nomadic wave, the Israelites harvested their fields in haste and stored the produce in hidden receptacles (Judg. 6:2). Rather than use an exposed threshing floor, Gideon was forced to thresh his harvested wheat in a barn where fleeces were dried (Judg. 6:37—40). Gideon was a well-to-do farmer, owning cattle and sheep, vines, and wheat fields. The ordinary Israelite, however, seems to have been poor. His main diet consisted of barley, and consequently the Israelites were contemptuously represented in the Midianite soldier's dream as a "cake of barley bread" baked on coals (Judg. 7:13).

The state of agriculture in biblical times may be deduced from the laws of land inheritance enumerated in the Pentateuch, the descriptions of the settlement of the tribes, the divisions of parcels of land among the various families, and the procedure of redeeming estates recounted in the Book of Ruth. These sources reveal Israelite agriculture as based on the small, single-family holding. It depicts an idyllic, prosperous village life, although workers were only hired at harvest time, and even the wealthy Boaz personally supervised the stacking of the grain after the winnowing.

In the course of time, however, a poor, landless class arose — as Scripture itself had foreseen: "the poor shall never cease out of the land" (Deut. 25:11). The unfortunates were the recipients of gifts to the poor: the gleanings, the forgotten sheaves, the corners of the fields, the poor tithe. The Book of Ruth reflects these practices, as well as the redeeming of fields to insure the continuity of family ties with the land. The almost sacred bond tying the Israelite farmer to his inherited land was characteristic of economic life during the biblical period. This relationship is an important element in the speedy recovery of local agriculture after every period of desolation.

One of the earliest Hebrew inscriptions known is an agricultural calendar from the 10th century found at Gezer (fig. 78). It contains the Hebrew months of the year by the agricultural activities, listing eight agricultural activities, four of them of a two-month duration and four of one-month duration. It reads as follows:

> The [two] months of harvest
> The [two] months of sowing
> The [two] months of late planting
> The month of reaping flax
> The month of reaping barley
> The month of reaping and measuring
> The [two] months of [vine] tending
> The month of summer [-fruit]

Although the purpose of the calendar is not clear and may have been a schoolboy exercise, nevertheless it supplies, in addition, indirect evidence to some type of formal instruction during that period.

Figure 78:   The Gezer Calendar, a record of the annual cycle of agricultural occupations, listing eight agricultural activities. Dating to the 10th cent. B.C.E

Israelite agriculture based on the independent family farm was, with the rise of the monarchy, threatened with collapse. Samuel warned the assembled people: "He [the king] will take your fields and your vineyards, and your olive yards, even the best of them, and give them to his servants" (I Sam.13:13). Although David owned royal estates over which he appointed officials (I Chron. 27:26–29), they were apparently conquered and annexed territories or else previously unworked areas which were developed by royal initiative. In the days of Solomon, boundaries were extended, and officials "who provided victuals for the king and his household" (I Kings 4:7) administered the royal estates. Agriculture prospered as was reflected in the Bible: "Judah and Israel dwelt safely, every man under his vine and fig tree from Dan to Beer-Sheba. . . " (I Kings 5:5).

Uzziah, king of Judah, called "lover of husbandry" was noted for owning fields and vineyards, and for building "towers in the wilderness and hewing out many cisterns" (II Chron. 26:10). Evidence corroborating this statement has been found through a survey in the Negev hill region. The archaeological survey revealed a series of small fortresses, usually with agricultural settlements near them, dating to the monarchy period (c. 10th–7th century B.C.E.). The settlements were either built near river plains using the terracing system of agriculture, or built on the slopes around the fortress with a cistern in the center. They contained a few Israelite houses and a closed courtyard which probably served for the cattle. It would appear that settlements of this type were guard posts and supply stations along the Negev caravan routes, probably in the time of three kings who ruled Elath: Solomon, Jehoshaphat, and Uzziah. During the reign of Uzziah agriculture and agronomy reached a peak of development, and were described by Isaiah as wisdom emanating from God, who had taught the sons of man excellent methods of plowing and reaping (Isa. 28:23–29) (see below). After the death of Uzziah, security deteriorated and a decline set in among the Israelite settlements in the lowland. Against this background, Isaiah prophesied better days to come, when settlements would extend through the lowland, when the farmer would sow his irrigated fields near the springs, and the shepherd tend his flocks without interference (Isa. 32:19–20).

The story of Naboth's vineyard, which was coveted by King Ahab, who wished to convert it into a vegetable garden, reflects agricultural conditions in the northern kingdom. Whereas the king respected the sanctity of a paternal inheritance to an Israelite farmer, Queen Jezebel, a Sidonian princess, could not appreciate it (I Kings ch. 21). With the passage of time, apparently, the poor, the widows, and the orphans were, in increasing numbers, evicted from their holdings, and the prophet denounced those "who join house to house, that lay field to field" (Isa. 5:68). Nevertheless, in the main, the right of inheritance to patriarchal estates was upheld, and when Jerusalem was actually under siege, Jeremiah, exercising his right of redemption, bought a plot of land (32:7—12).

The remarkable agricultural prosperity of the land of Israel during the First Temple period is indicated in Ezekiel 27:17, which lists the exports of Judah and Israel to the market of Tyre as wheat of Minnith (probably a place in Transjordan), "pannag" (which cannot be clearly identified), honey, oil, and balm.

With the destruction of the kingdom of Israel at the end of the 8th century B.C.E., Samaria was denuded of its Israelite population, and repopulated by the nations the king of Assyria transported from other districts of his empire. The new inhabitants, later called Samaritans, failed to farm their land properly. Perhaps the lions that attacked them (II Kings 17:25—27) had found a lair in the forests which encroached on neglected farms. There is no further information on conditions in Galilee, but evidently some Israelites must have remained there since Hezekiah communicated with them (II Chron. ch. 30), and Josiah extended his domain over them (II Chron. 34:6). A few biblical passages point to persisting desolation, and a prophecy predicted the restoration of cultivation in Samaria (Jer. 31:5).

Figure 79: Hebrew ostracon from Mesad Hashaviahu, late 7th cent. B.C.E., containing a letter of a poor reaper complaining before the governor (?) that an officer had confiscated his garment unjustly

THE PERIOD OF THE RETURN

Having destroyed the Temple, Nebuzaradan left in Judah only "the poorest of the land to be vinedressers and husbandmen" (II Kings 25:12), apparently tenant farmers or hired workers of the royal estates. He may also have left behind those familiar with local methods of soil cultivation, in order to prevent the further deterioration of the farms by unskilled and inexperienced labor. The impoverished Jews and the foreigners who settled in abandoned Jewish territory could not, however, maintain the terraced hill farms and orchards. When the exiles returned, they found the land forsaken and desolate. They proceeded to repair the terraces, to restore the agricultural installations, and to plant vines and fruit trees. Yet, due to their ignorance of how to exploit the rain water for hill cultivation, they failed to establish viable farms.

Somewhat later, conditions improved. Farming prospered, and the prophet Malachi regarded the changed situation as a manifestation of God's love for His people. Desolate Edom is contrasted with prospering Judah (1:2–3).

From the books of Ezra and Nehemiah it appears, however, that this optimism was premature, as a period of growing moral degeneration set in. Poor farmers were evicted from their lands by the rich, and a new land-owning class emerged. The new conditions loosened the bonds tying the farmer to his patrimony, and agriculture suffered. Now the foreigners, who had been forced to restore the lands seized from the Israelites, began to raise their heads. They obtained employment from the new owners and were often able to buy back the lands they had forfeited. Fields, vineyards, and orchards were neglected, and the woods again spread over arable fields. From these trees, the Jews were enjoined to cut branches and build tabernacles (Neh. 8:15).

As a result of the social and agrarian reforms instituted by Ezra and Nehemiah, the Jewish population became more securely settled. Although a significant portion of the land still belonged to the king of Persia, the Jewish settlement broke through its boundaries by extending northward toward Galilee. The meager historical source material for the period includes the Book of Judith, assigned to the early fourth century (the period of Arta-xerxes II, 404–359 B.C.E.). The setting of the book is the hills overlooking Jezreel. The Jewish settlements mentioned as existing in the vicinity (Judith 7:3–13) apparently formed the link between the inhabited areas of Judea and the colonies that flourished in Galilee in later generations.

AGRICULTURAL METHODS AND IMPLEMENTS

Both the Written and the Oral Laws reveal that, for long periods of time, the local inhabitants believed that they indeed lived in a land of milk and honey. Many wonder how so small a country, consisting mostly of mountains and desert, could sustain a population sometimes numbering several million, most of whom subsisted on agriculture. The answer lies in the energy of the farmers, their intensive cultivation of the soil, the firm bond tying them to their inherited land, and the many skills accumulated and handed down from one generation to another. Thus, Israelite agriculture progressed in the biblical period. The following are the techniques that were so successful in ancient days:

Plowing (fig. 80). This operation was considered crucial in producing a successful harvest. Done properly, it penetrated the soil deeply, and preserved the fertility of the land. Such deep penetration slowed the process of plowing, and thus only a relatively small area was prepared in a day. Isaiah noted that the soil was plowed twice before it was sown. The first time was to bare the soil to the penetration of rainwater, and the second to level the ground for planting (Isa. 28:24).

To preserve the fertility of the soil, a system of rotation was practiced in which land was alternatively sown and left fallow. It was not easy for the farmer to adapt himself to this cycle, which meant that he could plant his field only three years out of seven, the seventh being the Sabbatical year, but he knew that this was the only way to ensure continuous, abundant harvests. Only artificially fertilized fields could be plowed year after year with good results.

The plow was not essentially different from the implement used today in the Arab fallah's farm, except that the ancient instrument was sturdier and was capable of penetrating more deeply into the soil. It was made of wood and metal (bronze in earlier times; later of iron). Such implements have been uncovered in archaeological excavations in Israel. The metal part was funnel-shaped, ending in a sharp point. The plowshare was attached to the sharp wooden tailpiece which in turn was joined to the "knee," and was tied to the handle, a long pole that was attached to the yoke.

The plowman depressed the handle with one hand. In the other he held a long staff or goad with a nail at one end, which was used to goad the oxen and hold them in line. The other end was shaped like a shovel and served to clean the plow (see I Sam. 13:21). The animals drawing the plow were tied

Figure 80:   Arab plowing with a wooden plow similar to the ancient implement

to it by the yoke, which was a pole placed on the neck of the ox or cow. To yoke a pair of oxen, an additional pole was drawn under their necks while pegs joined the two poles together, thereby enclosing the heads of the oxen in frames. A broken pole could not be repaired, and the animal would have to be released. Hence "breaking the yoke" symbolized liberation (Jer. 2:20). Generally the yoke was made of wood; only in exceptional cases was it made of metal; accordingly, an "iron yoke" represented abnormal or tyrannical oppression (Deut. 28:48). A single ox was tied to his yoke by ropes, and the snapping of these bonds, too, became a metaphor for liberation (Isa. 58:6; Jer. 2:20).

A sturdy strain of oxen capable of bearing a double-poled yoke was used for plowing. The Torah regards the ox and the donkey as plowing animals (Deut. 22:10), and Isaiah mentions the use of donkeys for tilling the soil (30:24).

Planting. Fertilization also increased the productivity of the soil, and undoubtedly preceded the sowing of crops. The Bible makes no specific references to fertilization, but the analogy is frequently drawn between heaps of dead bodies and a heap of dung (e.g. II Kings 9:37). Apparently ashes also served this purpose (Ezek. 28:18).

The main crops were winter grains, which were planted at various times before the rains, and especially after the early rain. Usually the farmer distributed his sowing over various periods of the winter season (Eccles. 11:6), for if he planted all his crops together, a single adverse natural phenomenon could ruin them all. The normal planting season lasted from Tishri (October) to the end of Tevet (December).

The usual cycle in crop cultivation was plowing, planting and hoeing (fig. 81), with the last activity designed to remove noxious weeds. The main implement involved, the *ma'ader*, is somewhat different from the modern hoe. It consisted of two sticks tied together by a cord to form an acute angle. At the end of the shorter arm, a metal "tooth" was inserted. Such hoes frequently appear in Egyptian drawings. The *ma'ader* was used for digging in mountain areas where the plow could not be used (Isa. 7:25). Deep hoeing to prepare the earth for saplings was also known (Isa. 5:2).

Figure 81: *Ma'ader* (hoe), made of two sticks tied together with cord. Detail from fresco in the tomb of Rekh-mi-Re at Thebes, 15th cent. B.C.E.

Figure 82: Wall painting from Deir al-Madina, Egypt, showing a man harvesting with a sickle and his wife collecting the sheaves in a basket, 13th cent. B.C.E. According to biblical law, the gleanings were left for the poor

Harvest (fig. 82). The term *kaẓir* (harvest) applied to winter crops. There were two such harvests; first, the early ripening, various types of barley; later, the wheat and rice-wheat harvest (Ex. 9:31). At Passover, the *omer* (a measure) of barley was offered (Lev. 23:10; cf. II Sam. 21:9; II Kings 4:42). The Gezer calendar (see above) also lists barley as the first of the cereal harvests. Before the *omer* was offered, the new season's grain was not to be eaten (Lev. 23:14). Seven weeks later, the wheat harvest began with the offering of "the two loaves of bread" (Lev. 23:17).

At harvest time, the climate in Palestine is hot and dry. More than once the reaper was felled by sunstroke (cf. II Kings 4:18–20; Judith 8:2–3). He rose early to take advantage of the cool, morning hours, and he had to work quickly to avoid plunder, pests and the falling of the ripe heads of grain. In addition to his family, he sought to employ hired hands. The division of labor is depicted in the Book of Ruth. A supervisor would watch the workers. Girls were occupied with gleaning and also in tying sheaves. The owner supplied part of the food of his workers, bread dipped in vinegar. Only the wicked who exploited their workers failed to provide food (Job 24:10–11).

Even though the work was backbreaking, it was performed in a happy mood, to the accompaniment of joyous shouts (Ps. 126:5–6; Isa. 9:2). The poor, who gathered their gifts, also contributed to the festive atmosphere. Sometimes joy would be absent, when the land had been afflicted by drought (Deut. 11:17), or when the enemy attacked the reapers and pillaged the harvest (Isa. 16:7).

Harvesting Tools. The *"hermesh"* (Deut. 16:9) and *"maggal"* (Jer. 2:16) are mentioned in the Bible. It is almost certain that the two names signify the same object, the sickle. It had a short handle, in which there was inserted a curved blade with its short teeth bent backward. Archaeological excavations in Israel have uncovered flint, bone, bronze and iron sickles. When harvesting, the reaper grasped the stalks in his left hand. In his right he held the sickle, which he would "send out" (Joel 4:14) and pull back, so severing the stalk (Isa. 17:5; Ps. 129:7). When his left hand was full, he would lay the grain on the ground in bundles (Ruth 2:16), or else tie them together with a straw. The small heaps laid along the harvested rows would be gathered up by the sheaf-binder and held in his bosom (Ps. 129:7). They were then gathered into larger bundles, which were left lying on the ground, or else tied together in sheaves (Gen. 37:7–8). Once the grain was dry, it was collected in a large stack. An alternative practice was to heap the grain in various types of stacks to hasten or retard the drying process as desired. This stacking was the final destination of the grain prior to its being transported to the threshing floor.

The threshing floor stood near the city or village (I Kings 22:10), usually in a broad public place. There the grain was brought and spread out in a circle.

During the threshing, the grain was pounded to separate the kernels from the husks. This could be accomplished in several ways. A wooden board called a *morag* (fig. 83) about two by four feet in size, was used. Its underside was set with stones, mainly of basalt, so that when dragged by a pair of oxen, the weighted board would separate the grain. Since this tool was only adopted much later in Greece and Rome, there are grounds for assuming that it was the invention of the farmer in Erez Israel. This assumption may explain the exclamation of Isaiah (28:29): "This also cometh from the Lord of hosts; wonderful is His counsel and great His wisdom." In the preceding verses the prophet enumerates the threshing tools then in use. These included the normal *morag* as well as one with saw-like strips of iron set in it, and "cartwheels," which were discs made of stone or iron sharpened like a saw.

In contrast to these mechanical means, another method of threshing was to have oxen or other animals trample the grain (Deut. 25:4).

Figure 83:   The *morag,* a wooden board with small basalt stone discs set in it

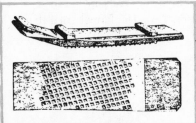

These methods were used to thresh wheat and legumes. More delicate grains were normally threshed with a stick (Isa. 28:29) as were small quantities of wheat (Judg. 6:11; Ruth 2:17).

Threshing separated the three components of the grain: kernels, chopped straw, and chaff. Winnowing, which consisted of throwing the threshed substances into the wind, caused the lighter elements to be carried away while the heavier kernels fell down in a heap. The implement for this process (Isa. 30:24) resembled a pitchfork with broad prongs. Next the kernels would be thrown up in the air by means of a shovel-like implement. This operation over, the harvest would be considered completed. The farmer would measure its size (Haggai 2:16) and stand guard over it till it was transferred to the barn (Ruth 3:7). The chopped straw left over from the winnowing would be kept for livestock feed, mortar, or compost.

Even after the final winnowing, the kernel heaps still retained waste matter. The grains would then be shaken horizontally in a sieve, a round device, to whose bottom a fiber net was attached. The heavier waste would fall through the threads, and the lighter gather on top of the kernels. The top waste would constantly be removed, until only the clean kernels remained in the sieve (cf. Amos 9:9). The kernels were then milled or crushed, and further cleaned with the aid of sieves with holes of various sizes, depending on the desired size of the finished product.

Irrigation. The agricultural prosperity of Israel is determined by the amount of yearly rainfall. This fact was already emphasized in the Bible, which noted that one of the advantages of the land was its non-dependence on irrigation, its being a land "that drinketh water as the rain of heaven cometh down" (Deut. 11:10–11), in contrast to Egypt, which was irrigated. Nonetheless, the danger of drought and famine was always present (Deut. 11:17). Scripture also designates Israel as a land "of brooks of water, of fountains and depths, springing forth in valleys and hills" (Deut. 8:7). However, there is no evidence that in biblical times there were any more than the few moderate and large water sources and the hundreds of small springs which now exist in Israel.

Many biblical passages use the simile of the well, spring, and river to symbolize plenty and security (Isa. 58:11; Jer. 31:11). In the rainwatered fields, grains and orchards could grow, but forlorn is "the garden that hath no water" (Isa. 1:30). Orchards, too, grow better when partially irrigated. Here is the source for the comparison of the person who trusts in God to "a tree planted by streams of water" (Jer. 14:8; Ps. 1:3). The farmer tried to provide auxiliary irrigation to his vines from a cistern hewed within the vineyard (cf. Isa. 27:3). Such cisterns are still preserved in many localities in the Judean mountains. In all regions of the country, installations for water gathering have been found, proof of the intensive exploitation of water resources in biblical times (see p.127).

Cisterns came into use in Erez Israel in the Canaanite period. An archaeological survey in the Samarian mountains found that most of the settlements of the Early Bronze period were placed near fountains, although unplastered rock-cut cisterns in soft nonpenetrable limestone already appear in this period. In the Middle Bronze period (especially in the 18th—17th century B.C.E.) settlements were placed all over the mountain, and cisterns were cut in hard, penetrable limestone. Thus the use of lime plaster for lining had begun to be widespread by this period, and new settlements could be established in regions lacking available sources of fresh water.

On entering Canaan, the Israelites took possession of cisterns hewed out by others (Deut. 6:11), and in the following period a private cistern was considered a common feature of the complete household (II Kings 19:31; Isa. 36:16), as substantiated by the excavations of contemporary sites. Various kings hewed out large public cisterns to promote animal husbandry (II Chron. 26:10) or as a defensive measure to ensure a supply of water during siege (Jer. 41:9).

The typical cistern of the Israelite period was cut into bedrock and consisted of a bell-shaped reservoir with a narrow opening at the top. While

Figure 84:   Water-wheel consisting of a wheel turning an axle to which a pail was attached by rope or chain

a diameter of just over four feet was common, much larger examples are known. The reservoir was usually plastered to prevent water seepage through the porous rock. Often a small basin was cut into the floor of the reservoir directly below the opening, presumably to catch impurities. Nevertheless, cisterns would eventually become extremely slimy at the bottom (Ps. 40:3; Jer. 38:6). In places where soil covered the bedrock, a circular stone-lined shaft led from the reservoir to the surface (see Waterworks). Rainwater was carried by drains leading from rooftops and other open places into the cistern through a hole in the shaft.

There were many other irrigation methods. In the regions rich in rivers and springs, like the Jericho, Jordan and Ḥuleh valleys, water flowed into the fields by gravitation and was directed through channels dug with shovels or pressed down by foot (cf. Deut. 11:10). Vegetable gardens, consisting mostly of rectangular beds enclosed by banks of earth were irrigated by water flowing in furrows. Trees were similarly irrigated (Ezek. 17:7; Song 5:13). A shallow pit dug round the tree was filled with the water which would sink deep into the ground and moisten the roots.

Gravitational irrigation is only possible where the water source is higher than the farm plot. Where the farmland was on a higher level than the well or spring, irrigation water was raised by mechanical means. One such water drawing device is described in Ecclesiastes (12:6), a wheel turning an axle to which a pail was attached by rope or chain (fig. 84).

11

TRADE AND COMMERCE

The geopolitical location of Erez Israel, set as it is in the heart of the Fertile Crescent, made it a pivotal link in the commercial activities carried on by land and sea between Egypt and the Arabian Peninsula in the south, and Phoenicia, Syria, Anatolia, and Mesopotamia in the north. It also played a part in the maritime-trade with the Mediterranean islands and with the commercial centers on the Mediterranean littoral (fig. 85).

The special position enjoyed by Erez Israel among the ancient lands was due to the existence of cities situated along the main arteries of communication which became important centers in international and internal trade.

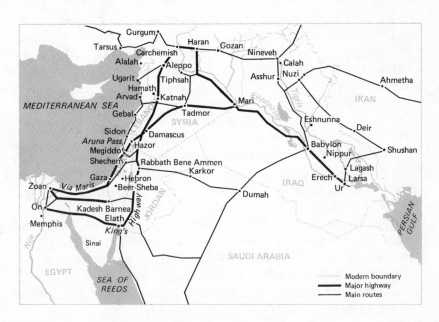

Figury 85:   Map of main routes of the Ancient East

The written sources in archaeological finds clearly show that trading was a favorite occupation by which a considerable proportion of the Canaanite population directly or indirectly earned a livelihood. A notable contribution to the development of the country's economic relations was made by the nomads who roamed the border areas of the permanently populated regions and along the main highways, engaging in transit trade (Gen. 37:25,28).

Since it was poor in natural resources and raw materials, Erez Israel's export trade was comprised of agricultural products and associated commodities. Foreign sources (in particular those of Egypt, which imported the products) and to some extent the Bible, emphasize that Erez Israel sustained itself by exporting cereals and flour, oil and wine, cosmetic and medicinal products extracted from plants (Gen. 43:11; Ezek. 27:17; Hos. 12:2) and, at a relatively later period, ore and finished metal goods. In contrast to its limited exports, the population of the land needed an unceasing stream of products, ranging from luxury goods to raw materials, such as timber and metal.

The destinations and composition of the commodities and the identity of the traders did not change with the conquest of Canaan by the Israelites. The latter did not actively participate in trade, either because of the tribal structure of their autarchic society and economy, or because access to the main arteries of commerce were obstructed by the indigenous population. Thus the Bible contains no evidence of the pursuit of trade or finance (allied areas even in ancient times). Nor do the laws of the Torah make much reference to commerce, the exceptions being the laws enjoining just weights, measures, and balances (Lev. 19:35–36; Deut. 25:13ff.), and stringent warnings against exacting interest from Israelites. However, these admonitions may reflect other spheres of economic activity, and a later period when the land was being divided among the tribes (see p. 9).

It is also probable that the sparse mention of trade is due in part to the negative attitude on the part of the writers and redactors of the Bible and of prophetic circles to commerce and to the foreigners who engaged in it: "As the merchant [lit. Canaan] keeps balances of deceit, he loves to oppress" (Hos. 12:8). The expression "Canaanite" became a synonym for a merchant. "Who has devised this against Tyre, the crowning city, whose tradesmen are princes, whose merchants [Canaanites] are the honorable of the earth?" (Isa. 23:8). Throughout the First Temple period (Isa. ch. 23; Ezek. ch. 27) and also in the early days of the Restoration (Neh. 13:16) the activities of these merchants were considerable.

THE PERIOD OF THE MONARCHY

Israelite participation in international economic activities and commerce began with the inception of the United Monarchy. The needs of the large kingdom were considerable and its political ties were extensive. Its control of lengthy sections of the important trade routes in Transjordan and along the coastal plain intensified the urge to profit from international commerce. In the days of David and particularly of Solomon, economic relations were developed with the kingdom of Tyre, one of the most important economic powers of the time. To carry out its extensive construction projects both within and outside the confines of Jerusalem, Israel needed building materials, metal, and other commodities, which were supplied and transported to Jaffa by the Tyrians in exchange for agricultural products: "And we will cut whatever timber you need from Lebanon, and bring it to you in rafts by sea to Jaffa, so that you may take it up to Jerusalem" (II Chron. 2:15).

The chronicler of Solomon's activities lays great stress on the place occupied by the royal trade. Indeed, it seems that the monarchy in Israel exercised a monopoly in this economic sphere. Solomon's Tyrian allies undoubtedly benefited from the Israelite control of the arteries of communication with southern Arabia and Egypt, for Solomon could direct the trading caravans to such destinations in his own kingdom and in friendly countries as he wished. Thus he profited not only from barter with Tyre, but also from the international transit trade.

The royal commercial apparatus in Israel was also able to initiate independent trading activities. According to the sources, Solomon's ships, built with Tyrian help in the port of Ezion Geber, took part in independent maritime commerce. Yet it is possible to draw an opposite conclusion from the same sources, for it is probable that the Tyrians insisted on being made partners in such ventures in exchange for their technical assistance and for the participation of their men in these expeditions: "King Solomon built a fleet of ships at Ezion Geber, which is near Eloth on the shore of the Red Sea, in the land of Edom. And Hiram sent with the fleet his servants, seamen who were familiar with the sea, together with the servants of Solomon" (I Kings 9:26–27; II Chron. 8:17–18). The ships sailed to and traded with Ophir, which is probably to be identified with Somaliland on the East African coast. On these voyages they brought with them precious metals and precious stones, as well as rare kinds of timber: "And they went to Ophir, and brought from there gold, to the amount of four hundred and twenty talents; and they brought it to King Solomon" (I Kings 9:28; II Chron. 8:18). "The fleet of Hiram, which brought gold from Ophir, brought from Ophir a very great amount of almug wood and precious stones" (I Kings 10:11; II Chron. 9:10).

According to one theory, Israelite-Tyrian ships also voyaged in the Mediterranean Sea as far as Spain (if Tarshish is explained as a place name); "For the king had a fleet of ships of Tarshish at sea with the fleet of Hiram. Once every three years the fleet of ships of Tarshish used to come bringing gold, silver, ivory, apes, and peacocks" (I Kings 10:22; II Chron. 9:21). However, another view maintains that "the fleet of ships of Tarshish" refers to a type of ship suitable for transporting metal, and hence alludes to the nature of the Israelite exports and the goods received in exchange.

Barter also occupied a place in Solomon's economic activities; the royal merchants purchased horses from Keveh (Cilicia), and chariots from Egypt, and marketed them as "a finished product" to the kings of Syria: "And Solomon's import of horses was from Egypt and Keveh, and the king's traders received them from Keveh at a price. A chariot could be imported from Egypt for six hundred shekels of silver, and a horse for a hundred and fifty; and so through the king's traders they were exported to all the kings of the Hittites, and for the kings of Aram" (I Kings 10:28–29; II Chron. 9:28). The enigmatic reference to "the kings of the mingled people" alongside "the governors of the land" as persons with whom Solomon had commercial relations either indicates that the United Monarchy traded directly with the Arabian peninsula, or may refer to contacts with nomads who engaged extensively in transporting goods from the south to the north (I Kings 10:15; II Chron. 9:14). The well-known story of the Queen of Sheba's visit to Jerusalem may reasonably be explained on the assumption that the queen of this south Arabian kingdom came to Jerusalem at the head of a trade delegation to establish closer relations with Israel (I Kings 10:1ff.; II Chron. 9:1–12).

The extensive space which the Bible devotes to Solomon is not accorded to the kings who reigned after him. This, however, does not warrant the conclusion that royal commercial activities ceased after Solomon's time. The continuation of these activities is attested to by the discovery of products of foreign lands in various archaeological sites, dating from the kingdoms of Israel and Judah.

Under Jehoshaphat of Judah there was a renewed attempt to sail ships from Ezion Geber. It failed owing to the destructive forces of nature: "Jehoshaphat made ships of Tarshish to go to Ophir for gold; but they did not go, for the ships were wrecked at Ezion Geber" (I Kings 22:49). This attempt is undoubtedly to be understood against the background of the relations which Jehoshaphat established with the dynasty of Omri in Israel and with the kindgom of Tyre. He may have been assisted in the building of his navy by the Tyrians. The close ties maintained by Omri and Ahab with the Tyrians are undoubtedly to be regarded as commercial relations. Apparently, the kings of Israel were associated with the activities of Jehoshaphat's navy in the Red Sea: "After this Jehoshaphat king of Judah joined with Ahaziah king of Israel, who did wickedly. He joined him in building ships to go to Tarshish, and they built the ships in Ezion Geber. Then Eliezer son of Dodavahu of Mareshah prophesied against Jehoshaphat, saying: 'Because you have joined with Ahaziah, the Lord will destroy what you have made.' And the ships were wrecked and were not able to go to Tarshish" (II Chron. 20:35–37). The use of the Hebrew root meaning "to join" indicates the significance of the relations between Jehoshaphat and Ahaziah. In several Semitic languages the use of the root denotes a commercial partnership, particularly in a maritime connection. According to I Kings 22:50, Jehoshaphat rejected Ahaziah's offer to cooperate with him in maritime commerce.

Additional evidence of trade that was conditioned by political circumstances is the presence of Aramean commercial agencies in Samaria in the days of Omri and (partly) of Ahab, and, after the latter's victory over Aram, of Israelite agencies in Damascus (I Kings 20:34). Furthermore the tendency toward development of trade in Israel and Judah, though not explicitly mentioned in the Bible, is evident in the expansionist ambitions of these kingdoms toward Transjordan and the west. The purpose of these attempts was to gain control of the trade routes in these areas and of the centrally located ports that promoted trade with Phoenicia, Egypt, and other countries on the Mediterranean littoral.

Biblical references to internal trade are sparse. Such trade was carried on in open places, in streets, squares, and marketplaces (Neh. 13:17–22), and in open areas near gates (II Kings 7:1). It apparently took the form mainly of barter, in which farmers, artisans, and others who offered the products of their labors participated. Merchants and peddlers also displayed their wares. The Bible mentions trade in oil (II Kings 4:7), wine, grapes, and figs (Neh. 13:15–16), fish (13:16), and animals (II Sam. 12:3, et al.), in addition to products such as pottery (Jer. 19:1) and clothing (13:1–2). These individual citations undoubtedly represent only a few of the potential articles of trade. As the standard of life rose among the inhabitants of the country, the articles of trade would inevitably increase in quantity and diversity.

12
MONETARY SYSTEM

The Hebrew word *kesef* is used in two connotations in the Bible. It may indicate the valuable metal silver: "The gold, the silver, and the copper, and the iron cannot be numbered..." (I Chron. 22:16); or it may be used to denote a means of payment: "...until an ass's head was sold for 80 pieces of silver, and the fourth part of a kab of dove's dung for five pieces of silver" (II Kings 6:25). These two meanings of the word throw some light upon the development of a monetary system in the ancient world.

The earliest trade was in the form of barter: items were exchanged by parties according to some accepted means of evaluation. An Egyptian monument (c. 2400 B.C.E.) pictures such barter among several people, each one holding a different item of commerce. Two of the individuals are shown engaged in an actual trade. According to the Torah, the ownership of any item could be exchanged by trade, with two exceptions: land within Erez Israel could not be sold in perpetuity (Lev. 25:23–24), and Hebrew slaves, both male and female, had to be freed after six years of bondage (Deut. 15:12ff.).

As trade developed, some intermediate object was employed to define the value of the item being acquired. Such intermediate objects had to be both valuable and not too common. Eventually, this system resulted in the issue of coins minted by some official authority, which set and guaranteed their value. The most striking and important feature in this process was the establishment of values for commercial trade by an independent yet responsible body. At first, such values were set by the individual, using his own judgment. However, as society and administrative institutions took form, the monetary authority of the ruling powers was accepted for purposes of commerce by all parties involved.

Of course, barter and direct trade have never been completely eliminated, and still exist today. While such barter was purely an individual matter at first, as states developed it frequently became part of the economic policy of the more highly organized countries. Echoes of this process are to be

168

found in the biblical description of affairs in Egypt during Joseph's time. He acquired all the land in Egypt for Pharaoh by bartering food and produce during the famine: "So Joseph gained possession of all the farmland of Egypt" (Gen. 47:20). In this way, the entire country became the king's property, and came under his strong central administration. Another form of trade on the part of a government appears during Solomon's reign. During this period, Palestine became the axis for trade between Egypt and Mesopotamia. Chariots produced in the north were passed on to Egypt by Solomon, who conveyed horses to the north in return (I Kings 10:28; II Chron. 9:28). Another example of governmental barter during the same period was the trade between Solomon and Hiram of Tyre. Solomon exported agricultural products, such as wheat and oil, and received in return wood from Tyre for the construction of the Temple in Jerusalem (I Kings 5:2–5).

In the nomadic pastoral society of the patriarchal period, sheep or cattle became the accepted means of evaluation for trade, since these constituted the main property which a family or tribe might have. Therefore, the term *mikneh*, from the root *knh*, meaning "property," came to refer to herds of sheep and cattle: "He acquired flocks and herds and a large household" (Gen. 26:14); or: "and all the wealth that he had amassed, the livestock in his possession" (Gen. 31:18).

As society moved from nomadism to established forms of settlement, the acquisition of immovable items such as land, houses, and burial grounds assumed greater importance. The purchase of such immovables brought with it a change in the method of payment, which now tended to be in monetary terms. Precious metals whose value was agreed upon by general consensus were used as a form of payment. Gold, silver, and copper served this purpose. The value of such metals was determined by weight (see below). "The field that Abraham had bought from the Hittites" (Gen. 25:10) near Hebron, and the Cave of Machpelah within it, was described in terms of monetary value as "a piece of land worth 400 shekels of silver" (Gen. 23:15). The price paid to Ephron the Hittite is further categorized as "the going merchants' rate" (v. 16).

A description of the acquisition of immovable property toward the end of the period of the monarchy is found in Jeremiah's purchase of a field: "And I bought the field at Anathoth from Hanamel my cousin, and weighed out the money to him, 17 shekels of silver. I signed the deed, sealed it, got witnesses, and weighed the money on scales" (Jer. 32:9–10).

The use of coins for purposes of payment became current in Erez Israel only in the 6th century B.C.E. They appear to have been used first at Lydia, where round pieces of amber have been found in the Pactolus River. They are imprinted with the seals of the kings of Lydia, who guaranteed their value (700–650 B.C.E.). These coins were the model upon which Persian coinage was based. The system then passed, by way of the Persian empire, to the Hellenistic cities along the Mediterranean coast.

13

SYSTEMS OF WEIGHTS
AND MEASURES

From the earliest period of their history the Israelites were sensitive to the necessity of having an accurate system of weights and measures, and an honest handling of them. Legislation in the interest of economic righteousness in general is found in Leviticus 19:35–36: "You shall not falsify measures of length, weight, or capacity. You shall have an honest balance, honest weights, an honest ephah, and an honest hin." The same idea is also found in Deuteronomy 25:13–16: "You shall not have in your pouch alternate weights, larger and smaller. You shall not have in your house alternate measures, a larger and a smaller. You must have completely honest weights and completely honest measures. . ." The Prophets, too, constantly denounced the use of false measures (Amos 8:5; Hos. 12:8; Micah 6:10).

An authoritative and accepted system of weights for buying and selling, building, measuring areas, and the like is a necessity of civilized life. Most of the first measures were natural or common physical phenomena, such as the palm of the hand, a day's journey, seeds of grain, and simple utensils. As time progressed, the measures were improved and made more precise, but they were still called by their ancient names. Various systems of measurement developed in the large cultural centers of Egypt and Mesopotamia from a very early period, and complex reckoning was carried out to determine the equivalence between the different categories, e.g. reckoning volume in terms of weight of area.

This type of reckoning was certainly known in Erez Israel, and an allusion to a system of equivalent reckoning is found in the Bible, in a verse which expresses acreage in terms of volume of seed requirement: "And he made a trench about the altar, as great as would contain two measures of seed" (I Kings 18:32).

The weights and measures in the Bible are in large part based upon the weights and measures which were accepted by the ancient peoples and retain the names by which they were known. In Erez Israel measuring

171

standards of several peoples were used simultaneously: Mesopotamian measures, the *kor, se'ah, shekel*; Egyptian measures, the *ephah, hin*; and measures whose names were borrowed from the Canaanites such as *letekh* and *kikkar*. Other measuring standards which have not been found among the neighboring countries were apparently established in Erez̦ Israel.

In biblical measures, it is customary to distinguish between natural measures (measures established in reference to parts of the human body, utensils, average sizes of burdens loaded on animals, etc.) and fixed and precise measures established by reckoning. In some cases the Bible explains the relationship between measures, but it is difficult today to establish their absolute values because as early as the days of the Second Temple the biblical measures were not precisely known, and later translators and commentators were inclined to identify them with their contemporary measures without specifying their exact values.

In the metrology practiced in the Ancient Near East, there were measures which differed in their absolute value but were identical in name. For example, in Egypt and Mesopotamia the short cubit was in use along with the long cubit, and there were also different weights, light and heavy, called by the same name, such as the *mina*. Double weights of this sort were also in use in Erez̦ Israel, as has been indicated in the Bible and corroborated by archaeological finds. Indeed, they were in use there almost until modern times. In addition, there were measures confined to specific localities. Ancient documents provide evidence of weights named for cities: "Alalakh weight," "Carchemish weight," and the like. The already mentioned difficulties are compounded by the problem of the durability of these weights, since it is likely that with the passage of time many changes took place in them.

The ascertaining of biblical measures and the determination of their values in terms of present day measures is done mainly on the basis of archaeological finds. In the excavations carried out in Palestine, many weights have been uncovered, as well as fragments of vessels upon which measurements of volume have been written. Linear measure can be reckoned according to ancient structures whose measurements are noted. In the neighboring countries – mainly Egypt, Syria, and Mesopotamia – actual measuring rods of wood and stone were uncovered, along with weights and economic documents, all of which are valuable aids in determining the biblical measures. However, it still cannot be known whether these measures are identical with biblical measures, and which of the various standards the Bible used.

LINEAR MEASURE

The units of length mentioned in the Bible, as well as those used by other ancient peoples, are derived from average measures of the length of human limbs. Names of measures based on the limbs of the body are in use in some languages even to this day.

It appears that in the early period it was customary to measure with the limbs themselves: the part of the arm from the elbow to the tip of the middle finger is the "standard cubit" [lit. by a man's forearm] (Deut. 3:11); the span was the distance between the tip of the little finger and the tip of the thumb with the fingers spread. The measurement of the handbreadth was the width of the four fingers, and the fingerbreadth was measured according to the width of the finger. As time progressed, absolute values and relationships were established for these natural measures, though these were still named after the parts of the body.

The large measures mentioned in the Bible are based upon crude estimates such as the range of the bowshot (Gen. 21:16), i.e., the distance which the bow is able to shoot the arrow. The Bible also uses the expression "a short distance" (Gen. 35:16; 48:7; II Kings 5:19), which seems to mean a journey of two hours. Greater distances were measured by days' journey (Gen. 30:36; 31:23; et al.).

Among the implements used for measuring small units of length, the Bible mentions "thread" (Jer. 52:21), "rope" (Amos 7:17), "measuring line" (Zech. 2:5; Jer. 31:38), "line of flax . . . and measuring reed" (Ezek. 40:3). It is likely that all or some of these implements were used regularly for linear measure. It should be noted that the rope served as a standard measurement of length among several ancient peoples.

Five small units of length are mentioned in the Bible. Their exact length is not explicit but their interrelations are generally established: "reed," "cubit," "span," "handbreadth," and "fingerbreadth." The most important and basic measure was the cubit. It appears that there were two values for the cubit which were in use in different periods. The short cubit is implicit in II Chronicles 3:3 in the description of the Temple, "in cubits of the old standard" (and not in terms of the longer royal cubit which was then in use). In the description of the future sanctuary in Ezekiel 40:5, the second or long cubit is mentioned: "and the length of the measuring reed in the man's hand was six long cubits, each being a cubit and a handbreadth in length." The cubit in this description thus contains seven handbreadths, and not six like the short cubit. This is the long Persian cubit, which was also in use in Mesopotamia, and which may have come into use in Erez Israel during the time of the Return.

Attempts have been made to ascertain the value of the cubit in terms of present-day measures by the study of ancient structures whose measurements are noted, such as the tunnel of Siloam dating to the reign of Hezekiah (see p.131); or on the basis of the measurements of buildings which, in the opinion of their excavators, were built in whole cubits, such as the walls of Hazor, Megiddo, and Gezer from Solomon's time (I Kings 9:15); or by estimating the volume of "the molten sea" which stood in the Temple (I Kings 7:23–26; II Chron. 4:2). However, all of these calculations are unreliable. Various scholars – some on the basis of comparisons with Egyptian and Mesopotamian standards, and some according to parallels from Hellenistic sources – have established their values. These estimations probably approximate the actual values of the measures,but they cannot be considered precise.

MEASURES OF VOLUME

As was the case with linear measures, human limbs were initially used to measure volume. The small units were: "handful" (Lev. 2:2; 5:12), which is the measure of the grasp of three fingers, *hofen* (e.q. Ex. 9:8), which is the entire palm of the hand; and *hofnayim*, which is two handfuls. Receptacles which the farmer used at home and in the field were also used as measures: the *omer* is a bundle of ears of corn; a skin (jar) holds a certain quantity of wine (I Sam. 1:24). The values of these measures cannot be established, for they were not precise. It is likely that various foods used to be prepared in fixed portions, and therefore the Bible notes quantities of food, liquid and dry, in numbers of portions, without designating the volume (I Sam. 25:18; II Sam. 16:1; et al.).

The units of volume mentioned in the Bible are: *homer* (e.g., Lev. 27:16; Isa. 5:10), *kor* (Ezek. 45:14), *letekh* (Hos. 3:2), *ephah* (Ex. 16:36; Ezek. 45:11; etc.), *bath* (Ezek. 45:11,14; II Chron. 2:9), *se'ah* (Gen. 18:6; I Sam. 25:18; etc.), *hin* (Ex. 29:40; Ezek. 45:24; etc.), *omer* (Ex. 16:16; Lev. 23:10–14; etc.), *'issaron* (Ex. 29:40; Lev. 14:21; etc.), *qav* (II Kings 6:25), *log*, which is the small liquid measure (Lev. 14:10,12,15,21,24).

The only method by which modern scholars can determine the values of these weights is to measure the volume of vessels discovered in excavations in Palestine whose capacity is marked on them, such as fragments of vessels with the words *"bath"* or "royal *bath"* written upon them. According to W.F. Albright's calculations, which are accepted by most scholars today, the "royal *bath"* has a capacity of 22 liters. Accordingly:

SCALE OF MEASURES OF VOLUME (DRY AND LIQUID)

Homer-kor	220 liters
letekh	110 liters
ephah-bath	22 liters
se'ah	7.3 liters
hin	3.6 liters
omer-'issaron	2.2 liters
qav	1.2 liters
log	0.3 liters

Aside from the inscriptions *"bath"* and "royal *bath,"* some potsherds were discovered during excavations with inscriptions which designate the type of goods and the quantity; however, for the most part, the names of the units of volume are missing from these inscriptions (a common practice in the Bible too; see I Sam. 25:18; II Sam. 16:1). A shard was found at Tell Qasila (fig. 86) probably bearing the inscription "To the king, 1,100 [measures of] oil, from Ahiyahu." The liquid measure is not explicit; in the

Figure 86: Hebrew ostracon of the 8th cent. B.C.E. from Tell Qasila, inscribed: "To the King, 1,100 [measures of] oil, from Ahiyahu."

opinion of Mazar, the *log* is intended. Another inscription, discovered in Kadesh-Barnea, reads 5 1, and according to M. Dothan, it designates five measures of oil (*hin*). Also discovered in Samaria were dozens of ostraca upon which measures of oil and wine are mentioned by the skin. The units of volume mentioned in the Elephantine papyri from the 5th century B.C.E. are *se'ah* and *qav*, the measure being designated by the first letter only.

AREA MEASURE

The main measure of area in the Bible is the *zemed* (I Sam. 14:14; Isa. 5:10), which refers to the area which a pair of oxen can plow in one day. Another system of measuring area was based upon the quantity of seeds sown in it (Lev. 27:16; I Kings 18:32), and, needless to say, this measurement was not precise. This system was prevalent in Mesopotamia, and was formulated in terms of "property measuring one *homer.*" The Bible uses more precise measurement in its description of a rectangular area, noting the length and width in cubits or parts of cubits, and adding the adjective "square" (Ex. 27:1; 28:16, et al.). Ezekiel also notes the areas of the entire complex of buildings in the Temple in cubits (Ezek. ch. 40).

WEIGHTS

The verb *shql* "to weigh" is shared by all Semitic languages; and generally the system of weights used by Semitic peoples is the same. Weights, for the most part, were made of stone, hence the Bible refers to weights generally as "stones." In Akkadian, weights are sometimes called "stones from the bag," that is stones placed in a cloth bag (Micah 6:11; Prov. 16:11, etc.). In Ugaritic, too, the word "stone" signified weights. However, many cast metal weights have been found, dating from the biblical period.

In some ancient countries, especially in Mesopotamia, the old unit of weight was a seed of grain. Although the Bible uses the names of early Mesopotamian weights, it does not mention this particular unit since the reciprocal relationship between Erez Israel and Mesopotamia in weights, as in measures of volume, appears only in a relatively late period.

Seven weights are mentioned in the Bible: talent, mina, shekel, *beka, gerah, pim,* and *kesitah.* A scale of the relationships between the first five weights mentioned can be established by a comparison of the Bible and other sources; the absolute and relative value of the *pim* can be determined from archaeological finds (see below). The seventh weight, the *kesitah* (Gen. 33:19; Josh. 24:32; Job 42:11), seems to be an archaic weight and the origin of its name and its metrological value are not known.

The basis of the biblical system of weights becomes clear by investigating the interrelationships of the three most important weights, the talent, shekel, and *gerah.*

The talent was the largest unit of weight in the Bible, and was already known by the same name in Ugaritic. The Hebrew name (*kikkar* = loaf) testifies to the round shape of the weights. The relation between the talent and the shekel becomes clear in Exodus 38:25–26. The half-shekel brought by 603,550 men amounted to 100 talents and 1,775 shekels. Thus the following calculations can be made:

RELATION BETWEEN THE SHEKEL AND THE TALENT

$$603{,}550 \text{ half-shekels} = 300{,}000 + 1775 \text{ shekels}$$
$$300{,}000 \text{ shekels} = 100 \text{ talents}$$
$$3{,}000 \text{ shekels} = 1 \text{ talent}$$

This system of dividing the talent into 3,000 shekels differs from the Mesopotamian system which divides the talent into 3,600 parts and is the same as the Ugaritic system where the talent is also divided into 3,000 shekels. From this it follows that the biblical division is based upon an ancient Canaanite tradition.

The shekel is the most basic weight, as its name, which means simply "weight," testifies. Thus, an expression such as "1,000 silver" (Gen. 20:16) can be explained as 1,000 shekels of silver; the name of the weight is omitted since it is self-explanatory. Abbreviations like these are also found in other Semitic languages. The fundamental nature of the shekel can also be seen in the fact that those weights which the Bible explains are defined only in terms of the shekel.

The *gerah* is also known in Akkadian, where its meaning is a grain of carob seed. The value of the Israelite *gerah* is the 20th part of a shekel (Ex. 30:13), unlike the Akkadian weight, which is the 24th part of a shekel. S.E. Loewenstamm noted that the ratio 24:20 is identical with the ratio 3,600:3,000, and therefore he holds that the division of the shekel into 20 *gerah* is based upon the same ancient Canaanite tradition according to which the talent was divided into 3,000 shekels.

The mina, which designates a weight of approximately 50 or 60 shekels (see below), is found in the Bible primarily in the late books (Ezek. 45:12; Ezra 2:69; Neh. 7:70,71). In the period preceding the destruction of the First Temple, the mina is mentioned only once, in the verse about Solomon's shields (I Kings 10:17). From this it is reasonable to assume that in ancient times Israelites reckoned only in shekels and talents, and the mina was not used except in unusual situations. It appears that this practice too had its roots in an ancient Canaanite tradition, for in Ugaritic writings many calculations are found involving shekels and talents and very few involving the mina.

The value of the mina is defined in Ezekiel 45:12 as equivalent to 60 shekels, like the Akkadian mina. However, there is reason to assume that Ezekiel's definition was influenced by his Mesopotamian environment, and that the Canaanite-Israelite mina was equivalent to only 50 shekels. First, it appears that there are two systems intertwined in Ezekiel's words. Portions of 15 and 20 shekels are appropriate for a mina of 60 shekels, as they equal a fourth and a third of it. Not so a portion of 25 shekels which is appropriate only for a mina of 50 shekels, of which it would comprise half. F. Thureau-Dangin found support for the existence of a Canaanite mina of 50 shekels in Ugaritic weights which contain 50 Ugaritic shekels. He regarded these as weights of a mina. According to this, the ratio of the Mesopotamian weight to the Canaanite weight would be 60:50, like the ratios 3600:3000 and 24:20 which were dealt with above. Support for this system can also be found in the passages which speak of payment of 50 or 100 shekels (Deut. 22:19, 29, etc.), which probably refer to payments of one or two minas. Moreover, there are signs that the Mesopotamian system of Ezekiel did not succeed in supplanting the Canaanite system. The Septuagint reads for Ezekiel 45:12: ' five shekels shall be five shekels, and ten shekels shall be ten shekels, and your mina shall be fifty shekels," and this version is significant. It provides evidence that, at the time of the translation, the mina consisted of 50 shekels.

The *beka* is mentioned twice in the Bible (Gen. 24:22; Ex. 38:26) and its value is explicitly determined as one-half a shekel. Its name is derived from the root meaning "to break, to divide," and its basic meaning is "a part." According to the reckoning of a mina as 50 shekels, the following table may be set up:

MEASURES OF WEIGHT AND THEIR RATIOS (mina=50 shekels).

	talent	mina	shekel	*beka*	*gerah*
talent	1				
mina	60	1			
shekel	3,000	50	1		
beka	6,000	100	2	1	
gerah	60,000	1,000	20	10	1

However, on the basis of Ezekiel 45:12 according to which the mina contains 60 shekels, and on the assumption that Ezekiel divided the talent into 60 minas, the following table may be set up:

MEASURES OF WEIGHT AND THEIR RATIOS (mina=60 shekels).

	talent	mina	shekel	*beka*	*gerah*
talent	1				
mina	60	1			
shekel	3,600	60	1		
beka	7,200	120	2	1	
gerah	72,000	1,200	20	10	1

This table is arranged according to the Mesopotamian system and contains nothing from the Canaanite-Israelite system except the division of the shekel into 20 *gerah* instead of 24.

In addition to being divided into the *beka* and *gerah*, the shekel is also divided into a fourth and a third (I Sam. 9:8; Neh. 10:33). There is support for this division both inside and outside Erez Israel. From Assyrian documents found at Calah it is evident that the shekel was divided there into many more sub-units, but there is no proof that this was so in Israel as well.

Also mentioned in the Bible is the *peres* (Dan. 5:25,28); Clermont-Ganneau has suggested that it is half a mina. This weight is also mentioned among bilingual weights (Akkadian-Aramaic) from the Persian period.

An additional complication establishing the value of the shekel is the fact that the Bible mentions at least three kinds of shekels: Genesis 23:16, a shekel of silver "at the going merchants' rate" is similar to the Akkadian

expression "in the merchant's mina"; Exodus 30:13, "shekel by the sanctuary weight"; and II Samuel 14:26, "shekels by the king's weight," that is,
shekels stamped by the royal treasury as proof that they are perfect. The
Elephantine papyri from the Persian period contain the expression "royal
weight." It cannot be determined whether these shekels were equivalent in
value, but on the basis of evidence from external sources, it appears that
there were differences among them.

Archaeological Finds. Many weights have been uncovered in excavations
carried out in Palestine — some with the weight marked on them, but most

Figure 87:   Basalt weight of the 9th–8th cent. B.C.E., with relief of winged
lion and Hebrew inscription *lshm'* (*le-shema* = (belonging) to Shema

without any notation. The shape of the weights, for the most part, is semi-circular (dome-shaped) (fig. 88a). There are also some cast metal weights that are rectangular and cube-shaped, and some that are oval or in the shape of animals (fig. 87). Most of the weights found in Palestine are from the end of the period of the monarchy (7th–6th centuries B.C.E.).

Very few weights and inscriptions with the word shekel written explicitly have been found in strata from the Israelite period. A bronze weight in the shape of a turtle was found in the coastal plain; on its reverse side it bears the inscription (according to the reading of A. Reifenberg) *plg sh[q]l*, and on the front *plg rb'yt*. Its weight is 2.63 gm. A weight of this sort (one-quarter shekel) is mentioned in I Samuel 9:8. Another bronze weight from Samaria, also in the shape of a turtle, bears the inscription 'five'' and this has been interpreted to mean five gerahs, that is one-quarter of a shekel. Its weight is 2.49 gm. Another weight from Samaria is marked on one side *rb' sh[q]l*, and on the other *rb' nzf*. Its weight is 2.54 gm (see below). Two ostraca containing calculations in shekels were found in Yavneh-Yam. Many weights found in excavations bear a special mark in the form of 𒅗 with another sign next to it which in general designates the number of units. These weights have for some time been considered shekels. They were discovered for the most part at localities in the kingdom of Judah: Gibeon, Jerusalem, Ramat Raḥel, Gezer, Tell Zechariah, Tell Jedideh, Lachish, En-Gedi, Tell Malḥatah, and Arad; and in the coastal plain; Tell Jamma, Nebi Rubin, Yavneh-Yam, and Ashdod. Only one weight of this type is known from the area of Samaria, and it was discovered at Shechem. Many others of unknown provenance are in private collections.

Scholars have been greatly divided as to the interpretation of the sign X which appears on some weights. The signs which generally appear alongside the symbol X are interpreted by all scholars as numbers which note the quantity of royal shekels contained in each weight.

Three other types of weights dating from the end of the kingdom of Judah have been discovered in Israel and their names are inscribed on them in full: *nzp, pym*, and *bq'*.

The word *nzp* does not appear in the Bible and is known only from the inscription of these Hebrew weights, and also from Ugaritic. It has most recently been explained as 5/6 of a shekel.

The *pim* is mentioned once in the Bible (I Sam. 13:21). *Pim* weights which were uncovered in excavations helped to clarify the obscure verse but not to explain the name. Clermont-Ganneau has suggested: *pi (shenayi)m* (according to Zech. 13:8), that is "two portions," i.e., two-thirds. E. A.

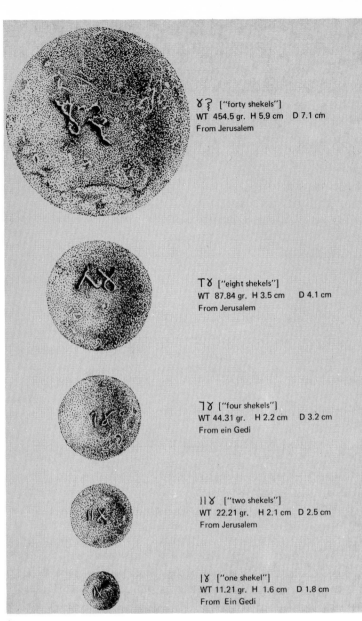

ﬡ ? ["forty shekels"]
WT 454.5 gr. H 5.9 cm   D 7.1 cm
From Jerusalem

beka ["half a shekel"]
WT 5.8 gr. H 1.3 cm   D 1.4 cm
mentioned in Genesis 24:22.
Provenance unknown

pim ["two-thirds of the shekel"]
WT 7.8 gr. H 1.3 cm   D 1.7 cm
mentioned in 1 Samuel 13:21
From Arad

ﬢﬡ ["eight shekels"]
WT 87.84 gr. H 3.5 cm   D 4.1 cm
From Jerusalem

nzp ["five-sixths of the shekel"]
WT 9.95 gr. H 1.6 cm   D 2 cm
From Mizpeh (Tell al-Nasba)

ﬧﬡ ["four shekels"]
WT 44.31 gr. H 2.2 cm   D 3.2 cm
From ein Gedi

||ﬡ ["two shekels"]
WT 22.21 gr. H 2.1 cm   D 2.5 cm
From Jerusalem

|ﬡ ["one shekel"]
WT 11.21 gr. H 1.6 cm   D 1.8 cm
From Ein Gedi

b

a

Figure 88:   Dome-shaped weights of the late Israelite period (a) and
drawing of the main weights bearing inscriptions (b)

Speiser held that its source is from the Akkadian *sinipu*, that it means two-thirds (of a shekel), and that in Canaan they borrowed the last part of the word from Mesopotamia, interpreted it as a third, and made it dual. Diringer and Barrois also think that the *pim* is two-thirds of a standard shekel but that Speiser is correct that the source of the word is foreign and that it has no meaning in Hebrew. Twelve such weights have been discovered, and their average weight is 7.8 gm.

The *beka* is the one unit of weight mentioned in the Bible whose value has been determined. It is half a shekel (see above). However, this value does not correspond to the *beka* weights found in excavations. In Israel, seven weights have been found with the name *beka* written on them. On some the name is written in full, and on some only the letter *bet* appears. Their average weight is 6.03 gm, more than the value of the half-shekel of 11.3 gm. The heaviest one is 6.65 gm and the lightest 5.55 gm. The *beka* has been discovered in pre-dynastic graves from the 4th millennium B.C.E. Petrie believes that it is an extremely ancient unit of weight used in Egypt for gold, and that its weight was 12.28–13.90 gm. If Petrie's opinion is accepted, the Israel *beka* would be half the weight of the weight which Petrie established as the Egyptian *beka*.

In addition to the above-mentioned weights, some 20 weights marked with numbers (ll, T, ∨∨) have been uncovered in excavations; their weights range from 1.52 to 7.05 gm. Recently, Scott has gathered all the above mentioned finds, sorted them into groups, and tried to determine their precise relationships to the perfect weights mentioned above. However, all attempts to determine the exact value of these small weights are unreliable, since there are no written sources about the detailed division of the Israelite shekel into small subunits.

A large number of weights have been discovered which contain no inscription, no number, and no sign whatsoever. Among them, it is worth noting two weights in particular. One was found at Tell Beit Mirsim, weighing 4.565 gm. In W. F. Albright's opinion it has the value of eight minas of 50 shekels each (that is the weight of 400 shekels). The second is a basalt stone weight from the area around Taanach which weighs 4.780 gm (fig. 87). This weight is decorated with the relief of a winged lion and in addition bears the personal name *Shm'*. In N. Avigad's opinion, the value of this weight is eight minas of 50 shekels, or 400 shekels, which, he believes, is a standard weight (compare "four hundred shekels of silver at the going merchants' rate" (Gen. 23:16)).

14
TAXATION

Biblical records do not contain a detailed account of fiscal policy in Israel nor does archaeology provide much opportunity to contribute toward such knowledge. However, the scattered references to direct and indirect taxes in the Bible, as well as in extra-biblical sources, are sufficient evidence of the existence of an organized revenue system during the time of the monarchy.

Even in the premonarchic period, when there was no need for regular taxation to support a central government or national army, the Bible provides examples of tax measures. While still in the desert on their way to Canaan, the Israelites were required to pay half a shekel per person for the construction of the Sanctuary. The tax, levied just once during this period, served a double purpose. It was used to finance the construction of the Sanctuary, while at the same time, the number of half-shekels collected constituted a form of census of the people (Ex. 30:11–16). The Bible defines this tax in terms of money for expiation, the tax having religious significance.

The concept of the shekel being used in payment of a tax to the government appears again at a later date, during the period of both the First and Second Temples. At Tell Qasila, near Tel Aviv, a shard has been found which is apparently a receipt or similar document connected with payment. It seems to make use of the term "shekel": "The gold of Ophir to Beth-Horon, sh[ekel] (?)." Nehemiah ordered a tax of one-third of a shekel per capita for the service of the Temple (Neh. 10:33), while a tax of one-half shekel per capita was levied at the end of the Second Temple period for purposes of refurbishing the Temple.

Immediately after the establishment of the monarchy by David attempts were made to set up a fiscal apparatus, undoubtedly based on the contemporary Canaanite practice of revenue collections. One such Canaanite system is known to us from the texts discovered at Ugarit in northern Syria. The taxes mentioned in these documents are the following: a tithe on grain, oil and wine; a tax on pasturing rights on crown lands; a general assessment on land and buildings; a levy on imports; corvée labor; and several kinds of occasional contributions. That a similar system of taxation existed in the non-Israelite parts of Erez Israel in the period of the Judges is indirectly attested to by "the manner of the king" (I Sam. 8:9—17). The Prophet's enumeration of a long catalogue of taxes which a king would impose upon the people includes, among others, a tithe on grain, wine, and flocks; a levy on fields, vineyards, and olive orchards; and forced labor.

The prerequisite for a sound and workable taxation policy is a census of the population. David ordered "a numbering of the people" (II Sam. 24:1—9), and while Joab, in his final report to the king, gave only the total number of all the able men "who drew the sword," it may be assumed that the object of the census was also to list the property of the individual householders for taxation purposes. Solomon perfected the system of taxa-tion by arbitrarily dividing the country into twelve administrative districts and by appointing over each one a "prefect" (I Kings 4:7—19). The reason for the division is clearly stated in verse 7: "Solomon had twelve prefects over all Israel, who provided food for the king and his household; each one had to make provisions for one month in the year." A special department, headed by a "chief officer of the corvée," was in charge of the overall collection of taxes and the drafting of men for forced labor (I Kings 4:6; 12:18). The division of the country into administrative units apparently remained in force throughout the biblical period (cf. the reference to "gov-ernors of the provinces," in I Kings 20:14). Although there is no direct evidence of the existence of individual revenue records, such data must have been available in the royal archives or in the local district offices (cf. Ex. 30:13). Menahem's levy of fifty shekels per capita on sixty thousand wealthy citizens in Israel (II Kings 15:19—20), Jehoiakim's assessment based on personal fortunes (II Kings 23:35), and Ezekiel's reference (45:16) that "all the people of the land" shall deliver "contribution" to the reigning "prince," could not have been effectively carried out unless there were records of individuals and their property in the possession of the govern-ment.

The paucity of references to direct taxation in the biblical records has led some scholars to the assumption that only in emergencies were the people called upon to pay a tax, while in normal times the expenses of the govern-ment were defrayed by the private resources of the king. This assumption is untenable. It is axiomatic that no state can maintain itself without the benefit of a regular source of income.

We may derive the regular imposition of direct taxes by the central authorities from the Samaria ostraca (fig. 15). These apparently recorded the quantities of wine and oil sent to the central tax official by the regional collectors. The *lmlkh* seals on jar handles (fig. 89) dating from the end of the kingdom of Judah indicate that these were standard size containers for the payment of taxes-in-kind.

In the Bible, the term *ma'aser* ("tithe") is used almost exclusively for the Temple tax. It seems, however, that originally the *ma'aser*, like the cognate Akkadian term meaning "tithe," referred equally to a state tax. This may be inferred from the statement (Gen. 14:20) that Abraham gave to Melchizedek, king of Salem, *ma'aser* of everything, and from the usage of the verbal form *ya'asor* to describe some of the taxes a king would impose upon the people (I Sam. 8:15,17). The actual amount of the *ma'aser* varied; it did not necessarily always consist of a tenth of the produce. Theoretically, the Babylonian tithe was a tenth of the crop, but in reality it sometimes amounted to one-fifth, one-fourth, and even as high as one-third of the harvest.

The term *mas'et* has several shades of meaning. But in Amos 5:11 the phrase *mas'at bar* definitely has the connotation of a tax on wheat. The Prophet is reproaching the tax collectors for taking excessive amounts of wheat even from the poor farmers. The Hebrew *mekhes* has its cognate in

Figure 89: Pottery jar-handle bearing seal-impression with four-winged scarab; above it appears the Hebrew word *lmlkh* = "(belonging) to the king," and below the place-name *Socoh*. Such impressions, but with three other place names, were either stamped by royal officials as a guarantee for the capacity of the jar, or belonged to standard-sized containers of oil and wine taxes, the four place-names thus being administrative centers where taxes were collected

Figure 90:   Close-up of the second register of the "Black Obelisk" of Shalmaneser III of Assyria (c. 9th cent. B.C.E.). According to the cuneiform inscription it shows "Jehu, son of Omri" paying tribute to the king

the Akkadian term meaning "import duty." We know that Israelite kings levied a toll on imported goods and on products in transit (cf. I Kings 10:14—15), and although the term *mekhes* is used in the Bible exclusively for cultic taxes (Num. 31:28,37—41), it is likely that the same word was also employed for import and export duties. In II Chronicles 17:5 it is reported that "all Judah" brought *minhah* (literally, "gifts") to King Jehoshaphat. It would seem that in this context *minhah* represents a special tax payment. According to a reference in Ezra 4:13 (see also 7:24), the Persian government imposed upon the people three kinds of levies called *mindah, belo,* and *halakh.* These are Babylonian technical terms for a variety of taxes.

The rural population paid their taxes in kind and the city dwellers in silver (for the latter cf. Ex. 30:11—16; I Kings 10:14—15; see also II Kings 15:20; 23:35; II Chron. 24:5). The agricultural products were delivered by the local tax collectors to the royal storehouses, which were situated in strategic places in the country (cf. I Chron. 26:24; 27:25—31; II Chron. 11:11; 32:27—29; 36:18; etc.). The precious metal was most probably melted down in the Temple or palace foundry (cf. Zech. 11:13), and then cast into a standard form for storage. As was the practice in the neighboring countries, taxes were paid on a yearly basis (cf. I Kings 10:14; II Chron. 24:5; see also II Kings 17:4). In times of economic stress Babylonian kings often proclaimed by special edicts a remission of debts and royal taxes. Whether this was also the case in Israel is not known.

15
CORVÉE

Corvée, the forced labor imposed by a conqueror on those conquered, or by the sovereign on the citizen body under his rule, is one of the most prominent indications of the central authority existing in the kingdoms of the ancient Near East. It was imposed in particular when vast building projects were undertaken for which a large quantity of manpower was required over lengthy periods. Various terms indicative of a corvée system are to be found in the context of landownership, trade, conditions of serfdom, etc.

The type of labor differed from place to place and in various periods men and women were employed for corvée labor, and even animals were drafted for special requirements. On the other hand, certain individuals, craftsmen, members of particular social strata, and occasional settlements might be exempted from the corvée, as a personal or collective privilege.

The many and diverse forms of corvée labor and the connected terminology and its derivation are also reflected in the biblical text. Three separate terms are used, but their original distinction is unclear. The term *mas oved,* "compulsory labor," sometimes *mas* alone, is derived from Canaanite or, in the opinion of some scholars, from Hittite. *Sevel,* a term found in the Mari documents, has a particular meaning as a labor unit for emergency use. *Perekh* is the type of corvée labor known in Mesopotamia. In the Bible this term is found only in the context of the slavery of the children of Israel in Egypt (Ex. 1:13; but see Lev. 25:43,46; Ezek. 34:4).

The slavery to Pharaoh in Egypt was a prolonged period of corvée labor by the Israelites. During the Israelite Conquest, corvée labor was one of the indications of the quality of the relations between the Israelites and the local Canaanite population. According to the biblical account, sometimes the Israelites paid tribute to the Canaanites, and sometimes the reverse was true (Gen. 49:15; Judg. 1:33, et al.). There are those who think that Joshua's compelling the Gibeonites to become "hewers of wood and drawers of water" (Josh. 9:21) is an example of the imposition of corvée labor.

Corvée labor became a permanent institution only in the period of the monarchy. According to II Samuel 20:24, the minister who was "over the levy" was one of the highest officials in David's regime. It seems that he was a foreigner, attached to the royal staff because of his expertise. The same official served Solomon and Rehoboam (I Kings 4:6; 12:18; II Chron. 10:18). Possibly, at first, only foreign elements in the country were obliged to submit to corvée labor (I Kings 9:20–22; II Chron. 8:7–9); only later was Solomon forced to demand compulsory labor from among the Israelite population, in order to carry out the vast building projects he had undertaken. There are scholars who hold that *mas oved* was the term applied to foreign manpower, and that *sevel* indicated an Israelite labor force. Yet such a distinction is not sufficiently clear, even if the corvée imposed upon the house of Joseph was called *sevel* (I Kings 11:28).

According to the Bible, Solomon sent thirty thousand men to hew cedars in Lebanon for the building of the Temple, in monthly shifts of ten thousand (I Kings 5:26–28). Similarly, he had at his disposal some seventy thousand ' bearers of burdens" and eighty thousand "hewers in the mountains" (I Kings 5:29ff.).

There is a hint of the continuation of the corvée tradition in the reign of Asa (I Kings 15:22). Asa built Geba Benjamin with stones taken by his subjects from Ramah: "Then King Asa made a proclamation unto all Judah; none was exempted. . ." (i.e., none could refuse the corvée). According to II Chronicles 34:13, King Josiah repaired the Temple with the labor of *sabalim* ("porters"). There was also corvée labor in the period of the return to Zion and the building of the wall around Jerusalem: "They that builded the wall and they that bore burdens *[sevel]* laded themselves. . ." (Neh. 4:11).

Part Three

TECHNOLOGY AND CRAFTS

16
RAW MATERIALS

From the many descriptive passages, allusions, and similes in the Bible we cannot but conclude that technical knowledge as well as artistic achievements were well developed in Israel at an early period. Unfortunately, in this particular area there are no actual remains which can be identified with the biblical descriptions. Archaeology can, however, help with some wider issues. Apart from providing parallels, to illustrate what would otherwise remain a difficult literary description, archaeology can grapple with a major problem: it can try to define the extent to which early Israelite technology was dependent on the surrounding cultures. To what extent were the technical and artistic achievements of Israel influenced by other ancient cultures and how much did Israel influence them? To what extent was Israelite art an expression of national growth? These questions are extremely difficult to answer, but the fact that archaeology has discovered parallels to biblical descriptions proves that Israel's technical and artistic achievements did not grow in a cultural vacuum, were linked to previous and contemporary cultures, and probably also influenced later technical developments in the region.

COPPER AND BRONZE

In the biblical account of the beginning of mankind there is a reference to Tubal-Cain, who lived eight generations after Adam. In a brief description of him the Bible states: "And Zillah, she also bore Tubal-Cain, the forger of every cutting instrument of copper and iron" (Gen. 4:22). By attributing the first smithery to Tubal-Cain the Bible in fact tells us that copper and iron-working was an extremely early development in the story of man. This view has been substantiated by modern research, which has found copper tools and other articles in use as long ago as the Chalcolithic period.

In Sumer, copper was already known about 3500 B.C.E. and it had become common there by 3000 B.C.E. Copper ore was probably obtained from Asia Minor or Central Asia. In Israel, too, the use of copper was introduced at an early period. A survey carried out by Benno Rothenberg in the Arabah, the great rift valley south of the Dead Sea, showed that there were copper mines in the area dating from the Chalcolithic period. Perrot, in his excavations around Beer-Sheba, found copper industries at Abu Matar and Bir Safadi. As no copper ore has been found near Beer-Sheba it is assumed that the raw material came from the mines in the Arabah area, some 60 miles distant. The fact that in the Chalcolithic period the settlement at Beer-Sheba was able to ensure a steady supply of ore from sources so far away shows that technical and political organization were well developed by then.

In addition to the mines which date back to the Chalcolithic period, a great number of copper mines and traces of copper smelting from a much later period have been discovered in the Arabah region and in southern Sinai. One such mine was explored by Nelson Glueck at Umm el-Amad on the east side of the Arabah Valley. It is cut into the face of the sandstone cliffs and extends some 100 ft. underground. At the far end, the beginnings of a number of galleries are visible. Five rock pillars were left standing at the entrance to the mine and other pillars supported the roof inside to prevent any caving in. The marks from the miner's picks can still be seen on the rock surface. Glueck ascribed the pottery he found there to the Iron Age and in consequence attributed the mines to Solomon, who needed the copper for the Temple, both for utensils and for decorations.

A fortified site with a large building, Tell al-Khalayfa (near the Gulf of Akaba), was identified by Glueck as the biblical port of Ezion Geber. The large building was thought to be a smelting center for the copper ore, and holes in the walls were identified as flues which allowed the strong winds coming down the rift valley from the north to fan the flames of the furnace. Thus Glueck attempted to reconstruct the biblical background for the period of Solomon and the Judean kingdom. The copper mines and the smelting centers, as well as the seaport used for trade with Ophir, gave the area a vital economic importance, which would explain why it was highly valued by the kings of Judah.

More recent research by Benno Rothenberg, however, has cast doubts on Glueck's conclusions. A temple discovered at Timna, at the foot of "Solomon's Pillars," was proved to be Egyptian, consecrated to the Egyptian goddess Hathor. It was built at the end of the 14th century B.C.E., and was destroyed about 1216–1210 B.C.E. A second temple was built on the ruins of the first, but it lasted only until about the middle of the 12th century. These two temples proved, for the first time, a connection between Egypt and the many mines, both at Timna and in the Arabah area. These findings complicate the establishment of a date for mining activities in the area. Nor is there evidence that the mines or smelting centers were in use after the 12th century. Moreover the Bible explicitly states that David set aside stores of copper for the Temple which he had taken as booty or received as gifts, and that it was from this store that Solomon fashioned the "copper sea" and the pillars and vessels of the Temple (I Chron. 18:8). As for the "smelting rooms" at Tell al-Khalayfa, the so-called "flues" are now recognized as being the sockets for long-rotted wooden beams which bonded the walls. Rothenberg has suggested that the site was a large forti-fied caravanserai, providing rest and food at an important crossroads in the north-south and east-west trade routes.

Ezion Geber, according to Rothenberg (but still very much disputed), should be sought at Jazīrat-Farʿūn (fig. 91), also known as the "Island of Pharaoh." Located not far from the northern end of the Gulf of Akabah, it has the only natural anchorage in the district, and is therefore the more

Figure 91:   Jazīrat-Farʿūn, also known as "Island of Pharaoh," tentatively identified with Ezion Geber, located in the northern part of the Gulf of Akaba

likely place for a port such as is mentioned in the Bible (II Kings 9:26; II Chron. 8:17). Traces of Iron Age casemate walls were also found at Jezīrat-Far'un, which would possibly connect the site with Solomon. Rothenberg's research has led to some questioning of the previously accepted opinion that the Arabah region constituted a great copper producing area in the time of Solomon, and that Timna was to be identified with "Solomon's Mines."

IRON

Iron is frequently mentioned in the Bible, not only as the metal from which many objects and utensils were made, but also as a metaphor for and a symbol of strength and toughness. As such it appears repeatedly in prophetic writings, for instance, "Because I knew that thou art obstinate, and thy neck is an iron sinew, and thy brow brass" (Isa. 48:4). In Jeremiah, the Lord promises the newly designated prophet: "I have made thee this day a fortified city, and an iron pillar, and brazen walls against the whole land. . ." (Jer. 1:18).

Even before this, in the Pentateuch, Moses used iron as a simile for its hard and unyielding property. He warns Israel that if they will not keep the commandments, God will punish them: "And I will break the pride of your power; and I will make your heaven as iron and your earth as brass" (Lev. 26:19). Moses also threatens the disobedient with "a yoke of iron" (Deut. 28:48).

Isaiah also gives some vivid descriptions of the ironsmith's craft: "Behold I have created the smith that bloweth the fire of coals, and bringeth forth a weapon for his work" (Isa. 54:16); "The smith maketh an axe, and worketh in the coals, and fashioneth it with hammers and worketh it with his strong arm" (Isa. 44:12). Whereas the term "smith" could refer to copper and bronze smiths, these two metals were not hammered but cast. Iron, on the other hand, had to be hammered and plunged into cold water in order to harden it and give it the desired qualities.

Like copper, the first workings of iron are ascribed by the Bible to Tubal-Cain, at the dawn of history. Iron tools and vessels are mentioned quite often in the biblical narrative. The land of Israel is "a land whose stones are iron" (Deut. 8:9); Og, king of Bashan, had a bedstead of iron (Deut. 3:11); vessels of iron were among the booty taken from the Midianites (Num. 31:22).

The Bible gives great prominence to the prohibition against using iron for hewing stone for the Temple altar (see above, p. 58). This prohibition was strictly adhered to by Solomon when he built the Temple. "For the House, when it was in building, was built of stone made ready at the quarry; and there was neither hammer nor ax nor any tool of iron heard in the House while it was a-building" (I Kings 6:7). The Rabbis explained it by saying that iron (i.e. weapons) shortens man's life while the Temple altar is designed to lengthen man's life. It would not be right to use an instrument of death in the creation of an instrument of life (Mid. 3:4).

The Bible also makes note of the "iron chariots" of the Canaanites living in the plain, which prevented the Israelites from conquering those districts (see p. 240). Most interesting, however, from the historical point of view, is the short description of the relations between the Israelites and the Philistines at the beginning of Saul's reign. "Now there was no smith found throughout all the land of Israel; for the Philistines said: 'Lest the Hebrews make them swords or spears'; but all the Israelites went down to the Philistines, to sharpen every man his plowshare, and his colter and his axe and his mattock. And the price of the filing was a pim for the mattocks and for the colters and for the forks with three teeth and for the axes; and to set the goads" (I Sam. 13:19—21). The above passage clearly shows that the Philistines kept a strict monopoly on the production of iron. This monopoly was broken only with the defeat of Philistine military power by Saul, and especially by David.

In David's time iron was plentiful, though it was still valued, for it is mentioned as one of the metals which the princes and the captains brought as a gift in preparation for building the Temple: "And they gave for the service of the House of God iron, a hundred thousand talents" (I Chron. 29:7). That gift of iron was needed, even though David had already prepared a vast hoard of iron for the building operations. "And David prepared iron in abundance for the nails for the doors of the gates, and for the couplings. . ." (I Chron. 22:3).

During the course of the years there must have been steady progress in the manufacture and working of iron in Israel, for during the reign of Joash (835—798 B.C.E.) craftsmen in iron are mentioned in connection with the Temple renovations carried out by Jehoiada (II Chron. 24:12). By the time the kingdom of Judah fell (597 B.C.E.), Israelite smiths and craftsmen formed an important separate class which Nebuchadnezzar took with him into exile: "And he carried away all Jerusalem, and all the princes, and all the mighty men of valour, even ten thousand captives, and all the craftsmen and smiths. . . ' (II Kings 24:14).

From this brief outline we see the importance of iron throughout biblical history. But iron was used in much earlier times; it was known in Mesopotamia as early as the 3rd millennium B.C.E. However, this was iron of meteoric origin, and was very soft. The tools and weapons made from it were not superior to bronze, and were more difficult and expensive to craft. It was only with the discovery of "steeling" the iron that it was possible to use it for tools and weapons. It seems that the process was first discovered by the Hittites in Asia Minor around 1400 B.C.E., and they kept the secret of their art for a period of some 200 years. During this period iron objects, mostly weapons, gradually penetrated into Syria-Erez Israel, but the metal was still of poorer quality than bronze. It was only around 1200 B.C.E., when the Hittite empire was destroyed and its craftsmen scattered, that iron weapons and tools came into common use in Erez Israel. Scholars take this period to mark the beginning of the Iron Age in the area.

There are two outstanding examples of iron-work of the period preceding the Iron Age. In Egypt, an iron dagger with an ivory handle decorated with gold and rock crystal was found in the tomb of Pharaoh Tuth-ankh-Amon (c. 1350 B.C.E.). The dagger must have been highly prized and seems to have been a present from a foreign country. And at Ugarit, in Syria, a beautiful axe has been found, which was probably used for ceremonial purposes. The blade is of iron, but the socket is of copper inlaid with gold. The natural shrinkage of the copper when cooling clamped the blade so tightly that no riveting was necessary. The weapon is dated to about 1300 B.C.E. There is also some literary evidence from Egypt concerning iron chariots. In the account given in Papyrus Anastasi I (c. 1250 B.C.E.), a royal Egyptian messenger arrives in Jaffa, a bustling Canaanite town, filled with craftsmen of all kinds. Here he has his chariot repaired by iron workers.

It is generally accepted today that it was the Philistines who brought the new art of iron manufacture to Canaan, when they occupied the coastal plain c. 1200 B.C.E. Archaeological excavations have turned up iron implements at nearly all the Philistine sites excavated. At Tell al-Far'ah, usually identified with Sharuhen, in the southwest of Israel, a large cemetery dating from the 13th to the middle of the 12th century B.C.E. has been excavated. No Philistine pottery was found, and all the metal objects discovered were made of bronze. However, in another cemetery in which Philistine pottery was dominant, metal objects of both bronze and iron were found. The iron objects were weapons and jewelry. Iron tools, usually more common than the above, are, of course, not to be expected among funeral offerings.

Another site, also in Philistine territory at the southern end of the coastal plain, is Tell Jamma (Jemmeh). The location of the site and the pottery found there show it to have been a Philistine town. Sir Flinders Petrie, who excavated the site in 1926–27, found four furnaces at Tell Jamma, which he claimed were used for smelting iron ore. Despite the fact that the furnace for smelting iron was well known in biblical times (Deut. 4:20; I Kings 8:51; Jer. 11:4), this view is also being challenged today as no traces of iron slag are apparent. Rather these are thought to have been furnaces for heating iron bars which must have been imported, and which were then worked to make tools, weapons, and other objects.

A large number of agricultural tools of iron and weapons were found at Tell Jamma. These include hoes, plowshares, picks, sickles, adzes, daggers, spearheads, and arrowheads (see p. 239–240). Similar objects have been found at other sites associated with the Philistines. (Surprisingly, though, no ironware has been found to date in the first two Philistine layers at Tell Qasila near Tel Aviv. Only in the third Philistine layer were objects of iron discovered.) Especially interesting is the iron plowshare which was found at Tell al-Fūl, which is identified with Gibeath-Shaul (Gibeah of Saul). In all probability it was a Philistine outpost before Saul defeated the Philistines at the battle of Michmash and built his palace-fortress there. The large amounts of iron slag found at Ashdod, a major Philistine center dating from the 9th–8th century B.C.E., indicate that even in later centuries the Philistines continued to manufacture iron. The biblical descriptions which link the Philistines with iron-working are therefore borne out by archaeological excavations.

That iron remained a valuable metal is shown by two additional pieces of evidence. In the palace of Sargon II (king of Assyria, 722–705 B.C.E.), 330,000 lbs. of unworked iron bars were found. During the reign of Sennacherib, Sargon's successor to the Assyrian throne, Hezekiah, king of Judah, was forced to pay tribute in order to allay the Assyrian threat to the Judean kingdom. This tribute included a number of daggers of iron which are specifically mentioned.

GOLD

Of all the metals in the Bible, the most frequently mentioned are gold and silver. Whereas the latter frequently served as currency, the former was used mainly for ornamentation and kept for its intrinsic value. The Bible uses several different words for gold and various adjectives to describe it.

Although the meaning of these descriptions is not clear today, and was already being questioned in the Talmud (Yoma 44b–45a), it does seem that there were different types of gold. The differences lay in the degree of purity of the metal, the color, and the place of origin.

In Erez Israel itself there were no gold deposits and the metal had to be imported. One of the sources for gold, already mentioned above in connection with the Israel-Tyrian expedition, was Ophir (I Kings 9:27–28). To this day the exact location of Ophir has not been definitely established by scholars. At Tell Qasila near modern Tel Aviv an inscription was found on a pottery sherd, reading "gold of Ophir for Beth-Horon."

Hebrew was not the only language which had a variety of terms and descriptions for gold. Other Near East languages show the same tendency; it is especially noticeable in Egyptian. The mining of gold by the Egyptians in ancient times was so extensive as to constitute almost a monopoly of its production. Gold mining was state run, and goldsmiths either bought their material from the state or worked in the temples under the supervision of the priests. Silver was usually present in the gold, forming an alloy which varied in color according to the percentage of silver content. But color effects were also produced artificially in Egypt by coloring the gold itself, or coloring the surface of base metals to give the appearance of the appropriate gold alloy. The variations in color of the different alloys or artificially prepared gold were used with good esthetic effect in ornamentation.

Different methods were used for working gold, and examples of the main techniques can be found in the Bible. The gold could be melted and cast to form a figure or solid object. The earliest gold objects were cast in open molds of stone or baked clay. Later two-piece molds came into use. Casting was probably the method employed for making the Golden Calf (Ex. 32:4; see p. 268). Alternately, owing to the softness of the metal, gold could be worked into thin sheets. It could then be applied to cover wood, bronze, ivory, or other materials. Very often the gold sheets were used to make gold wire or thread. This method is mentioned in the Bible for use in the Tabernacle: "And they did beat the gold into thin plates, and cut it into threads to work it in the blue, and in the purple, and in the scarlet, and in the fine linen, the work of the skillful workmen" (Ex. 39:3).

Gold could also be beaten into a required form, and this method of working the metal is also found in the Bible. The cherubs and the gold candelabrum for the Tabernacle were made of beaten gold. The cherubs were made of one piece, together with the lid of the Ark, while the candelabrum was beaten in one piece out of a talent of gold (Ex. 25:17–19, 31–40).

The purposes for which gold was used can be roughly divided into four categories, which again can be found in the Bible: a) as objets d'art, with or without practical use, e.g. cups and bowls; b) for jewelry; c) for decoration, such as covering for walls or chairs; d) for cultic purposes.

As with the other materials, also with gold we find that certain objects discovered by archaeology are strongly reminiscent of biblical themes, while others provide us with parallels or background to biblical descriptions. Actual gold objects described in the Bible have, however, not survived.

Many scholars believe that gold was the first metal to be worked by man, preceding even copper. While this has not been demonstrated sufficiently, and is almost certainly not true of Egypt, nevertheless gold was used in a very early age. Some of the gold craftmanship of ancient Sumer and Egypt has never been surpassed.

There is, for example, a lovely and well-known figure of a ram, some 20 inches high, from ancient Ur. It is made of gold and electrum (which is an alloy of gold and silver), mounted on a wooden core. The fleece is made of overlapping pieces of shell and lapis lazuli. The ram stands on its hind legs and its head is caught in the branches of a bush. The figure, which dates back to before 2500 B.C.E., recalls the biblical episode recounted in Genesis, where Abraham, who was preparing to sacrifice his son Isaac on the altar on Mount Moriah, was held back by a heavenly voice at the last minute. Abraham "lifted up his eyes and looked, and behold, behind him a ram caught in the thicket by his horns" (Gen. 22:13). Because of the resemblance to the biblical story, the ram of Ur is often called the "Ram caught in a Thicket."

Ornaments of gold occur frequently in the Bible. The servant of Abraham gave a ring and two bracelets to Rebekah when he met her at the well (Gen. 24:22). The Israelites brought their gold earrings to Aaron in order to make the Golden Calf (Ex. 32:2–3). The gold ornaments taken as booty from the Midianites are listed as "jewels of gold, armlets and bracelets, signet rings, earrings, and girdles" (Num. 31:50). In the later period of the Judges, Gideon used the golden earrings, crescents, and pendants taken as spoil from the Ishmaelites to make an *ephod,* a garment of gold which he hung as a trophy in his home town Ophrah (Judg. 8:24–27; see p. 000). David, in his elegy on Saul, mentions the ornaments of gold with which Saul clothed the maidens of Israel (II Sam. 1:24).

Examples of most of the ornaments mentioned can be found among the many gold and electrum ornaments found at Tell al-'Ajjūl (fig. 92), some four miles southwest of Gaza. There are earrings and signet rings, bracelets,

Figure 92:   Gold jewels and pendant incised with Hathor head, from Beit Eglaim (Tell al-'Ajjūl), c. first half of the 2nd millennium B.C.E.

pendants and crescents, and other types of ornaments. Although gold ornaments have been discovered in other parts of Israel, the finds at Tell al-'Ajjūl
are the most numerous and varied. They date from the early part of the 2nd
millennium to about the 15th century B.C.E.

In a pit on the plain west of Tell al-'Ajjūl, Petrie discovered an immense
quantity of black ash, the remains of burnt garments. Amid this ash was
goldwork which had obviously been most carefully destroyed. Bracelets had
been cut into scraps, and the terminals, in the shape of serpents' heads
whose eyes still gleamed when found, had been severed. The bright plating
of gold had been stripped from everything and broken into the smallest
fragments. Gold-plated studs and nails were all loosed from woodwork
which had been burnt. Lumps and globules of gold were found, the melted
remains of the inferno. Found together with the gold were two basalt tripod
stands which had been smashed on the spot, as shown by the fact that not a
single fragment was missing. Many horses' teeth and chips of bone were also
found. There must have been a complete destruction of property, gold and
silver, at the spot. Although the period in which this destruction took place
is well before the Israelites (Petrie dates it to the beginning of the 2nd

millennium B.C.E.), it is a remarkable Canaanite example illustrating the biblical ordinance of the *ḥerem* (doom) — the punishment of complete destruction. When the inhabitants of a town are found convicted of idol worship they are to be put to the sword and all their belongings gathered together and burnt (Deut. 13:13–19).

A specific case when the *ḥerem* was applied to a single person is described in the Book of Joshua (7:1,16–26). Achan had taken some of the forbidden spoils of Jericho for himself. When the crime was discovered, Achan together with all his family and possessions, including the stolen property, were led out of the camp and stoned to death. All was then burned. The pit at Tell al-'Ajjūl proves that the *ḥerem* was not peculiar to Israel but was already practiced by the Canaanites, though for what crimes we have no way of knowing.

In the Late Bronze Age period there was a marked influence of Mycenaean culture on the art of the Near East. This was particularly noted along the eastern littoral of the Mediterranean. At Mycenae and in the surrounding sites a large number of gold articles have been discovered, among which are ornaments such as pendants and necklaces of gold. Particularly interesting are some gold discs found in a woman's grave at Mycenae (16th century B.C.E.). It is a likely possibility that these discs were golden sequins which were sewn on a dress. This would be a remarkable illustration of the góld ornaments with which Saul clothed the maidens of Israel (II Sam. 1:24). Although there is an intervening period of some 500 years from the date given for the Mycenae sequins and the period of Saul, the sequins show that the idea of covering a dress with gold discs was already current.

It is clear that Philistine pottery decidedly follows the Mycenaean tradition in its shapes and distinctive decorations. The connection between the ceramic ware of the Philistines and the Aegean was established at the beginning of this century by Mackenzie, who excavated at Beth-Shemesh in 1911–1912. Certainly, if the Philistines carried on the Mycenaean cultural traditions, they would not only include ceramic ware but also other artistic objects. It was such golden objects which reached Israel in the form of war booty, and it is to these that David may refer.

Gold overlay was used in the Tabernacle in the wilderness, where the surrounding wooden boards were covered with gold. As pointed out gold overlay was made possible owing to the softness and easy workability of the metal. This was an ancient form of the art.

In Egypt, gold foil and sheet gold were widely applied to such objects as columns, doors, obelisks, and bas-reliefs, in addition to small objects. The

Bible tells that gold overlay was also used extensively for covering idols (see pp. 274–77).

Among the gold objets d'art mentioned in the Bible are gold cups. "And all King Solomon's drinking-vessels were of gold" (I Kings 10:21). In a very much later period Ahasuerus entertained the people with gold vessels: "And they gave them drink in vessels of gold – the vessels being diverse one from the other – and royal wine in abundance" (Esther 1:7).

Gold cups or drinking bowls were used by kings and royalty throughout the ages. Beautifully worked cups of gold have been found in Mycenae and the surrounding sites, which date from the 16th–15th century B.C.E. Gold bowls which possibly served a similar purpose have been found at various sites. Numerous examples of gold cups of Persian provenance include beautiful golden rhytons, cups fashioned in the shape of an animal head. One wonders whether these are the "vessels diverse one from the other."

IVORY

Ivory was rare and precious. The impression gained from both the Bible and modern research is that the use of ivory was reserved for royalty and the aristocracy. Large hoards or collections have been found all over the Near East. The objects in them were fashioned mainly from elephant tusks, although rhinoceros horns are known from early times in Egypt.

Compared with iron, biblical information about ivory is sparse. In the Bible, ivory became a symbol for lavishness and indolent living. It is first mentioned in connection with Solomon, whose fleet, together with that of Tyre, brought back ivory and other rarities. "For the king had at sea a navy of Tarshish with the navy of Hiram; once every three years came the navy of Tarshish, bringing gold, and silver, ivory and apes and peacocks" (I Kings 10:22). We do not know what use Solomon made of the ivory; only his throne is mentioned as having been made of that material.

The next mention of ivory is in a well-known aside on Ahab: "And the ivory house which he built..." (I Kings 22:39). This "house of ivory" is probably included in the dire prophecy of Amos: "And I will smite the winter-house with the summer-house, and the houses of ivory shall perish" (Amos 3:15).

It is generally thought that the manufacture of ivory artefacts originated in the Near East; certainly ivory work was an art in which the Canaanites, and later the Phoenicians, excelled. In a prophecy on Tyre, Ezekiel exclaims: "Many isles were the merchandise of thine hand, they brought thee for a present horns of ivory and ebony" (Ezek. 27:15). There were two main sources of supply of elephant tusks. One was from Africa and the other from north Syria, where the Asiatic type of elephant existed until the 8th century B.C.E. The natural limitation in size of the raw material restricted its use largely to ornamentation, mainly small carvings or inlays. An object like a chair would be made of slim, long pieces with carvings or inlay. Small-scale ivory sculptures usually show a greater freedom and more naturalistic trend than examples in other media.

Although works in ivory are known as a developed art in Erez Israel and Egypt as early as the Chalcolithic period (end of the 4th millennium), the craft flowered in the Late Bronze Age (15th to 14th century B.C.E.). Well before the age of Solomon, ivory had become a medium for sophisticated art. The ivory hoard from Megiddo (VII) (fig. 25), paralleled by that from Ugarit and other ivories, reflects many influences from various cultures and shows the formation of a Canaanite art which was later taken over by the Phoenicians and Israel. Egyptian, Hittite, and Mycenaean themes and forms were incorporated in what became the typical art of the region.

Our knowledge of the art in Israel comes mainly from the ivories found at Samaria (fig. 14), but these are by no means isolated examples. Greatly similar ivories have been found all over the Near East, especially at Arslan-Tash in northern Syria and at Nimrud (biblical Calah). These ivories are indicative of contemporary styles of decorative art favored by the Israelite aristocracy, and reflect the art of the 9th–8th centuries B.C.E. Crowfoot, who excavated at Samaria, saw an immediate source of comparison in the style and subject of the ivories with the decorations of the Temple of Solomon. Apart from the sphinxes portrayed which, according to Albright, provide the clue to the form of the biblical cherubs, there are decorative pieces with flower and palm designs (fig. 93), which remind one of the descriptions of the designs used by Solomon to decorate the doors and walls of the Temple: "And he carved all the walls of the house round about with carved figures of cherubim and palm-trees and open flowers within and without. . . and as for the two doors of olive-wood, he carved upon them carvings of cherubim and palm-trees and open flowers and overlaid them with gold" (I Kings 6:29–32).

Although the Bible does not mention ivory inlay, for the Temple structure was overlaid with wood, wood carvings were obviously a related art. The gold overlay which the Bible mentions here is also similar to ivory work, so that ivory decorations can serve as an excellent indication of what

Figure 93:   Ivory plaque from Ahab's palace at Samaria, decorated with palmettes

was accomplished in wood and gold. Among the ivories of Samaria are decorative pieces with flower designs and palms. Variations of these designs are also to be found among the Nimrud ivories, so that these may provide clues to the decorative designs used by Solomon in the Temple.

To judge from the profuse number of ivory fragments found at Samaria, there can be little doubt that they came from the "house of ivory" which Ahab built. They must have been used for interior decorations and for inlays for furniture. Those pieces which were recovered were mostly small plaques, carved in low or high relief or open work. A number were small sculptures carved in the round. Many of the ivories were decorated with colored insets of glass and paste, or gold leaf. Details were often deeply grooved and filled with colored insets. The majority of the plaques are Egyptian in subject and treatment, but they clearly portray the independent art peculiar to the Phoenicians and Israel. They show sphinxes, lions, stags, an Egyptian figure, Heh, who symbolized longevity, the child Horus sitting on a lotus plant, and decorative border designs. The Samaria ivories are the only evidence we have of the artistic tastes of the rulers of Israel in the 9th–8th centuries B.C.E.

The great similarity in style and themes of some of the Nimrud ivories suggest that these were spoils carried off by Sargon II, king of Assyria, when he sacked Samaria in 722 B.C.E. An ivory palm design is almost the exact copy of one from Samaria. There are also examples of the "woman at the window" though these have been found at various other sites too (see p. 38–39).

Ivory also reached Assyria in the form of gifts from the satellite kingdoms. We know, for instance, that ivory was included among the treasures sent by Hezekiah to Sennacherib.

Barnett, one of the greatest authorities on ancient ivories, states: "The ivories of Ahab and the Phoenician art ... can be seen to be intimately bound up with the early history of the Israelites. It was partly in reaction against the pagan symbolism of these works of art, related to the fertility cult of Astarte ... that the prophets campaigned so bitterly ... By study-ing these ivories the background of the Bible can be enlarged and illustrated and better understood."

POTTERY

From the archaeological point of view, the most common yet the most important single factor in assessing newly excavated information is pottery; its importance cannot be overestimated. The use of pottery as the source of archaeological knowledge and conclusions was first introduced by Sir Flinders Petrie, and later was developed by W. F. Albright.

Pottery is used for fixing the dates for the strata of a mound. A pottery vessel is extremely fragile, but once broken, the sherds remain practically indestructible. This indestructibility is what makes it so common an artefact in archaeological excavations. The numerous shards found at every site are of the greatest importance for the evaluation of the character and period of the site. Once the absolute date of a potsherd is established, based on its form, decoration, and method of manufacture, the stratum in which it was found can be dated. For cultures and periods containing few or no written remains, which are the primary source of absolute chronology, the presence of pottery can serve as a substitute to establish a chronology.

Pottery is a highly versatile art form. It is made of clay and thus is easy and inexpensive to produce, yet it lends itself to forms and designs which can reach artistic heights. Thus it mirrors the technological and artistic achievement of an age. From the examination of pottery types and decora-tions, techniques of working the clay and firing the pots, one may seek to deduce the direction of cultural influence and the connections between countries and people, whether through trade, migration, or conquest. Pot-tery may also provide evidence of changes in the ethnic composition of the population at a site. An abrupt change in pottery type may denote the presence of a new ethnic group, whereas a gradual change would reflect a more or less static picture from the ethnic point of view.

In the Bible, pottery occurs in different contexts. Pottery vessels were used for cooking (Lev. 6:21), as containers for liquids (Num. 5:17), and as containers for scrolls (Jer. 32:14). Many specific household utensils are mentioned in the Bible, but we cannot always be certain which ones were made of pottery and which of metal, nor can we be quite sure of their form, although their purpose usually provides a reliable clue to their general shape.

The prophets knew the art of pottery manufacture and often alluded to it in similes or metaphors. There is an example in Jeremiah: "The word which came to Jeremiah from the Lord, saying: 'Arise, and go down to the potter's house and there I will cause thee to hear My words.' Then I went down to the potter's house, and, behold, he was at his work on the wheels. And whensoever the vessel that he made of clay was marred in the hand of the potter, he made it again another vessel, as seemed good to the potter to make it. Then the word of the Lord came to me saying: 'O house of Israel, cannot I do with you as this potter?' saith the Lord. Behold, as the clay in the potter's hand, so are ye in My hand, O house of Israel" (Jer. 18:1–6).

Second Isaiah points out the relationship of man with God: "But now, O Lord, Thou art our Father. We are the clay and Thou our potter, And we are all the work of Thy hand" (Isa. 64:7). "Woe unto him that striveth with his Maker, As a potsherd with the potsherds of the earth! Shall the clay say to him that fashioneth it: 'What makest thou?' Or: 'Thy work: it hath no hands'?" (Isa. 45:9). The potsherd is an ideal simile in all these cases, because man also comes from the earth.

Pottery appears for the first time in the Neolithic period, 5th millennium B.C.E. The earliest examples were found at Jericho (thus called ceramic culture of Jericho) and are handformed, coarse and sun-baked. They include bowls and storage jars decorated with burnished red slip painted with triangular zigzag lines. In the later phase appear incised herringbone and zigzag designs, and the rest of the pot is painted. This type appears mainly near the Yarmuk River (Shaar ha-Golan and is thus called Yarmukian culture). In the Chalcolithic (4th millennium B.C.E.) and Early Bronze (3rd millennium B.C.E.) periods, primitive potters' wheels first appear.

Several potters' workshops and kilns have been discovered in excavations in Erez Israel. Two early and good examples have been found at Tell al-Far'ah and Lachish. The former, dating to the Early Bronze period, had a potter's wheel, kilns, piles of clay and *degraissant*, shaping and polishing tools, and discarded vessels. The latter was found in a cave. It dates from the end of the Late Bronze period, but must have remained in use well into the early Iron Age; that is from about 1300–1050 B.C.E. Slag and unbaked shards at the entrance pointed to the use of the cave as a pottery workshop. A cave was an ideal place for making pottery because it was so much cooler than outside, a fact which permitted the slower drying of the clay before it was put in the furnace. In the cave itself were several pits and depressions. One of these pits probably served as an emplacement for the potter's wheel, while the potter sat on a stone slab found nearby. Other pits contained potter's tools and trial pieces, as well as finished vessels. On the floor of the cave were heaps of raw material — clay, crushed lime and shells, charcoal, and lumps of red and yellow ocher which were used for painting the pottery. In one of the pits, a small mortar for grinding the ocher was discovered. Two large stones were also found which must have been parts of the potter's wheels. The lower side had been ground smooth by the turning movement on the socket stone which was set in the pit in the ground. The potter's kiln was not found, although there were some indications of its position in the far recesses of the cave.

With the passage of time, pottery manufacture grew more sophisticated, and a wide variety of styles developed. (see chart, pp. 278–79).

GLASS

Glass is mentioned only once in the Bible, where it is said of divine wisdom that "gold and glass cannot equal it; neither shall the exchange thereof be vessels of fine gold" (Job 28:17).

Glass is found in nature in the form of obsidian (volcanic glass), and obsidian implements have occasionally appeared in Erez Israel in deposits of the Neolithic and Chalcolithic periods. The obsidian probably was imported from Anatolia and Armenia.

Most glass, however, is manufactured from various raw materials. Ancient glass is usually a compound produced by the fusion of silica (sand, flint, or quartz) with an alkaline (soda or potash) and calcium (limestone or chalk). The color is determined by the addition of metallic oxides. Other properties of the glass are the result of controlling temperature, duration of heating, and proportions of the various compounds.

Glazed beads and similar objects were first made in the Near East in the 5th millennium B.C.E., but the earliest use of man-made glass does not antedate the 3rd millennium, when the first glass beads were made in Mesopotamia and Egypt. The invention of glass vessel making dates to the mid-2nd millennium B.C.E. These early vessels were formed on a core, since glass blowing was unknown before the early Roman period. The core was made in the shape of the desired vessel, and viscous glass was applied to it.

Then the surface of the vessel was decorated by threads of differently colored glass applied in decorative patterns. The vessel was finally rolled on a flat stone until the decorative threads sank into the still viscous matrix. Handles and bases were added afterward. The core had to be strong enough to withstand the heat of the molten glass, and friable enough to be removed after the glass cooled.

The earliest core-formed glass vessels appear, almost simultaneously, around 1500 B.C.E. in both Egypt and Mesopotamia. There are, however, indications that this technique was invented in the Hurrian lands of northern Mesopotamia, and was then introduced into Egypt. The colors of the glass used in this early period indicate that the artisans sought to imitate precious stones, like the blue of lapis lazuli, and turquoise. The Egyptian glass industry flourished particularly in the Tell el-Amarna period, and the remains of a glass factory were excavated at Tell el-Amarna by Sir Flinders Petrie. Mesopotamian glass vessels have been found at Alalakh in northern Syria, but not in Erez Israel or the rest of Syria. In contrast, Egyptian glass vessels were exported to Erez Israel, Syria, Cyprus, and at times as far as the Aegean islands.

Several sites in Erez Israel have yielded Egyptian glass vessels of the 14th–13th centuries B.C.E. A rich collection of such vessels was found in the small Canaanite Fosse Temple at Lachish; others were found in the temples of Beth-Shean and Tell Deir 'Allā (ancient Sukkoth). Egyptian glass vessels were also found in tombs at Tell al-'Ajjūl, Beth-Shemesh and Dhahrat el-Humraya near Jaffa, and in Gezer and Megiddo. There is no positive evidence that glass vessels were made in Canaan in the Late Bronze Age.

Other techniques, like casting glass in molds, glass-cutting, and engraving, were also introduced in the mid-2nd millennium B.C.E. A homogeneous group of blue glass pendants fashioned in the shape of a nude female (possibly a fertility goddess) has been found widely distributed throughout many areas of the Middle East, including Erez Israel (Beth-Shean, Megiddo, and Lachish). Others have been found in Cyprus, around the Aegean, and, less frequently, in Egypt. Their origin is either in northern Mesopotamia or Syria, and they date to the 15th–13th centuries B.C.E. A group of molded discoid glass pendants, well known from Nuzi and Ashur, was found in the Late Bronze levels of Megiddo and Beth-Shean. These may be imports from northern Mesopotamia. Glass vessels made of "mosaic glass" were also known in Mesopotamia and Egypt in the 14th century B.C.E., but have not yet been reported from Syria or Erez Israel.

A complete decline in glass making set in toward the end of the 2nd millennium B.C.E. It is only in the second half of the 8th and the 7th centuries B.C.E. that glass vessels are found again. Core-formed glass reappeared in this period in Mesopotamia, and molded and cut-glass bowls and other luxury vessels of light green, blue, and violet glass were found in the royal Assyrian palaces at Nimrud. Engraved on a glass bottle found at the last site is a lion and the cuneiform inscription: "Palace of Sargon, king of Assyria."

Molded and cut-glass vessels of this type have not yet been found in Erez Israel, but a tomb at Achzib yielded a core-formed vessel of the 7th century B.C.E. Glass inlay pieces of the late 9th and 8th centuries B.C.E. were found together with the celebrated ivories in the palace of the kings of Israel at Samaria. It cannot be ascertained whether the glass of these pieces was of Syrian or other provenance, perhaps imported together with the ivory. Similar inlay pieces were found at Nimrud and at Hadata (Arslan Tash) in northwestern Mesopotamia.

The Phoenicians undoubtedly had a share in trading and distributing glass throughout the Mediterranean area in this and subsequent periods, but whether they had a role in producing glass vessels remains the subject of conflicting views.

Archaeological finds indicate that an active glass production center began to manufacture small vessels late in the 7th century B.C.E. These vessels were popular in all Mediterranean countries between the 6th and 4th centuries B.C.E. Their color schemes are reminiscent of Egyptian vessels of the 18th–19th Dynasties, but their shapes are mostly Greek in inspiration. Recent studies seem to point to Rhodes as their place of origin. Vessels of this type were also found in Erez Israel, i.e. an early 6th century B.C.E. tomb at Gibeah (north of Jerusalem), excavations at Athlit, Achzib, Hazor, Beth-Shean, and En-Gedi, and Ammonite tombs in Transjordan.

Molded and cut-glass vessels continued to be made in the Persian period. Such vessels are known from Iran and Mesopotamia. The remains of an alabastron of this type were found in a tomb at Athlit.

STONE

The Bible does not mention stone implements as such, but does list various utensils which have been revealed, in archaeological finds, to have been made of stone. The very earliest implements devised by man were made of stone, and his skill in working with this material was undoubtedly connected with the fashioning of flint tools.

Stone working required a knowledge of two operations: the drilling of the inner area of the vessel, and the smoothing or polishing of both the inner and outer surfaces. The latter operation probably derived from two other skills — the grinding of cereals and the honing of flint utensils.

Beginning with the Chalcolithic period and perhaps even earlier, we find evidence of a drilling tool having been used on stone clubheads which have a hole bored at either end. An Egyptian fresco dating from the Old Kingdom shows a stoneworker's shop. The artisan is using a drill, his apprentice is holding the stone block steady, and two other men are smoothing and polishing the surfaces of vessels both within and without. The Egyptian tool is composed of a pointed drill bit placed within a wooden haft. In the days of the Old Kingdom, the drill had a double-weighted cord attached to it. The craftsman would press down with one hand on the upper portion of the drill, while the other hand would swing the weights attached to the cord. As they swung, they would exert additional pressure on the drill bit.

A few sharp, pointed pieces of bronze and iron have been found in Erez Israel, and they may be identified as drill heads. It is not known whether the weighted cord was used there, although weights of stone or clay have been found, with grooves showing marks of something having been tied on them; these are considered to be drill weights.

The various stone implements found in excavations appear to be locally made for the most part, although implements of basalt and limestone were probably fashioned on the site of the stone strata. Despite the weight of the objects, there was a trade in stoneware between areas in Erez Israel rich in basalt and areas lacking that stone. Certain stone implements having a specific use, such as cosmetic items, were made of stone that was not found in Erez Israel and were imported.

Stone implements are less valuable in their contribution to our knowledge of human civilization than are clay or glass vessels, for the development of stoneware is not as well-defined, except for the stoneware of predynastic and Old Kingdom Egypt, and the very special case of the alabaster utensils found in Egypt and Erez Israel.

WOOD

In Hebrew the word *ez* means both "tree" and "wood" (also "stick"). The Bible speaks of special craftsmen who worked in the various branches of wood manufacturing (Ex. 31:5; II Sam. 5:11; I Chron. 22:15, et al.). The

Bible also mentions several types of wood which were treated for various purposes; gopher wood (Gen. 6:14), cedar wood (Ezra 3:7), acacia wood (Ex. 38:1), juniper wood (I Kings 6:34), almug wood (I Kings 10:11), and olive wood (I Kings 6:31). Apparently, cedars and cypress trees were used primarily for the construction of ornate buildings, while the other types were used mainly in the construction of furniture, and other articles and utensils. Cedars and almug wood were imported from abroad, mainly during the period of the monarchy, while acacia and olive trees were common in Palestine.

The Bible lists a number of pieces of wooden furniture which were used in the Temple and the Tabernacle: the table of display (Ex. 25:23—30), the Ark (Ex. 25:10—14), the altar for burnt offerings (Ex. 38:1), and the incense altar (Ex. 37:25); and various wooden household utensils, such as mortars, dishes, spoons, etc., are mentioned in connection with the laws of uncleanness and purification (Lev. 15:12).

Wood was also used for axe and spear handles. Stone heads were attached to the wooden handles by tying them together with sinews or ropes, while metal blades of various shapes and uses were attached to wooden handles by tying them with cords, by driving one end into the wood, or by making a hole in the metal into which the wood was inserted and riveted.

Wood also appears in connection with the criticism of idol worshipers, when the Bible indicates that they are worshipers of wood and stone, the work of men (Deut. 4:28).

Only a small number of wooden objects from the biblical period have been discovered in excavations in Israel, because of the process of decay. The richest finds of wooden furniture and vessels, including tables, bowls, combs, jugs, and toilet boxes, were in the Middle Bronze tombs in Jericho and other places.

Archaeological studies reveal a variegated use of wood in the construction of houses in Erez Israel. It includes the building of huts from branches which were cut down and left in their natural state, the use of lumber in the consolidation of frames of buildings, in the covering of wooden structures, as columns for reinforcing walls, for the roofing of clay, stone, or straw buildings, and for making doors and windows.

TEXTILES

Because vegetable or animal fibers disintegrate in wet climates, not many fabrics of biblical times have survived. Biblical references to garments and fabrics are not helpful in providing information about them, for they are not specific.

The description of the curtains to be made for the Tabernacle does provide exact dimensions: "The length of each curtain shall be 28 cubits and the breadth of each curtain four cubits." Further on, a length of 30 cubits is mentioned, but the same width of 4 cubits (approximately 6 ft.) remains, which suggests that this was a standard width for weaving curtain fabric. The materials to be used were fine twined linen, blue and purple and scarlet stuff, and goats' hair. Embroidery, including cherubim to be worked on the inner curtains and veil, was to decorate the fabric. In addition to the linen, wool, and goat's hair used for the Tabernacle curtains, gold thread was to be added to the garments worn by the priests. Moreover, the priestly tunic was to be woven of linen in a "checkered" pattern. Biblical references to fabrics and garments would seem to reflect a civilization that was well acquainted with the processes of spinning, weaving, and tailoring fabrics, so that there was no need to explain a technique or custom in detail.

Although few examples of textiles have been preserved in Erez Israel, more have been found in the dry climate of Egypt. As fabrics were frequently imported by boat or camel caravan during the biblical period, one may surmise that some of these samples may have come from Erez Israel, or that the fabrics used there were similar to the Egyptian textiles. Some of the specimens preserved are 6 ft. in width (see above); others are narrow tapes. They include fabrics of wool and of linen, of plain and of patterned weave. The weaving was uniformly simple, but the workmanship was, in many cases, extraordinary. The colors of the textiles which have survived are not limited to the "blue and purple and scarlet" of the Bible, but cover the entire spectrum.

In the ancient Middle East, as in all parts of the world, the vegetable fibers, flax and cotton, were the first to be spun into yarn for weaving. These fibers had to be cultivated by people who stayed in one place long enough to sow and reap, and they were luxuries in lands where the economy was based on flocks and herds, and where clothing was made of hides and leather.

It was probably the vegetable fibers themselves which suggested the idea of spinning to ancient man, for when they are wet, they turn as they dry. Flax turns in the direction of the center part of the letter "S"; cotton turns in all directions, but more in the "Z" direction. In Egypt, where flax was the principal fiber, spinning turned in the "S" direction, and this method of spinning spread through all the countries under Egyptian influence. In contrast, in India, where cotton seems to have originated, spinning followed the "Z" direction, and this method traveled west over the trade routes.

Flax was a flourishing crop in Egypt, and the Pharaohs gave garments of fine linen as gifts, together with gold and jewels (Gen. 41:42). Egyptian linen was soft and pliable; clothes made of it were comfortable to wear, and linen sails did not cut themselves in a gale (cf. Ezek. 27:7). This pliability was produced by steeping the flax in running water in order to decompose the woody parts of the stem and separate the fibers. In contrast, flax laid out on the roofs to be retted by the dew (Josh. 2:6) produced fibers which were stiff and brittle. The term "fine twined linen" probably referred to the quality and method of preparation in running water, since there is little difference in the diameter of linen fibers from various places in the Near East.

Cotton grew in many lands, but it seems to have been spun only in countries with a damp climate, which helped keep the short (1¼ inches at most) fibers together during the spinning process. Isaiah 19:9 probably refers to Upper Egypt or the Sudan; the climate of Lower Egypt was too dry to permit cotton to be spun there.

In earlier biblical times, linen and cotton were generally used undyed. However, cotton could be dyed with indigo (Esth. 1:6). Whereas linen was difficult to dye, occasional blue threads were woven either in warp or weft for decorative purposes, and some examples have been found in the Dead Sea Scroll Caves.

Since sheep and goats were raised in many areas of the Fertile Crescent, wool was frequently used for textiles. Wool varies in its natural color. In Asia Minor it is clear white; in the Caucasus and northern Mesopotamia it ranges from clear white to yellow and tan, medium and dark brown.

In addition to the many natural colors of wool, it was also customary to dye the fibers. A combination of red and blue dyes with a variety of natural colored wool could produce any color of the spectrum. In Erez Israel dyers were concentrated in certain towns. At Tell Beit Mirsim, Albright identified a house containing stone vats and weights as a dyers' workshop. Similar vats were found at Gezer, which was an important dyeing center.

Whereas vegetable fibers were spun from the Stone Age, wool began to be spun (rather than being used as sheepskin or as pressed felt) only in the Bronze Age, and more commonly in the Iron Age. Wool was spun in both the "S" and "Z" directions, since the fibers have no inherent turn of their own.

Three kinds of looms were commonly used in biblical times, two vertical and one horizontal. According to Herodotus, the Egyptians were the only ones to use their particular type of vertical loom, whereas many peoples used the Greek vertical loom.

The horizontal loom was the type carried by nomadic peoples. It consisted of two beams held in place by four pegs driven into the ground. The weaver sat in front of the loom, which was generally narrower than the Egyptian vertical model, for the width had to be limited to the reach of the weaver's arms, or in some cases, to the reach of two weavers sitting side by side. This obviously was the loom mentioned in Judges 16:13–14, used by Delilah when weaving the seven locks of Samson's head into her web; otherwise Samson would have had to be sleeping while sitting up.

Another type of thread mentioned in the Bible as being used for special garments was gold thread. Exodus 39:3 explains the process of preparing this costly stuff. Drawn wire, such as that used for filigree work (*ibid.* v. 16) was beaten thin and cut into strips. A hank of such gold thread was found at Dura on the Euphrates. Textiles from Ereẓ Israel and Syria used the metal thread flat.

LEATHER

The principal biblical Hebrew word for leather (*or*) also denotes skin and hide, so it is difficult to establish the exact meaning of the biblical references. Skinning is mentioned in the Bible in connection with sacrifices, but details concerning the processing and working of leather are lacking. It may be assumed that in biblical times, tanning was essentially a simple process of drying the hide in the sun.

Biblical references to articles made of leather include curtains and coverings made from the skin of goats and rams, clothing (Gen. 3:21), and a skin bottle for storing and transporting water or wine (Josh. 9:4,13). From archaeological finds and various ancient written records it is known that leather was also used for chariots, weapons, and as a writing material.

Excavations in Ereẓ Israel have yielded various tools which were connected with the processing of leather. In Tell al-Naṣba and in Tell Beit Mirsim, knives were found which probably served to skin animals. Two Aramaic ostraca found in En-Gedi (6th century B.C.E.) deal with the tanning of leather. Other than a pair of sandals (see p. 228), no leather objects dating to the First Temple period have been found in Ereẓ Israel.

17

TOOLS AND UTENSILS

DOMESTIC TOOLS

Household Furnishings

Archaeological evidence regarding household goods and equipment is rather one-sided, consisting of pottery vessels found in houses and graves excavated in Erez Israel, dating as far back as the Neolithic period (see Pottery). Stone mortars, hand mills, and metal tools are common finds. In contrast, few goods made of more perishable substances such as wood, leather, woven materials, and basketry have survived the centuries.

The Middle Bronze Age tombs of Jericho yielded important evidence concerning the wooden furniture of the period. Tables were found in several tombs, built of a single plank standing on three legs, two placed at one end of the plank, and one in the middle of the opposite end. (Three legs provide more stability on uneven ground than four.) Square wooden stools, a rectangular stool to seat two, and a wooden bed were also found in these tombs. The bed frame preserves signs of stringing, and the stools seem to have had cord seats. The style of the furniture reveals Egyptian influence. The same tombs were also furnished with carved wooden bowls and toilet boxes decorated with bone inlays. Inlays of similar boxes have been found in Erez Israel in many sites of the 18th–16th centuries B.C.E. To the 14th–13th centuries B.C.E. belong ivory-inlaid furniture found at Megiddo; this was probably royal property.

This type of furniture was probably foreign to the semi-nomadic Israelites, but once in Canaan, they adapted themselves to the local customs, as is evident from biblical references to various items of furniture. The typical furniture of a room in Erez Israel in the 9th century B.C.E. is listed in II Kings 4:10, where the woman of Shunem suggests that her husband build "a little chamber on the roof" for the prophet Elisha: "... let us set for him there a bed, and a table, and a stool, and a candlestick."

217

The Bible also mentions banqueting beds with ivory inlays (Amos 6:4). Pieces of beautifully carved ivory inlays were found in the royal palaces of the kings of Israel at Samaria (late 9th and 8th centuries B.C.E.). These ivories, which are of Phoenician and Egyptian influence, probably belonged to various pieces of furniture, including banqueting beds of the type well known from Assyrian excavations of the same period. Bronze angle pieces and the fittings of a bed and a stool were found in a grave of the Persian period at Tell al-Far'ah (Sharuhen), southeast of Gaza.

Domestic household equipment also included pottery footbaths. Several oval footbaths (maximum dimension 2 ft.) were found at Samaria (8th century B.C.E.). Similar footbaths of the Israelite period were found at Tell al-Naṣba, and at Megiddo.

Items of basketry must have been an important component of household goods. Several whole and many partially decomposed baskets survived in the arid caves of the Judean Desert. One extraordinary find is a straw sieve, 15 in. in diameter, probably used for sifting grain, which dates to the Chalcolithic period (4th millennium B.C.E.); other baskets, as well as water goatskins, date from the time of the Bar Kokhba revolt (132–35 C.E.). Remains of basketry have also been found in the Middle Bronze Age tombs of Jericho.

Cooking Utensils

Diet in Ereẓ Israel during the biblical period consisted of foods supplied by the local agricultural society. Most agricultural produce was grown by farmers living in permanent settlements, while meat was provided by cattle- and sheep-raising nomads. Some wild plants were also gathered.

Food was prepared by baking, boiling, frying, or roasting, or by a combination of these methods. Cooking or baking was generally done in the courtyard or the kitchen, either in a hearth or an oven (see above, p. 51). In seasons of intensive agricultural labor the workers camped in the fields (Gen. 37:17), while in other seasons they returned to their homes each night. Accordingly, cooking utensils were developed for use in both the permanent kitchen and the field encampment.

As a rule, cooking utensils were made of earthenware (Lev. 6:21). Special attention was given to the preparation of these utensils, which had to be able to withstand heat. The clay was mixed with coarse solid matter, such as pebbles, shells, or shards, in order to reduce the porosity of the utensil and to prevent its cracking under heat. Metal cookingware was rare in the biblical period. However, the term *sir* specifically means a copper pot (cf. Ezek. 24:11).

Cooking vessels were of simple practical forms, and usually lacked decoration. The bases of the vessels were rounded and wide, in order to bring as much surface as possible into contact with the fire and to allow the heat to be distributed equally over the entire container. As vessels were not placed on the ground or on a flat surface, but on stones, on a stand, or on any noncombustible object which would hold them over the flame, the bases did not have to be flat.

Excavations in Erez Israel have revealed various methods of supporting cooking vessels. The simplest was a small pit in the ground with an opening at the side, which permitted feeding and fanning the fire. A more sophisticated method was a low mound of rocks arranged in the shape of a horseshoe. The fire was fed through the opening and the utensil was placed on the rim. On the floors of rooms and kitchens at many sites small pits have been found which were coated with clay seared by the fire which continuously burned within them. Each of these pits also had an opening through which the flame could be tended. Beginning with the Early Bronze Age, well-made portable stands of baked clay appear. Their shape was that of a thick, high horseshoe with a flat base that enabled them to stand on a level surface. On the rim were at least three protrusions for supporting the cooking pot.

From the Early Bronze Age onward, handleless vessels with the width of the base greater than the height appear. These pots stood on stands while cooking, as well as during the meal, when the cooked food was scooped out with another vessel and served. In the Israelite period (Iron Age) various types of cooking vessels were common, some without handles, some with two handles, and some with more than two handles. In addition, smaller cooking vessels with only one handle were widely used. Apparently, vessels without handles were placed in the permanent pits or on fixed stands, where they could remain standing while the food was ladled into bowls for eating. Vessels with two or more handles were used in a slightly different manner: by means of a rope tied to the handles, they were hung from a tripod, with the fire beneath them. These vessels may have been used during the seasons of outdoor labor. The smaller single handled vessels served for cooking and pouring, the cooked food being ladled into the eating vessels after its removal from the fire. Possibly, these vessels were used for thinner foodstuffs in contrast to the larger cooking vessels.

While fruits and certain vegetables were eaten fresh, lentils and legumes, such as kidney beans, broad beans, and chick-peas, were prepared for consumption by cooking them in water (as were eggs) and mixing them with other vegetables and seasonings, such as onions and garlic. Meat was a scarce commodity. Mutton, goat meat, or fowl were most commonly eaten, but sometimes veal or other types of meat were prepared. Meat was served principally at special festive meals in which the entire family or tribe took part. One way to prepare meat was to boil it in water with seasonings. Softened by boiling, meat could easily be separated from the bones. Other methods of preparation included roasting on the open flame, baking in the oven, or frying in oil. It is not known whether meat was salted or smoked, but it is possible that these procedures were practiced.

While cooking hearths were open, baking ovens were usually closed. The Hebrew word for "to bake" and its derivatives specifically refer to the baking of bread (Gen. 19:3; Lev. 26:26; Isa. 44:15) and cakes (Ex. 12:39; I Kings 17:12–13), including the preparation of the bread of display (Lev. 24:5) and baked offerings (2:4ff.). Baking, like cooking, was from the earliest periods an integral part of the everyday household chores. Only in later periods was baking somewhat industrialized and done by specialists, or in national bakeries.

The simplest method of baking involved placing the dough on glowing coals which baked it from below, while coals were also spread on top of the dough to bake it from above (Isa. 44:19). In a second method a bowl was placed upside down over the fire and when it was sufficiently heated, the prepared dough was placed on it for baking. Excavations of Middle Bronze Age settlements have yielded specially designed baking trays which are perforated in order to preserve the utensil for a long time and prevent the bread from sticking to it.

The baking oven was a relatively sophisticated piece of equipment. Ovens made of clay or built of brick or stone have been found in various shapes — cylindrical, hive-shaped, semicircular and square (see above, p. 51). Dough was stuck to the inner wall of the oven. A fire heated the oven from the outside, thus baking the bottom of the bread, while a fire inside the oven baked the top of the bread. A more perfected oven had two levels; the fire was kindled in the lower level, while the dough was placed on the floor of the upper level. Ovens operated in this manner served the needs of industrialized baking. As portrayed in ancient Egyptian paintings, an oven of this type was operated by two people; one fanned the flame and the other inserted and removed the bread. The oven had three openings: one for feeding the fire, the second for inserting and removing the bread, and the third for fanning the flame and letting out the smoke in the oven. The oven was heated with dried dung, with wood that had been gathered or chopped from trees and then dried, or with charcoal.

Deuteronomy 8:8 lists the seven types of produce grown in Erez Israel: "A land of wheat and barley, and vines and fig-trees and pomegranates; a land of olive-trees and honey." The basic nutritional element in the diet of Erez Israel was cereals, and wheat and barley were cultivated crops. In addition, a stew made of lentils or beans was common. Other vegetables were eaten less frequently. In contrast to Egypt, where melons, cucumbers, onions, and garlic were cultivated (Num. 11:5), in Erez Israel these vegetables grew wild and were picked as needed. (They were cultivated only in the post-biblical period.) Sesame seeds were also gathered wild and were used for cooking or for their oil.

Grapes were grown mainly for the production of wine, although they were also eaten fresh or were dried in the sun to produce raisins which could be preserved for substantial periods of time. Grapes were processed to produce a thick liquid, called grape honey, made by treading the fruit in special vats. The liquid produced was not left to ferment, but was boiled in order to evaporate the water content, leaving behind a thick liquid resembling honey.

Figs were eaten either fresh or dried, the dried figs being strung into a chain or pressed into a hard cake or block. After sufficient drying, the fig block was sliced and eaten like bread. Pomegranates were usually eaten fresh, although occasionally they were used in the preparation of wine for medicinal use. Dates were eaten fresh or were sun-dried. Like grapes, dates were made into a sweet, thick drink called date honey. This was prepared by soaking the fruit in water for some time, during which it would disintegrate. Then the liquid was cooked down until thick and sweet. Olives were generally used to make oil (see below), although some were eaten after being preserved in tasty and fragrant spices, which removed their naturally bitter flavor. The Bible also mentions apples, nuts, pistachios, and almonds. These were not cultivated, but grew wild. Considered delicacies, they were imported for table use by the wealthy.

Almost all food was seasoned with salt (Job 6:6), which was the most commonly used spice. Salt served the additional function of symbolizing the making of a covenant (II Chron. 13:5), or the destruction of a city (Judg. 9:45). It was obtained in two ways: the most common method was mining, as at Sodom, although it was also produced by evaporating sea water and removing the salts from the sediment. The raw salt was rinsed in fresh water, purified, and then crushed until fine.

The flavor of food was also enhanced by spices derived from plants: garlic, onions, coriander, cumin, and black cumin. More delicate spices for special feasts were imported from Arabia and India, and were considered merchandise of the highest value. Among such spices were various types of pepper and ginger.

During the biblical period, birds' eggs and wild bee honey were also eaten. The latter was sufficiently rare to have been considered among the finest of foods ("honey out of the rock" in Deut. 32:13; Ps. 81:17). This wild honey figures prominently in the story of the wedding of Samson at Timnah (Judg. ch. 14), where Samson, having found honey amidst a swarm of bees in the carcass (more plausibly, skeleton) of a lion he had previously killed, wagers thirty festal garments on the riddle "out of the eater came something to eat, out of the strong came something sweet" (Judg. 14:14). The Philistines, unable to solve the riddle, have Samson's wife learn the answer: "What is sweeter than honey, what is stronger than a lion?" (*ibid.* v. 18). Samson, enraged, slaughters thirty men in Ashkelon to pay the wager, and departs. Bees' honey was also found in the forest, where it was eaten by Jonathan in violation of his father's oath (I Sam. 14:24–30).

Dairy items were generally made of sheep or goat milk in Erez Israel, since cattle was scarce there. However, Mesopotamian sources, such as the "Banner of Ur," and various Egyptian steles dating back to the 4th millennium B.C.E. attest to the use of cow's milk in those lands. In Ur, cows were milked from behind, and in Egypt from in front of the udder, with the cow's rear legs tied together.

Milk was one of the characteristic products of Erez Israel (Ex. 3:8; 33:3; Joel 4:18). It was drunk fresh, or was cooked with other foods, and was also a component of medicines and ointments. Because of their importance, milk and its by-products served as offerings to gods and kings. Milk was used in pagan cults where a kid would be cooked in its mother's milk. This practice was forbidden to the Israelites (Ex. 23:19; etc.).

The Bible mentions butter and various cheeses as milk-derived products. Butter was made by churning milk in special vessels, examples of which have been found at Beer-Sheba dating to the Chalcolithic period. The butterfat was separated as a result of the churning, and the excess liquid was evaporated in order to produce butter which was used principally for cooking and frying. Cheese was made from milk soured in special molds. The hard lumps which were formed were dried in the sun or evaporated by cooking (Job 10:10). A softer cheese was made in cloth bags filled with soured milk. The thin liquid filtered through the cloth while the soft cheese curds remained in the bag. The Hittites used cheese as an offering in their cult.

Several types of wine are mentioned in the Bible: a sparkling or foaming wine (Ps. 75:9); the wine of Helbon (Ezek. 27:18); spiced wine (Song. 8:2); and the wine of Lebanon (Hos. 14:8). The type of wine was determined by the grapes from which it was pressed, the time allowed for fermentation, and the age of the wine. While most wine was produced from grapes, it was also made from raisins, dates, figs, and pomegranates.

Erez̲ Israel was known for its fine wines and advanced methods of production. Some indication of this may be gained from the widespread occurrence of presses in archaeological excavations throughout the country. A good example of a rock-cut winepress from the biblical period, found at Gibeon, has a broad surface for treading the grapes and several collecting vats. The vintage would be brought to the winepress where the grapes were spread on the broad upper surface of the press and tread upon by foot, in order to squeeze the liquid from them. This liquid flowed down through a drainage channel into a vat in which the precipitates settled. From there it flowed to a second vat where it was collected. The drainage system was constructed so that the liquid flowed into the collecting vat only when the precipitation vat was filled. Thus, the heavier sediments such as waste matter, seeds, and skins had time to settle at the bottom of the vat, while the juice flowed into the collecting vat. The new wine was then transferred to vessels which were sealed and placed in a cool place to stand until the juice fermented by the action of the yeast in the fruit, becoming wine. Spices were added to improve the aroma and taste, and the color could be improved by steeping crushed grape skins in the wine. Sometimes aroma was added by rubbing the winepress with wood resin. The resulting wine was poured into liquid measures, the *bath* (II Chron. 2:9), and the *hin* (Ex. 29:40; Samaria ostraca). It was stored in vessels of uniform size in the treasuries of the royal and wealthy families.

Wine was recognized as an intoxicant having a stimulating effect upon the human disposition. One who had taken Nazirite vows was, therefore, not permitted to drink it or to make any use of vine-derived products (e.g.; Num. 6:3). The Bible mentions houses which were visited for the purpose of drinking and becoming intoxicated (Song 2:4).

Another product of the vine was vinegar, which was produced by additional fermentation of new wine. It was used for seasoning foods, pickling vegetables, and medicinal purposes.

Figure 94:   Oil press. The
round stone crushes and
squeezes the olives while
rolling

Oil was produced mainly from olives in presses designed for this purpose.
There were three stages in its production. First, the hard olives were crushed
into a soft paste. This was then squeezed, the crude oil flowing out as a
result of the pressure. Finally, the crude oil was stored in vessels or vats for
some time, while the sediments and water from the olives settled and the
pure oil rose to the surface. The oil was then collected in vessels for storage
or use. Oil production was advanced in Erez Israel, as is attested by much
documentary evidence, and the discovery of many olive presses in various
locations, and particularly of the Hellenistic period. The earliest press excavated in the country was found at Tirat Yehudah near Lydda. This press has
been reconstructed and transferred to the garden of the Israel Museum.

Oil was used as a condiment for various dishes, to fry foods, especially
meats, and as a component in certain dishes. Specially purified oils mixed
with spices were used as ointments (Song 1:3) or for medicinal purposes.
Sesame oil, produced in a similar way, was particularly fine. Like wine, oil
was used as an offering to the gods and for payment of taxes to kings.

CLOTHING

The biblical terms for clothing refer to a variety of items which cover the
body for warmth or for reasons of modesty. The terms are also used extensively in figures of speech: "Put on thy beautiful garments" (Isa. 52:1), is a

symbol of greatness; "He put on garments of vengeance for clothing" (Isa. 59:17), is a symbol of revenge; "For he dressed me in clothes of triumph" is a metaphor for victory and good fortune (Isa. 61:10); "They shall wear shame" (Ps. 35:26), is a metaphor for failure and defeat; and "Let your priests be clothed with triumph" (Ps. 132:9), is a metaphor for success and prestige.

On many occasions, clothing emphasized a person's status, position, or task: "Royal apparel . . . which the king is accustomed to wear" (Esth. 6:8), with which another man (Mordecai) would be honored or favored. A hairy cloak was probably a hallmark of Nazirites and ascetics: "Neither shall they wear a hairy mantle to deceive" (Zech. 13:4). During the period of mourning a widow wore a characteristic garment: "She put off from her garments of widowhood" (Gen. 38:14). Prisoners apparently also had special clothing: "He changed his prison garments" (II Kings 25:29). The official uniform (holy garments) worn by priests in the service of God was of great importance: "And thou shalt make holy garments for Aaron" (Ex. 28:2). Just as the beauty of a garment symbolized a man's greatness, tearing the clothing, or wearing poor and dirty clothing or sackcloth, indicated a lowered station or mourning.

The Bible mentions articles of clothing appropriate to specific parts of the body: a cloth miter or turban to cover the head (Ex. 29:6; Zech. 3:5); metal or leather helmets, and head coverings used in warfare for protection (I Sam. 17:5; II Chron. 26:14); a dress-like garment, apparently with closed seams, used by both men and women to cover the entire body from the shoulders to the ankles (I Kings 11:30; Ex. 12:34); the tunic, a short, closed garment, covering the top part of the body, worn by both men and women (Gen. 37:3; Lev. 16:14; Song 5:3); the coat, a long outer garment open at the front (I Sam. 15:27; 24:5; II Sam. 13:18); breeches, covering the loins, worn by the priests (Ex. 28:42; Ezek. 44:18); the girdle, a belt for fastening the coat or dress around the waist (Ex. 29:9; Lev. 8:7); and the shoe, made of skin and attached with laces, strings, or straps (Gen. 14:23; Isa. 5:27).

Clothes, particularly the dress-like garment and the tunic, were considered essential though expensive articles, both because of their value, which was related to the work that went into producing them, and because they helped indicate a man's status, position, character, and living style. It is for this reason that the Bible and royal documents frequently list the quantities of clothing given as gifts (Gen. 45:22), or taken in war (Judg. 14:12). Kings had keepers of the wardrobe (II Kings 22:14), and the Temple in Jerusalem had a special wardrobe room.

Figure 95:   Asiatics wearing kilts or aprons in a wall painting of the 19th cent. B.C.E. at Beni Hasan, Egypt

Archaeological finds provide additional information regarding Israelite clothing, for it may be assumed that the Patriarchs dressed in similar fashion to their neighbors. The clothing of the period, illustrated in the Beni Hasan wall painting of the 19th century B.C.E. (fig. 95) shows Asiatics wearing kilts or aprons, which hung from the waist to the knees or below. Some were apparently of wool, perhaps dyed in various colors and decorated with embroidery; others were of a smooth white cloth. This clothing probably sufficed while working. The painting also shows both men and women wearing tunics which covered the body from the shoulder to the ankle. Many of them appear to be made of long, narrow lengths of colored and embroidered wool. Others, of a smooth, white material, appear to be made of a single piece of cloth. With only one exception, all the tunics leave the right shoulder bare; one even leaves much of the left shoulder bare as well, and is held in place by a tape which goes around the neck. One of the women is dressed in a colored tunic made of narrow strips, which covers both shoulders, but since she is standing behind two other women it cannot be ascertained if the tunic had sleeves. In any event, it had more embroidery (geometric designs) than the other garments depicted; perhaps this had something to do with the status of the wearer.

The biblical narrative of the period of the conquest and settlement of Canaan contains only occasional references to clothing. The spoils taken by Achan included a Shinar mantle (Josh. 7:21), probably a mantle brought from southern Mesopotamia. The story of the Gibeonites includes mention of worn garments and shoes (Josh. 9:13); the Song of Deborah cites dyed garments of embroidery (Judg. 5:30); the chapter describing Samson's wedding feast makes note of 30 linen garments and 30 changes of clothing (Judg. 14:12,13), and raiment (*ibid.,* v. 19). The robe is mentioned in I Samuel 2:19; 18:4; and elsewhere, and would appear to be an outer garment worn by important persons. It may have been similar to the garment depicted on a Babylonian boundary stone (end of the 12th century B.C.E.), on which the king is shown wearing a short, collarless, outer garment which covered the shoulders and had short sleeves.

Pictorial representations from the 13th–11th centuries B.C.E. are relatively scarce, and so is our knowledge of Israelite costumes. Several of the ivory fragments from Megiddo (see p.205) portray contemporary dress, but since the subjects are the king and his royal entourage, they do not necessarily indicate anything about Israelite clothing. One ivory shows a barefoot woman wearing a wig whose tresses flow over her shoulder. A tunic reaching down to her ankles appears to be made of a single square piece of cloth with fringed edges and sleeves reaching below the elbows. Embroidery around the neckline forms a triangle in front. Over the tunic the woman wears a sleeveless garment, also made of a single piece of fabric, fringed along its edges, completely open in front, and having scalloped edges top and bottom.

Another ivory fragment depicts two women wearing similar overgarments, this time closed in the front, and overlapping at the knee. Beneath this garment, both women wear tunics, either woven or embroidered in colors, with wrist-length sleeves, tied at the neck with a narrow tape. Both women are barefoot. One woman wears a veil covering her hair, but leaving her ears exposed, and hanging down to her hips. The bottom edge is decorated with designs and fringes. A turban is wound above the veil. The other woman, a musician, has her head uncovered, and her hair hanging loose on her shoulders.

The men shown on the ivory fragments wear an outer garment draped around their bodies in such a fashion as to leave the right shoulder and arm bare, while the left arm is covered to the elbow. These garments are similar to those depicted in the Beni Hasan paintings of Asiatics. Under these garments the men wear tunics with embroidered geometric patterns. Undoubtedly they also wore kilts under the tunics. During work, only kilts were worn, as is evident in the etching found at Megiddo and from a relief found at Moab (13th–12th centuries B.C.E.). The Megiddo ivory shows them wearing skull-caps covering their hair but exposing their ears. Only the soldier is bareheaded. This is true of the Moab relief as well. Egyptian representations of Syrians of the 13th–12th centuries B.C.E. show a thin, colored cord wound around their heads, with the ends hanging to their shoulders.

Both biblical references and archaeological finds are more numerous during the period of the monarchy. While poor people evidently had only one garment (cf. Ex. 22:26; Deut. 24:13), the wealthy possessed a variety of clothing. Undoubtedly kilts were worn, although they are not specifically mentioned, nor are they apparent in contemporary representations which show only fully clothed people. Assyrian reliefs showing Israelites bringing tribute to the king of Assyria in the days of Jehu depict tunics similar to those of the early Israelite period.

Isaiah 3:18–24 contains the most extensive list of clothing and ornaments worn by the women of Jerusalem during the middle of the 8th century B.C.E. Unfortunately it is very difficult to identify many of the items in this catalogue of finery.

Sandals and Shoes

The Hebrew word *na'al* is applied to both a shoe and a sandal, and appears about 20 times in the Bible. A separate term, *se'on*, found in the Book of Isaiah (9:4), is interpreted as the high boot worn by a soldier. Shoes were designed for protection against cold and dampness in winter and against hot sand and sharp stones during the summer.

Shoes also had symbolic significance. The renunciation of levirate marriage obligations involved removing the shoe (Deut. 25:9; Ruth 4:7–8). To be "unsandaled" was to be dispossessed (Deut. 25:10), and to cast one's sandals upon property signified possession (Ps. 60:10; 108:10). Taking off one's shoes at a holy place was a mark of respect (Ex. 3:5; Josh. 5:15), and is still practiced by the Samaritans, Karaites, and Muslims when they enter their temples. To go without shoes was an outward sign of mourning (II Sam. 15:30; Isa. 20:2–4; Ezek. 24:17,23), while to put on one's sandals indicated readiness for a journey (Ex. 12:11).

As noted above, there is no way of distinguishing types of footwear in the biblical terminology, but monuments and archaeological finds in Erez Israel and in neighboring countries provide pictorial information of this nature. In Egypt, the customary sandal was made of a single piece of leather cut to the shape of the foot, and tied on with thongs or cords. The slate palette of Pharaoh Narmer depicts such sandals in the First Dynasty (c. 3100–2890 B.C.E.), and that style remained in general use, with minor variations in the manner of attaching the thongs, through the Middle and Late Kingdoms and even thereafter. During the period of the Middle Kingdom (c. 2133–1785 B.C.E.), sandals of painted wood were buried in tombs. The shoes found in the tomb of Tuth-ankh-Amon (c. 1344–1335 B.C.E.) differ from others only in that their soles were decorated with figures of human beings. Tombs from the beginning of the Late Kingdom have yielded

shoes of men, women, and children, with woven straw soles. A shoe workshop is depicted in the fresco in the tomb of Rekh-mi-Re, the vizier of Upper
Egypt in the reign of Thutmose III (c. 1490–1468 B.C.E.).

Clay models of Hittite shoes of the 19th century B.C.E. were found in
Tell Kultepe (Kanish). These were high shoes with pointed, turned-up toes.
Similar footwear has been found in Anatolia and northern Syria from the
2nd and part of the 1st millennium B.C.E. In Mesopotamia, from the 3rd
millennium onward, the thonged sandal was common, but it had high
counters in the back, reaching across the heel.

The earliest representation of shoes in Erez Israel was found on a colored
wall fresco at Teleilat Ghassul (4th millennium B.C.E.), but it is far from
clear, and all that can be distinguished on a painted panel is some kind of
low-cut boot. The Beni Hasan painting from the early 19th century B.C.E.
depicts a group of Asiatics wearing sandals made of soles fastened by various
methods — some with ankle and crisscrossed straps, others with an additional strap encircling the ankle. The women wear an above-the-ankle boot
trimmed with a white band around the top. The Black Obelisk of Shalmaneser III (854–842 B.C.E.) depicts Jehu of Israel or his messenger
bearing tribute to the king. The men wear shoes with upturned, pointed
toes; their height and method of fastening cannot be determined. One
should not draw conclusions about the type of footwear worn in Israel from
this picture. It is possible that during the period of the monarchy, Israelites
wore shoes of both Hittite and Mesopotamian style, as was the custom in
Syria at that period.

Samples of shoes from the period after the destruction of the Second
Temple were found in the Judean Desert caves. One specimen, from the
cave in Wadi Murabba'at, is considered to date from the First Temple.

WEAPONS OF WAR

Weapons make their appearance far back in the history of mankind. They
were needed to protect man from wild beasts, to provide meat for his
consumption, and to serve as a means of defense, or attack, vis à vis his
human enemies. Thus, weapons have occupied an unusually important place
in man's cultural development, and, as a concomitant, the framework of war
in which they were used appears to have been a constant companion of
man's social history.

The wars in which the Israelites engaged during the biblical period were many and varied: wars of conquest and colonization, defensive wars against neighboring aggressor nations during the period of the Judges, wars to stabilize and/or extend Israel's boundaries, wars in which the kings of Judah and Israel sought to maintain their kingdoms, and, finally, the hopeless stand against the expansive thrusts of powerful empires. Indeed, war was such a frequent occurrence, and the years of peace were so few, that the Bible makes particular mention of peaceful periods (e.g. Judg. 3:11; I Kings 5:4; II Chron. 14:5).

Since warfare, by definition, involves two or more groups, a study of weapons cannot be limited to one country. The inquiry must be extended to an entire region in which the component countries were involved in defensive or offensive measures one against the other. Moreover, in terms of archaeological research, it is clear that the weapons of one country are often found in excavations in another land, having been brought there as spoils of war or having been used by an occupying garrison. One must also consider that the history of weaponry is not a single strand, but reflects the intermingling of mutual influences; the development of a sophisticated weapon calls for the creation of improved defensive armament, and vice versa. A better suit of armor, for example, was the reaction to the development of stronger bows, which shot arrows with greater velocity over a longer firing range. In turn, new forms of battle-axes appeared in reaction to improved body armor. It is, therefore, clear that a study of weapons in the biblical period must include their use both in Erez Israel and in the neighboring countries.

Methods of offensive and defensive warfare developed side by side in the ancient Near East (see also Fortifications). The development of weapons was dependent upon the supply of raw materials, such as stone, metal, and wood: the technical strides of the period, e.g., the creation of a metallurgical industry, the manner in which wood was treated, and that in which different materials, such as wood and metal, were joined; and the need, i.e., whether methods of warfare developed by one country necessitated corresponding improvements by a rival country.

Pre-Biblical Period: The Early Bronze Age

The beginning of the move from a rural to an urban environment and the consequent development of more sophisticated armies in the Early Bronze Age brought with it an improvement in weapons; the first metal weapons appear at this time. Several types of bows are known in this period: the simple double-convex Egyptian bow; the early Mesopotamian bow, shaped like a simple curve; and the composite bow, developed by the Akkadians in the second half of the third millennium. Arrows were hollow reed shafts, their bases usually feathered; arrowheads were at first made of flint and later of metal. Tubular leather quivers with circular bases have been found in Egypt.

The spear was used for hand-to-hand combat (Num. 25:7–8) while the javelin, a smaller and lighter weapon, was thrown from a distance (I Sam. 18:11). Spearheads found in Palestine (Kefar Monash and Tell al-Hasī) are triangular with a protuberant midrib and a tang terminating in a hood, which was fitted into the staff. The sword, battle-ax, and mace were the principal weapons used on the battlefield, but technical limitations precluded the production of long and tough metal blades and the use of the sword as the basic weapon. At this time, swords were straight, double-edged, and pointed, an average of 10 in. in length. They were designed mainly for stabbing as if they were daggers. A second type of sword, the sickle-sword, developed in Mesopotamia in the second half of the third millennium B.C.E., was used for striking. There were two types of axes: the cutting ax and the piercing ax, developed as an answer to the metal helmet. Technically, axes are divided into two groups according to the manner in which they were attached to the wooden staff: both shaft-holed axes and the tanged axes were developed in this period.

The Sumerian infantry, for which there is the most information on military dress in this period, wore sleeveless leather vests with metal studs, presumably the earliest known coats of mail. Their metal helmets were slightly pointed, and they carried large rectangular shields of wood and leather (?) to which a metal disk was attached.

Chariots were not weapons in themselves, but were used as mobile firing bases. For this purpose they had to fulfill two basic requirements: stability and speed. These contradictory functions influenced the development of the chariot, which was first evolved by the Sumerians at the beginning of the 3rd millennium B.C.E. Two-wheeled and four-wheeled chariots are evident at this time, both drawn by two pairs of horses.

The Age of The Patriarchs: The Middle Bronze Age

The latest type of bow, the composite bow, was developed in Akkad late in the 3rd millennium. While the highly technical skill that the bow required is not evident among the nomads who penetrated and conquered Syria and Mesopotamia, the appearance of the fully developed composite bow at the beginning of the Late Bronze Age shows that composite bows were in use before then. Most of the data on bows comes from Egypt. The conservative

Egyptians continued to use the simple double-convex bow, as seen in the wall paintings at Beni Hasan, and the Asiatics in the same painting also carry this bow. Also portrayed is a workshop for the manufacture of bows, and the use of the bow in battle. Quivers did not change much, and the same type of quiver is carried by Egyptians and by one of the Asiatics in the Beni Hasan wall painting.

Spears and javelins are divided into two types according to the method of attachment to the wooden staff: the tanged head and the socketed head. Tanged javelin heads have been found mainly in the tombs of the semi-nomadic peoples of Middle Bronze Age I. The blade is typically leaf-shaped, with a long tang ending in a hook. Also found were pointed metal skewers with long hooked tangs, which were either the butt ends of the javelin or perhaps the heads of pikes. These pikes may have been used as weapons (II Sam. 2:23) or to stick the weapon into the ground when not in use (I Sam. 26:7). The socketed javelin head appears at the time of the Hyksos. Both the javelin head and the socket were cast in the same mold, the socket being wrought into shape afterward.

The sickle-sword, used for striking, was modified in the Middle Bronze Age, when it was made in a mold and the handle was attached to the hilt by a metal rivet. The length of the handle was twice as long as the blade. Several well-preserved examples have been found at Byblos, Shechem, and in Egypt. The dagger-sword was also developed in this period. Those of Middle Bronze Age I, found mostly in tombs, are straight and narrow, with a prominent central spine. The hilt was made together with the blade, and had up to ten rivets. From their length of approximately 12 to 15 in. it can be assumed that they were used for striking and thrusting. While the sickle-sword was used for striking, broader and shorter daggers for stabbing also appear at this time (Middle Bronze Age II B–C). In accordance with their function, they were strengthened by ribs and a central spine. The hilt was made together with the blade and a crescent-shaped stone or metal piece served as a pommel.

While the development of the sword as the main weapon of the infantry lagged because of technical difficulties, the battle-ax that replaced it in hand-to-hand combat made rapid technical advances. The blade of the lugged, tanged ax is narrower and longer than previously, and the cutting edge is shaped like a crescent and is wider than the rest of the blade. Such weapons were used by the Egyptian army as piercing axes until the beginning of the New Kingdom. The triple-tanged ax was used at the beginning of the Middle Kingdom in Egypt mainly as a cutting ax.

Demand for a special ax for piercing metal helmets gave rise to the "eye-ax," used in the 21st–20th centuries B.C.E. The three tangs of this ax ended in a semicircular shaft, thus forming two "eyes." Such axes were used in the 12th Dynasty period and in Palestine, Syria, and Anatolia; a group of ceremonial gold "eye-axes" have been found at Byblos. In Syria and Palestine in the 19th century B.C.E., the "eye-ax" was developed into the "duck-bill" ax, which had a longer blade, a narrower cutting edge, and narrower oblong "eyes." which gave the ax its name. The haft was curved to prevent its slipping from the hand. Such axes were found mainly in Syria, and one of the Asiatics in the Beni Hasan wall painting carries one. Shaft-holed axes, the typical piercing battle-ax, appear in Syria and Palestine in the 18th century B.C.E. and were used throughout Middle Bronze Age II. The forerunner of this ax was used in the Akkadian army. It has a long and very narrow blade, with a shaft no wider than the blade. Technical changes usually consisted of a strengthening of the shaft and a better means of connection between the haft and the blade.

Data from the Middle Bronze Age provide no information on the development of personal armor and chariots. However, the highly technical advances made at the beginning of the Late Bronze Age could not have been developed in a vacuum, and presumably the personal equipment of this period was similar to that of the succeeding period.

The Late Bronze Age
The composite bow, which was made of wood taken from birch trees (?), tendons of wild bulls, horns of wild goats, and sinews from the hocks of bulls, was the only type of bow used by archers in this period. The highly technical skill required for its manufacture made it the weapon of imperial armies and of the wealthy ruling class of the city-states. The two basic types of bow, triangular and bi-concave, were both used during the same period. The triangular bow is shaped like a shallow isosceles triangle with a wide-angled peak. The arms of the bi-concave bow curve near the ends, at the points to which the string is attached. A special bow case was attached to the Egyptian chariot, the bow being the main weapon of Egyptian charioteers. The charioteer had a quiver attached to the right side of the chariot and sometimes carried additional ones on his shoulders. Quivers, made of leather with a shoulder strap, remained long and cylindrical, and each contained 25 to 30 arrows. Arrowheads were leaf-shaped with a central ridge. To train soldiers in the operation of the bow, on foot or while driving a chariot, special programs were devised, in which ranges and target shooting were employed (I Sam. 20:20–22).

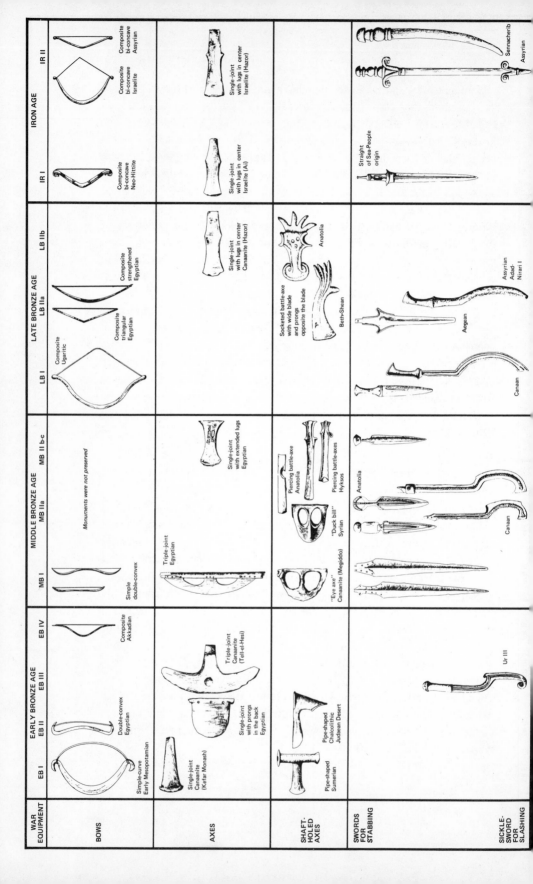

| | EARLY BRONZE AGE | | | | MIDDLE BRONZE AGE | | | LATE BRONZE AGE | | | IRON AGE | |
WAR EQUIPMENT	EB I	EB II	EB III	EB IV	MB I	MB IIa	MB II b-c	LB I	LB IIa	LB IIb	IR I	IR II
BOWS	Simple-curve Early Mesopotamian	Double-convex Egyptian		Composite Akkadian	Simple double-convex	*Monuments were not preserved*		Composite Ugaritic	Composite triangular Egyptian / Composite strengthened Egyptian		Composite bi-concave Neo-Hittite	Composite bi-concave Assyrian / Composite bi-concave Israelite
AXES	Pipe-shaped Sumerian / Single-joint Canaanite (Kefar Monash)	Single-joint with prongs in the back Egyptian	Triple-joint Canaanite (Tell-el-Hesi)		Triple-joint Egyptian	Single-joint with extended lugs Egyptian			Single-joint with lugs in center Canaanite (Hazor)		Single-joint with lugs in center Israelite (Ai)	Single-joint with lugs (Hazor) Israelite (Hazor)
SHAFT-HOLED AXES	Pipe-shaped Chalcolithic Judaean Desert				"Eye axe" Canaanite (Megiddo)	Piercing battle-axe Anatolia / "Duck bill" Syrian / Piercing battle-axes Hyksos		Socketed battle-axe with wide blade and prongs opposite the blade Anatolia / Beth-Shean				
SWORDS FOR STABBING					Anatolia / Canaan			Aegean / Canaan		Assyrian Adad-Nirari I		
SICKLE-SWORD FOR SLASHING		Ur III									Straight of Sea-People origin	Sennacherib Assyrian

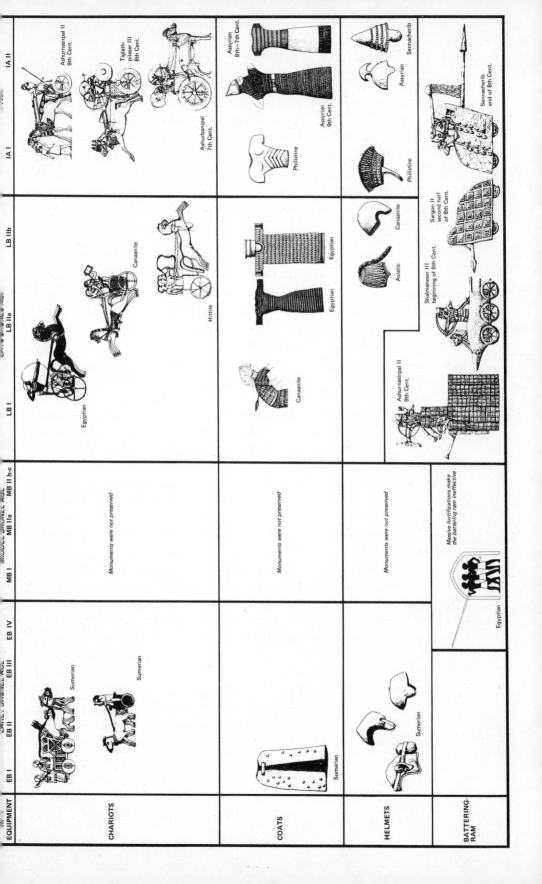

This table chart shows military equipment across archaeological periods. The column headers read (left to right): EQUIPMENT, EB I, EB II, EB III, EB IV, MB I, MB IIa, MB II b-c, LB I, LB IIa, LB IIb, IA I, IA II. Period group labels include EARLY BRONZE AGE, MIDDLE BRONZE AGE, LATE BRONZE AGE.

Row labels (top to bottom): CHARIOTS, COATS, HELMETS, BATTERING-RAM.

CHARIOTS:
- Sumerian (EB II)
- Sumerian (EB III)
- "Monuments were not preserved" (MB I – MB II b-c)
- Egyptian (LB I)
- Canaanite (LB IIa)
- Hittite (LB IIb)
- Ashurnasirpal II 9th Cent. (IA I)
- Tiglath-pileser III 8th Cent. (IA II)
- Ashurbanipal 7th Cent. (IA II)

COATS:
- Sumerian (EB I)
- "Monuments were not preserved" (MB I – MB II b-c)
- Canaanite (LB I)
- Egyptian, Egyptian (LB IIb)
- Assyrian 8th–7th Cent. (IA II)
- Assyrian 9th Cent., Philistine (IA I)

HELMETS:
- Sumerian (EB I–II)
- Sumerian (EB III)
- "Monuments were not preserved" (MB I – MB II b-c)
- Canaanite, Asiatic, Egyptian (LB IIb)
- Philistine, Assyrian (IA I)
- Assyrian, Sennacherib (IA II)

BATTERING-RAM:
- Egyptian — "Massive fortifications make the battering ram ineffective" (MB II b-c)
- Ashurnasirpal II 9th Cent. (LB I)
- Shalmaneser III beginning of 8th Cent. (LB IIa)
- Sargon II second half of 8th Cent. (LB IIb)
- Sennacherib end of 8th Cent. (IA I)

Spears and javelins did not change much from those of the Middle Bronze Age. They were used by the infantry of all armies, especially by the assault phalanx. They were the main weapon of Hittite charioteers, while Egyptian charioteers used the bow, as is clearly seen in the reliefs portraying the battle of Kadesh.

Improvements in the melting and casting of metal are evident in the swords and daggers of this period. For the first time, the complete weapon — blade, hilt, and handle — was cast in a single mold, making for a stronger weapon. The sickle-sword remained the main type of sword, but the relative sizes of the hilt and handle were in a 1:1 ratio. Daggers were straight and narrow, the handle becoming part of the blade. The handle of both the sickle-sword and the dagger was molded with side flanges, the resulting recess in the center of the handle perhaps being filled by plates. At the end of the period, due to the influence of the Sea Peoples, a straight, long sword took the place of the sickle-sword. The two main types of battle-axes continued in this period.

The Egyptians still used the tanged ax-head with extended lugs for better attachment to the wood haft. This ax-head, with a crescent-shaped cutting edge, was used throughout the period, with only minimal changes. The blade was shortened and the cutting edge narrowed. The socketed battle-ax, used mainly by armies of the northern countries, underwent slight changes. The blade was widened and prongs were attached to the socket opposite the blade. This type of ax disappeared at the beginning of the Iron Age.

The development of the piercing battle-ax and the composite bow necessitated a development in personal defense. Body armor was composed of leather or rough cloth, to which oblong scales made of thin leaves of bronze were attached. The size of the scales varied according to their position on the coat. According to the Nuzi tablets, each coat of the chain mail contained 400 to 600 scales. Such armor had several disadvantages: weight, high cost, and the weak points created by joints at the sleeves, between the scales, and at the collar (I Kings 22:34). Chain mail was used by charioteers and archers, as well as for protection of the chariots and horses. Several outfits have been found in Egypt, Syria, Erez Israel and Mesopotamia, and they are represented in the wall reliefs of the Egyptian kings, especially in the chariot reliefs of Thutmose IV (1425–1417 B.C.E.) and those of Ramses II (1304–1237 B.C.E.) portraying the battle of Kadesh.

Several types of helmets were used by the Late Bronze Age soldiers. The Canaanites wore a round metal helmet that covered the back of the neck but exposed the ears, as represented on the carved ivory plaque from

Megiddo. The Asiatics who fought Thutmose IV wore slightly pointed helmets covered by feathers or decorated leather, with a tassel attached to the crown and knotted at the back like a plait. The Hittite helmet as represented on the King's Gate at the Hittite capital, modern Boghazköy, is pointed with well-defined ear and neck shields and a long tassel. Another type of Hittite helmet is shown in the reliefs of the battle of Kadesh, in which Hittite charioteers wear round helmets covering the neck and exposing the ears. The Pharaoh had a special battle helmet known as the Blue Crown.

The development of armor resulted in a reduction in the size of the shield, which was composed of a wooden frame covered with leather. The Egyptians used a small oblong shield with a round top. A metal disk was later added at the top. The Hittites carried a shield shaped like the number eight. The Canaanite shield was small and rectangular and was later replaced by a small round shield.

The chariot reached a high point of development in this period. It was brought to Egypt by the Hyksos, and the Egyptian chariots of the 16th–15th centuries are imitations of the Canaanite ones. The Egyptian chariots were light, with two wheels, a pole, and a yoke to which two horses were harnessed. The earlier chariots were lighter, with four-spoked wheels and an axle-rod placed near the rear of the body. The frame was constructed of wood and partly covered with leather or light wood. The pole ran underneath the body for additional support, and a double-convex yoke was nailed at the forward end. Chariots of the 14th–13th centuries B.C.E., such as that of Ramses II, were heavier, with six-spoked wheels and an axle-tree at the rear of the body. The Egyptian chariot was built to carry a driver and an archer, and a bow case and quiver were attached to it. While Canaanite chariots were copied by the Egyptians at the beginning of the period, under Egyptian rule in Canaan, Egyptian chariots were copied by the Canaanites, as seen in an ivory plaque from Megiddo.

Hittite chariots, as represented on the reliefs of Ramses II portraying the battle of Kadesh, were heavier, with six-spoked wheels and an axle-tree placed under the middle of the chariot or near the rear. Two horses were harnessed to it, and a driver, a javelin hurler, and a shield bearer rode in it. While the Egyptians employed their chariots as mobile bases for the archers, the Hittites used them as mobile bases for the infantry, which was armed with javelins and capable of fighting without the chariots.

The principles of warfare as known today were also employed in the ancient Near East. The techniques included surprise attack, ambush, concentration of power, exploitation of maximum mobility, and the combined use of various forces. Battles usually were fought on the main roads, such as the battle of Megiddo between Thutmose III and the Syro-Palestine coalition headed by the king of Kadesh. Prior to this battle in the summer of 1468 B.C.E., Thutmose III and his army, which included chariots and infantry, camped at Yehem (?), where the Pharaoh received the latest intelligence information concerning the king of Kadesh and his allies, who were reportedly waiting for him near Megiddo. A staff meeting with the Egyptian commanders was held and the three possible approaches to Megiddo were discussed. The commanders preferred to march along the easier routes, the southern one, via Taanach or the northern one via Djefti. They argued against the use of the main route via wadi 'Aruna, because the way becomes narrow and they would be forced to march "one man behind the other, and one horse behind the other." Thutmose III, however, decided to take the more dangerous route on principles of honor and for the sake of achieving a tactical surprise. The entire Egyptian force marched in a long procession through the pass, without encountering any resistance or harassment; it regrouped, chose the ground on which the battle would be fought, and won the battle. Then the Egyptian army, instead of pursuing the fleeing Canaanites, began to loot the camp. Thus the Canaanites managed to take refuge in Megiddo, and it took the Pharaoh seven more months of siege to conquer the city and break the rebellion.

Further data concerning the conduct of war are given in the Egyptian description of the battle of Kadesh on the Orontes. In the summer of 1286 B.C.E. Ramses II marched to Syria to check the advance of the Hittites, taking with him four brigades. Before he crossed the Orontes, two Bedouins came to his camp and gave him false information – that the Hittites were camping at Aleppo to the north of Kadesh. Acting on this information, Ramses II divided his forces and headed for Kadesh with only two brigades, those of Amon and Re. He arrived at Kadesh with the leading Amon brigade, and while he encamped, his scouts discovered the Hittite army hidden beyond the city of Kadesh. The Hittite chariots then attacked, destroyed the Re brigade while it was marching unawares toward the city, and then struck north, breaking into the fortified camp of the Pharaoh. Only the leadership and valor of Ramses and the employment of his reserve brigade saved the Egyptians from total defeat.

A mere glimpse of the military tactics of the armies is given in the descriptions of these two battles. However, they reveal that these armies were aware of the advantages of surprise attack, the importance of military intelligence, deployment of armies marching into battle (with or without a defended flank according to the terrain and the time of day), the division of the army into separate chariot and infantry units, and military discipline.

The Period of The Judges and the United Kingdom: The Iron Age

After a period of decline, the bow was used as in the Late Bronze Age. The composite bow was found in all armies. Changes in the shape of quivers and arrows were marginal. Arrowheads lost their protruding spine and some of those found in Erez Israel and Syria carried inscriptions, such as "the arrow of 'Abdlabi'at." The sling, essentially a shepherd's weapon, also appears on the battlefield, as in the confrontation of David and Goliath (I Sam. ch. 17).

The spear and the javelin, along with the sword and the bow, were the basic weapons of the infantry. Deborah lamented that her army was not prepared because it lacked spears: "Was there a shield or spear among forty thousand in Israel?" (Judg. 5:8). The main type was a shaft-holed spearhead with a long blade and a very broad midrib. The description of Goliath's armament (I Sam. 17:5–7) includes mention of a special hurling javelin, with a finger-loop like a "weaver's beam" on the shaft. Under the influence of the Philistines, the sickle-sword changed into a long, straight iron sword used for cutting and thrusting. Since the smiths at that time were all Philistine, the Israelites were not able to produce similar swords (I Sam. 13:19). The new type of sword, described in Judges 3:16, replaced the sickle-sword as the basic weapon.

The Philistines brought with them weapons that had been developed in the Aegean. In the wall reliefs of Ramses III (1198–1166 B.C.E.) at Medinet Habu, each group of Sea Peoples wore slightly different helmets and armor, perhaps as a tribal distinction. The Philistines wore feather-crested helmets, while the other groups wore horned helmets, or helmets with disks and horns. The body was protected by a coat of armor made of numerous metal strips laid at angles to each other, thus forming inverted V's or V's, depending upon the tribe. The lower part of the body was protected by a kilt with two strips of leather (?) forming a cross in the front.

The Philistine army fought in groups of four, each soldier armed with either a long sword or a pair of spears, and protected by a round wood and leather shield. In hand-to-hand combat, the duelist, like Goliath, was protected by a man-sized shield carried by a special shield bearer. The bow and the battle-ax were not included in the Philistine arsenal. While the bow remained a decisive weapon on the battlefield, the long, straight-bladed sword took the place of the ax.

It is interesting to compare the dress and weapons of Goliath with those of David. The former had, besides a sword (I Sam. 17:51), "a helmet of brass upon his head, and he was clad with a coat of mail, and the weight of the coat was 5,000 shekels of brass. And he had greaves of brass upon his legs, and a javelin of brass between his shoulders. And the shaft of his spear was like a weaver's bow; and his spear's head weighed six hundred shekels of iron; and his shield bearer went before him" (I Sam. 17:5–7). David was clad in Saul's "apparel, and he [Saul] put a helmet of brass upon his head, and he clad him with a coat of mail. And David girded his sword upon his apparel" (I Sam. 17:38–39).

While the Egyptian army continued to use the same type of chariot as was used in the Late Bronze Age, the Philistines employed a heavy chariot with six-spoked wheels and a crew of three, armed with hurling javelins like the Hittite charioteers. The Israelite tribes, when settling in the hill country, "drove out the inhabitants of the hill country, for he [Judah] was unable to drive out the inhabitants of the valley, because they had chariots of iron" (Judg. 1:19). The tribal army of Deborah and Barak was victorious over the chariots of Sisera in a battle in the Jezreel Valley (Judg. 4:13–15). David and Solomon were the first to form chariot squadrons in the Israelite army, and Solomon built special cities for chariots (I Kings 10:26; II Chron. 1:14). At the same time, Solomon was the main trader in horses and chariots between Egypt and the Hittites (I Kings 10:28–29).

The technique of night attack can be seen in the description of the battle between Gideon and the Midianites (Judg. ch. 6–8), the latter being mounted on camels. The army of Gideon encamped "beside En-Harod; and the camp of Midian was on the north side of them, by Gibeath-Moreh, in the valley." After the Israelites had assembled, Gideon chose only 300 of them, for a surprise night attack requires only a small number of men. Before the attack, Gideon reconnoitered outside the Midian camp. His plan of attack was simple, with the 300 men divided into three companies under the leadership of Gideon, an agreed signal and the battle cry of "For the Lord and for Gideon." After a timetable for the attack was set, the Israelites attacked the enemy camp during the changing of the guard. The attack was executed according to plan and the enemy was put to flight. Gideon asked the Ephraimites to block the retreat of the Midianites across the Jordan, while he and his army pursued the fleeing enemy until it was destroyed and the Midianite kings captured.

The Kingdoms of Israel and Judah: The Iron Age

The military organization of this period is known from the wall reliefs found in the palaces of the Assyrian kings. The prophet Isaiah describes the character and great strength of the Assyrian army (5:26–28), which was a model for the other armies of the ancient Near East. The army was divided into three forces – infantry, cavalry, and chariots – as described in the Bible: "And muster an army like the army that you have lost, horse for horse, and chariot for chariot" (I Kings 20:25); "For there was not left to Jehoahaz of the people save fifty horsemen and ten chariots and 10,000 footmen" (II Kings 13:7). Besides his special weapons, each soldier had a basic armament of a sword, a coat of mail, and a helmet. The design of this basic armament was slightly changed from the reign of one king to the other. The iron sword was long and straight with a double edge, and the handle was constructed to fit to the fingers. It was carried in a sheath shaped like the sword, and a floral decoration was occasionally added near the opening and the base. The sheath was hooked to the belt on the left side and held in place by a leather strap that circled the left shoulder. The coat of armor, shaped like a sack with an opening for the head and short sleeves, was full-length in the 9th century B.C.E. A special scarf of scales, used by archers, connected the helmet to the armor. In the 8th and 7th centuries the chain mail dress was shortened into a shirt. The shape of metal helmets varied from conical and pointed to feather-crested, according to the troops wearing them and the reigning king.

The infantry (I Kings 20:29) was divided into four groups: archers (Jer. 50:14; I Chron. 12:2), slingers (II Kings 3:25), spearmen (I Chron. 12:9), and auxiliaries. While the spearmen, the assault troops of the army, defended themselves with shields which were rectangular, round, or curved with a round top, depending upon the period, the archers and the slingers were without shields, and special shield bearers were attached to their companies. The infantry took part in battles in the open field and in assaults on fortified cities with no change in their equipment. The cavalry only participated in open field engagements and were equipped with either bows or spears. While mounted spearmen defended themselves with round shields, mounted archers, who needed the use of both hands in combat, were protected by mounted shield bearers. The cavalry operated either as independent units or as a mobile defense for the chariots.

Chariots, the main assault force, underwent many changes in Assyrian military history. The earliest known ones, those of Ashurnasirpal II (883–859 B.C.E.), were heavier than those of the preceding period. Each had six-spoked wheels of medium size, an axle-rod at the rear of the body, and a heavy pole. Two horses were harnessed to it and a third, riding as an outrigger, was held in reserve. The crew consisted of a driver, who also served as a spearman, and an archer. A shield bearer was added to the king's chariot. The chariots of Tiglath-Pileser III (745–727 B.C.E.) are heavier still, and the wheels are larger, with eight spokes. A driver, archer, and shield bearer rode in the chariot, the latter protecting the others with two round shields. The number of horses and, correspondingly, of yokes was increased to four. The tendency of the kings following Tiglath-Pileser III was to build heavier chariots. In the time of Ashurbanipal (668–630 B.C.E.), the crew numbered four — a driver, an archer, and two shield bearers.

A complicated description of the battle between Ahab and Ben-Hadad of Aram is given in I Kings 20:1–23. This battle took place in the Samarian Hills, and the Arameans blamed their defeat on the fact that the Israelite God "is a God of the hills; therefore they were stronger than we; but let us fight against them in the plain, and surely we shall be stronger than they." Subsequently, a second battle was fought in the plain of Aphek in the Golan (I Kings 20:23–30). The two armies faced each other for seven days before finally joining battle, which the Arameans again lost.

MUSICAL INSTRUMENTS

The Bible is the foremost and richest source for knowledge of the musical life of ancient Israel until some time after the return from the Babylonian Exile. It is complemented by several external sources: archaeological relics of musical instruments and depictions of musical scenes; comparative material from neighboring cultures; and post-biblical sources.

A truly chronological ordering of the biblical evidence on music is hardly possible, since a relatively late source frequently attributes certain occurrences to an early period, in which they could not have existed. A case in point is the chronicler's reports about the ordering of the Temple music by King David. Many details — above all the prominent status of the levitical singers, which almost overshadows that of the priests — are probably a projection back from the chronicler's own time, and may even be nothing more than an attempt to furnish the levitical singers with a Davidic authorization in order to strengthen their position. It is therefore more prudent to draw a synthetic picture, in which most of the facts can be assumed to have existed for at least a considerable part of the time.

The mythical dimension of music is represented in biblical tradition only by the story of Jubal, who was "the ancestor of all who play the *kinnor* and *ugav*" (Gen. 4:21; for names of instruments see below). Another relic of the same kind may well be found in the allusion in God's speech to Job to the day on which the creation was finished, whereupon, "the morning stars sang together and all the Sons of God raised a shout of acclamation" (Job 38:7).

Most of the biblical evidence concerns the place of music in the cult. Music is conspicuously absent in the narrative concerning the Tabernacle, where the bells (perhaps only rattling platelets, see below) on the tunic of the high priest had no musical function but only an apotropaic one. The trumpets served mainly to direct the movements of the multitude and to arouse God's "remembrance," a function common to both cultic sacrifice and war (Num. 10:1–10). In the transport of the Ark to Jerusalem by David, which is accompanied by the playing of lyres, drums, rattles, and cymbals (II Sam. 6:5; I Chron. 13:8), the context is that of a popular fete, not an established cult ritual. Even the description of the inauguration of Solomon's Temple in the first chapters of I Kings lacks an explicit reference to music. Only the trumpets are mentioned in the reconstitution of the Temple services in the time of Joash (II Kings 12:14).

However, in the earlier stages of religious organization, centered around inspirational-ecstatic prophecy, the role of music was understandably important (cf. I Sam. 10:5, and the story of Elisha's musically induced

Figure 96: Engraved panel from an ivory casket, from Tell el-Far'ah, c. 13th–12th cent. B.C.E., showing a banqueting dignitary dressed in long garments, entertained by a dancer accompanied by a double-pipe player

prophetic seizure in II Kings 3:15). David's playing and singing before Saul has a related psychological aspect (I Sam. 16:16ff.).

At coronations the trumpets were blown as part of the formal proclamation (II Kings 11:14), and the spontaneous and organized rejoicings after victory in war were accompanied by women who sang, drummed, and danced (cf. The Song of the Sea, and the women's welcome of David and Saul in I Sam. 18:6–7). Music at popular feasts is described in Judges 21:19ff. Finally, the musical accompaniment at the feasts of the rich and, of course, at the king's court is also described several times, often with a note of reproach (II Sam. 19:36; Isa. 5:12; Amos 6:5; Eccles. 2:8). The musical expression of mourning is implicit in the verses of David's lament for Saul and Jonathan and explicit in the mention of the male and female mourners who repeated specially composed dirges (II Chron. 35:25). Folk music includes the songs and rhythmic shouts of the workers in the vineyards (probably the grape treaders) alluded to by the prophets.

In Chronicles, the musical element suddenly appears as the most prominent part of the service, with detailed and repeated "duty rosters" of the levitic singers and instrumentalists, as planned by David and established by Solomon. Since the lists of the returned exiles from Babylon, in Ezra and Nehemiah, include a number of families of Temple singers (e.g. Ezra 2:41; 3:10), it can be assumed that at least toward the end of the First Temple there was already some kind of organized cult music in Jerusalem. On the other hand, there are grounds to believe that the role of music in the First Temple was minimal. In the sanctuaries outside Jerusalem it was probably much more prominent (I Sam. 10:5; Amos 5:23).

After the return from Babylon, music was gradually given a place in the Temple services. It consisted of a large body of one or two types of stringed instruments; a small number, or a single pair, of cymbals; and a large choir. The trumpets of the priests always remained separate, fulfilling a ritual but not really musical function.

About 19 identifiable terms for musical instruments appear in the Bible. Some scholars hold that other terms, notably those appearing in the headings of the Psalms, also refer to instruments; it is, however, more probable that they provide instructions regarding a particular melody.

The *halil* (I Sam. 10:5; I Kings 1:40) is a double-pipe wind instrument, probably having one melody and one drone pipe, and a single-reed (clarinet) type mouthpiece. The double-tongued mouthpiece was less well-known in the ancient Near East, and made its appearance only during the period of the New Kingdom in Egypt, while the single-reed type was

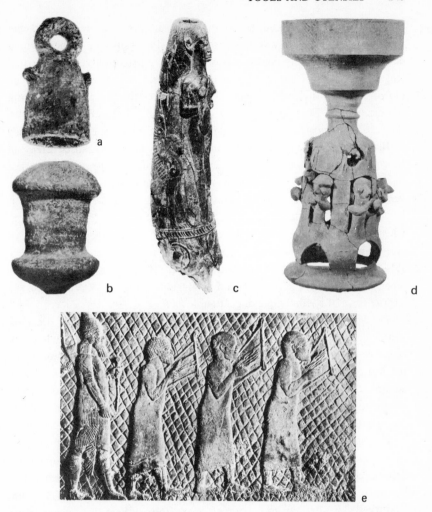

Figure 97:   Music instruments from the biblical period. (a) Bronze bell of
the 10th—9th cent. from Megiddo. The two shoulder-like protuberances
hold an iron pin, from which an iron clapper, now missing, was suspended.
Height: about 6 cm; (b) Pottery rattle from Beit Shemesh, first half of 1st
millennium B.C.E. Height: 3½ inches (8.5 cm); (c) Ivory horn, decorated in
relief, from Ugarit, c. 14th cent. B.C.E. Present length about 60 cm, internal
diameter of mouth hole about 1.5 cm; (d) Pottery incense stand of the 10th
cent. B.C.E., from Ashdod. Its openings are decorated with figures who
play, respectively, cymbals, a double pipe, a frame drum and a lyre;
(e) Close-up of wall relief from the palace of Sennacherib in Nineveh,
showing three captive lyre players, probably from Lachish, in the charge of
an Assyrian soldier

common even in the Old Kingdom. No examples have survived of the Egyptian *ḥalil*, for it was made of the hollow stalks of rushes, which decompose easily, but pictures show the thin pipes to have been of equal length, with a ⊓ -shape cut near the upper end of the reed; this was the blowing hole, which was completely covered by the mouth while playing the instrument. The right-hand pipe had holes in it and carried the melody, the left-hand pipe lacked holes and probably played a single, drone tone.

Illustrations of a musician playing the *ḥalil*, have been discovered in Erez Israel and northern Mesopotamia. An Egyptian illustration shows the pipes separated from one another. A small stone instrument shaped like a *ḥalil*, with two holes, was found at Gezer (14th—13th centuries B.C.E.?); however, it may have been a toy. Various sites have yielded short bone-whistles with a single hole; it has been suggested that they were used to imitate bird calls for hunting purposes. On an ivory box found at the Tell al-Far'ah (Sharuhen) (end of the 13th century B.C.E.) is an illustration of a piper and dancers. The candle-stand at Megiddo (stratum IV; 9th century?) has the form of a woman playing a double-*ḥalil*.

The *ḥazozerah* is identified with the trumpet and was made of precious metal, generally silver. It is mentioned 30 times in the Bible, where its introduction in Israelite ceremonies is attributed to Moses. The silver trumpet Moses was commanded to make (Num. 10:2) served ritual, war, and administrative-organizational functions. Since these instruments were made of ornamental silver, they were frequently seized as spoils of war, which may explain why none have been found in excavations in Erez Israel.

The *kinnor* is a stringed instrument in the lyre family, having a body and two arms, joined together by a yoke. It is the noble string instrument of Semitic civilization; it was played by David, and thus was held in particular honor by the Levites. An Egyptian tomb fresco at Beni Hasan (early 19th century B.C.E.) depicts a musician among a group of Semitic nomads. Ivory plaques from Megiddo (early 12th century B.C.E.) show a musician playing before the king. On a Philistine (?) vessel from Megiddo (11th century B.C.E.) there is a drawing of a musician walking among animals. At Calah, an ivory box of the 9th century B.C.E. bears illustrations of women playing the *kinnor* and the *ḥalil*. A cultic object found at Ashdod (8th—7th century B.C.E.), and metal bowls of Phoenician origin found at various sites (apparently from the 7th century B.C.E.), show both men and women musicians. The reliefs of Nineveh, depicting the victory of Sennacherib of Assyria (7th century B.C.E.), indicate that musicians were among those taken captive at Lachish (fig. 98).

The Canaanite type of *kinnor,* which was undoubtedly that played by the Israelites, is asymmetric, with a box-shaped body and one arm shorter than the other. The instrument probably had an average length of 20–23 in., and sounded in the alto range, as evinced by surviving specimens from Egypt. The latter copied the form and even kept the Semitic name of the instrument.

The *mena'anayim* are mentioned only in II Samuel 6:5, where they are listed among the instruments played during David's transport of the Ark to Jerusalem. The parallel narrative in I Chronicles 13:3 substitutes the term *meziltayim* ("cymbals"). Etymological analogy ("shaking") makes it highly probable that the term can be applied to the pottery rattles found in numerous excavations. The appearance of these rattles at the beginning of

Figure 98:   Hexagonal clay prism of Sennacherib, king of Assyria, bearing a cuneiform inscription describing the military campaigns of Sennacherib against King Hezekiah of Judah and against Philistia in 701 B.C.E. The prism, which is one of three complete prisms found so far, is the most detailed Assyrian description of an episode related to the Bible. It describes Sennacherib's siege and conquest of 46 cities in Judah, and the booty taken from them, including "male and female musicians/singers"

the Late Canaanite period is associated with temple cults. Later they are found as tomb offerings. During the Israelite period, these rattles are found only in private dwellings, and may be considered to be toys. After about the 7th century B.C.E., these rattles disappeared and were replaced by the newly invented metal bell (*pa'amon*).

The *meziltayim* (Ezra 3:10) and *zilzalim* (II Sam. 6:5) probably refer to cymbals. Bronze cymbals (cf. I Chron. 15:19) were found in excavations at Hazor, Beth-Shemesh, Tell Abu-Hawam, Megiddo, Achzib, etc., and date from the 14th to the 8th century B.C.E. They were shaped like plates with a central hollow boss and a metal thumb-loop; their average diameter was about 4.5 in. Cymbals were played by the Levites in the Temple. The *mezillot* of horses (Zech. 14:20) are probably the metal ball-jingles depicted on Assyrian reliefs.

An unclear term, the *minnim* (Ps. 150:4), presumably was a stringed instrument, perhaps the lute.

The *nevel* (II Sam. 6:5; I Kings 10:12) is a type of lyre, perhaps originating in Asia Minor, differing from the *kinnor* in its larger size and therefore deeper tone. The Bar Kokhba coins show it in a schematized form. It was the second main instrument in the Temple orchestra. The *nevel asor* (or briefly *asor*; Ps. 33:2; 92:4; 144:9), may have been a slightly smaller *nevel* with ten strings.

The *pa'amon,* usually defined as a bell, is mentioned only in connection with the service of the Tabernacle (Ex. 28:33–34; 39:25–26). It was made of gold and was attached to the tunic of the high priest, alternating with the ornament called *rimmon* ("pomegranate"). However, as bells came into use in the Near East apparently only in the 7th century B.C.E., an alternate explanation is that the original *pa'amonim* may have been metal platelets.

Most bells found in Erez Israel are small, made of bronze, with an iron clapper. The earliest found were made to be held in the hand; shortly thereafter small bells designed to be attached to garments began to appear.

The *shalishim* are mentioned only in I Samuel 18:6–7, where they are played by women. If they are related to the Ugaritic term *tlt* ("metal"), one may surmise that they were cymbals or metal bowls designed to be struck.

The *shofar* is identified with the horn of the ram or the wild ovine, and may be synonymous with the *keren* and *keren ha-yovel*. It is the only biblical instrument to have survived in Jewish usage. In the Bible it functioned as a signaling instrument, especially in wartime; its famous appearance at the siege of Jericho (Josh. 6:6–20) must be understood in this sense, and not as a magical noisemaker. The *shofar*-like sound at the receiving of the Ten Commandments (Ex. 19:13–19; 20:18) had a similar function.

The *shofar* is one of the most ancient of instruments. Primitive man would sound threatening notes on an animal horn in an attempt to subjugate natural forces, animals, human enemies, and even gods. To date, excavations dating from the biblical period in Erez Israel have not yielded a *shofar* or even a depiction of one. Other blown instruments or objects, such as a seashell adapted for blowing (Hazor, 9th century B.C.E.), and an elaborately carved ivory horn (Ugarit, 14th century B.C.E.), are not to be identified with the biblical *shofar*.

The *tof* was a shallow, generally undecorated, round-framed drum, about nine inches in diameter. It was frequently played by women and was associated with the dance (e.g. Ex. 15:20–21; Judg. 11:34). In Egypt a square drum was also played.

The meaning of *ugav* is still unclear, but it is very probably not the wind instrument which medieval exegesis held it to be. Perhaps it can be identified with the harp which, like the lute, was never an integral part of the Canaanite and Israelite orchestra.

Other instruments are listed in Daniel 3:5, which describes, in Aramaic, an orchestra at the court of the Babylonian king. It includes the *karna, mashrokita, kaitros, sabbekha, pesanterin, sumponyah*, "and all kinds of instruments." *Karna* is the horn, and *kaitros, sabbekha,* and *pesanterin* are Aramaized versions of the Greek *kithara, sambyke,* and *psalterion. Mashrokita* is a whistling or piping instrument; *sumponyah* parallels the Greek *symphoneia*, which, in itself, means only "the sounding together." It is highly probable that the term does not stand for an instrument at all, but means the concerted sound of those mentioned before. The end of the sentence, "and all kinds of instruments," would thus be nothing but an explanatory gloss.

RELIGIOUS ARTIFACTS

The Temple of Solomon: Major Utensils

The Cherubs. Within the Holy of Holies of Solomon's Temple were two cherubs which faced each other across the Ark. Their outstretched wings reached the wall on either side and touched each other in the middle (I Kings 6:27; II Chron. 3:11). The wings of the cherubs screened the Ark cover (I Kings 8:6–7; II Chron. 5:7) and formed the throne of God.

These are not the only figures of cherubs known to us from the Bible. In the story of the Garden of Eden, God stationed cherubim at the entrance to the garden to guard the way to the tree of life after the expulsion of Adam and Eve (Gen. 3:24). The prophet Ezekiel relates a parable about a cherub in reference to the downfall of the king of Tyre (28:13ff.). The cherub who dwelt in Eden, the garden – or mountain – of God, sinned in his overwhelming pride against God and, as a punishment for his transgression, was hurled down from the mountain of God. In the Genesis version, the story of the Garden of Eden was demythologized, and the sin and punishment of man were substituted for that of the cherub.

In II Samuel 22:11 and Psalms 18:11 a cherub, perhaps a personified wind, serves the Lord as a Pegasus: "He mounted a cherub and flew." In Ezekiel's vision of the chariot throne (ch. 1), the expanse on which the throne reposes appears to be supported by four strange composite creatures which chapter 10 identifies as cherubim (cf. I Chron. 28:18).

The figures of the cherubim were also appropriated for cultic symbolism. They were used for decorative purposes: (a) embroidered on the veil separating the "holy place" from the "most Holy" (Ex. 26:31; 36:35), and on the curtains of the Tabernacle (Ex. 26:1; 36:8); (b) carved on all the inner and outer walls (I Kings 6:29), the doors of the inner and outer sanctuary (I Kings 6:32,25), and the panels of Solomon's Temple (I Kings 7:29,36); and (c) carved on the walls and doors of the Temple envisioned by Ezekiel (41:18–20,25).

The Bible itself contains variant descriptions of the cherubim. The two cherubim in the Tabernacle and in Solomon's Temple have two wings apiece (Ex. 25:20; I Kings 6:24,27) and one face (Ex. 25:20). However, in the chariot vision of Ezekiel the symmetry of four predominates: Each of the four cherubim has four wings and four faces (1:6). Two of their wings, spread out above, touch one another, and the other two cover their bodies. Their four faces include one of a man, probably in front, a lion on the right side, an ox on the left side, and an eagle (Ezek. 1:10). Later, however, Ezekiel includes the face of a cherub among the four faces and omits that of the ox (10:14). The cherubim, moreover, have legs and "each one's feet were like a calf's foot; and they sparkled like burnished bronze. Under their wings on their four sides they had human hands" (Ezek. 1:7–8). In the Temple vision of Ezekiel, the cherubim engraved on the walls and doors are said to have only two faces, a man's face and a lion's face (41:18–19). This apparent contradiction may be explained as a result of Ezekiel's borrowing the motif of a "two-faced" cherub from the paradigm of the Tabernacle in Exodus or from Solomon's Temple, or it may be the result of his describing a two-dimensional picture on a flat surface rather than the three-dimensional one of his chariot vision.

The etymology of the Hebrew word for cherub has been subject to several different explanations, e.g., as a metathesis, or inversion of letters, of "chariot" (cf. Ps. 104:3 with II Sam. 22:11 and Ps. 18:11); or as a derivation from the Aramaic term "to plow," which is based on Ezekiel's substitution of the face of a cherub (10:14) for that of an ox (1:10), which plows. The most plausible derivations is from the Akkadian *kāribu/kurību,* an intercessor who brings the prayers of humans to the gods.

Figures of winged creatures are well-known from the art and religious symbolism of the ancient Near East. Two winged beings flank the throne of Hiram, king of Byblos, and winged bulls were placed at the entrance of Babylonian and Assyrian palaces and temples. They also appear on the pottery incense altars from Taanach and Megiddo. Winged sphinxes, griffins, and human creatures are represented in the art and iconography of Carchemish, Calah - Nimrud (see front cover), the Samarian ivories, Aleppo, and Tell Halaf.

The Ark. The Ark was the chest in which the Tablets of the Covenant were kept. According to the description in Exodus 26:10–22 and 37:1–9, which relate how Bezalel, upon the instruction of Moses, built the Ark, the length of the Ark was two and a half cubits (4 ft. 2 in.), and its width and height were a cubit and a half (30 in.). It was made of acacia wood and was overlaid both inside and out with pure gold. A crown of gold surrounded it above, and four golden rings were attached to its feet, two on each side; into these were inserted the staves used to carry the Ark while traveling in the wilderness. An Ark cover *(kapporet)* which was made entirely of gold in the same dimensions as the Ark, covered the aperture on top. The two cherubim that "screened" the Ark and its contents were set at the two ends of the Ark cover (cf. Gen. 3:24; Ps. 5:12; 91:4).

Sacred chests containing holy objects or images of deities are also to be found among other peoples. Several scholars have compared the ark to the *Markab* or *'Atfah,* a type of elongated chest adorned with ostrich-feathers, to the *Maḥmal,* a pyramid-shaped box sent by Arab princes, with gifts, to a pilgrim procession to Mecca, or to the *Qubbah,* a kind of tent of the pre-Islamic period, tapering to a point and made of red leather, which is found among several Arabian tribes. All these are borne on camels and have a certain sanctity attributed to them. Like the Ark, the *'Atfah* — and in ancient times, the *Qubbah* — was brought to the camp, but only when decisive wars were being fought or when an enemy threatened grave danger. However, the *'Atfah* functioned chiefly as the seat for a young girl with flowing hair and bared bosom, whose purpose was to incite the young men to conquer or die fighting. Clearly there is no resemblance between the function of the Ark and the *'Atfah*. The *Maḥmal*, on the other hand, is not taken out to war.

Some scholars have compared the Ark to the chests (the lower part of which was generally boat-shaped) which were brought out of the temple by the Egyptian priests at festivals, and on which statues of the gods were placed.

The coffin of Tuth-ankh-Amon (mid-14th century B.C.E.) shares one of the features of the Ark. The lid of the Ark was made of pure gold, out of which the two cherubs were hammered, the whole forming one piece. The third inner coffin of Tuth-ankh-Amon was also of solid gold, about an eighth of an inch thick. It weighed nearly 250 lbs. The lid had been wrought, by direct hammering, into a finely modeled portrait figure of the boy king, in high relief. This type of hammered work in gold, as practiced and brought to perfection in Egypt, must have been known to the Israelites.

The Menorah. The Bible relates that the large hall (*heikhal*) of the Temple was furnished with three sacred objects: the golden altar (see p. 59), the golden table (I Kings 7:49; but cf. II Chron. 4:8, which lists ten golden tables; this discrepancy may reflect descriptions of the Temple at different periods), and the ten golden candelabra, standing five to the right and five to the left of the entrance to the Holy of Holies (I Kings 7:49; II Chron. 4:7).

The term *menorah* (plural: *menorot*) denotes a stand on which lamps are arranged. In biblical times, the well-to-do, not content with lamps which were to be found in every home, provided themselves with lampstands (II Kings 4:10; cf. Dan.5:5).

The treasuries of Solomon's Temple were filled with precious objects which had begun to be collected in the days of David (II Sam. 8:10—11), and which were consecrated to the Lord although they were not used in the cult. The passage in Chronicles enumerating the gifts prepared for the Temple by David before his death refers to *menorot* of gold and silver in the Temple treasuries (I Chron. 28:15; cf. verse 12).

The Bible gives details of the form and ornamentation of two *menorot*, both made of gold – the *menorah* of the Tabernacle (Ex. 25:31–40; 37:17–24) and the *menorah* described in the vision of Zechariah 4:1–6, 10–14. A pattern of the Tabernacle *menorah* was, it is related, shown by God to Moses at Mt. Sinai (Ex. 25:40), as was the pattern of the Tabernacle and all its furniture (25:9). Six branches, three on each side, curved upward from the *menorah*'s central shaft, which stood on a base (25:31; Num. 8:4) whose precise shape cannot be determined. Each of the branches was ornamented with three carvings of cups shaped like almond-blossoms, each subdivided into a knop and a flower. The shaft was ornamented with four such cups. Under every two branches a knop was carved on the central shaft, making a total of three knops "for the six branches going out of the *menorah*" (Ex. 25:35). These three knops were probably an integral part of the cups on the central shaft and not, as some hold, in addition to its four cups. The fourth cup was at the top of the central shaft, above the places where the branches joined it. The uppermost cups of the branches were similarly at the top, all of them being the same height as the cup of the central shaft. The flowers on these uppermost cups served as receptacles for the seven lamps.

The entire *menorah* was formed from one ingot of gold and was of "beaten work" (Ex. 25:31), whereas its appliances, also of gold, were carved separately (25:37–38). The *menorah* was placed in front of the veil *(parokhet)* "on the south side of the Tabernacle opposite the table" (Ex. 26:35; 40:24). When the lamps burned they gave "light upon the space in front of the menorah" (Ex. 25:37; Num. 8:2–3), that is, the spouts of the lamps and the wicks faced northward, so that their shadow was cast on the wall. The measurements of the *menorah* are not given in the text.

No actual specimen of a *menorah* of the kind used in the Tabernacle, nor of one with a different number of branches, has turned up in archaeological finds. Only reproductions of the *menorah* of the Second Temple are extant. The artistic and architectonic elements of its description, however, are undoubtedly based on an actual art style and derive from reality. Some scholars contend that the *menorah* represents a stylization of the tree of life. This, however, is only a supposition.

In the Temple built by Solomon the ten *menorot* of gold, five along the northern and five along the southern wall of the outer hall (I Kings 7:49; II Chron. 4:7), were ornamented with carvings of flowers and furnished with appliances of gold for tending the lamps (I Kings 7:49–50). The number of lamps on each *menorah* is not stated. All the golden vessels in Solomon's Temple, including the ten *menorot*, were destroyed at the end of Jehoia-

Figure 99: Incised *menorah* of the Second Temple period found in excavations at the Jewish Quarter in Jerusalem. The *menorah*, which is considered the most accurate evidence of the seven-branched *menorah*, has six branches, three on each side, curved upward from the *menorah*'s central shaft, which stands on a triangular base. Each of the branches is ornamented with cups, each one divided into a knop and a flower

chin's reign by the Chaldeans who broke into the Temple (II Kings 24:13). Hence, none of these vessels is mentioned in Ezekiel's visionary Temple (Ezek. 41:1–4), whose description is apparently based on the actual appearance of the Temple in Jerusalem after Jehoiachin's deportation.

Since the outer hall of Solomon's Temple, which measured 40 by 20 cubits (I Kings 6:2,17), was too large to be adequately illuminated by only ten lamps, it is likely that each of the ten *menorot* had not one but several lamps, arranged on branches, and it is not improbable that they were seven in number. Further support for the similarity between the *menorot* of Solomon's Temple and the *menorah* of the Tabernacle is to be found in the fact that both were ornamented with carvings of flowers, and both were made of pure gold (7:49: *zahav sagur,* which is apparently the equivalent expression for *zahav tahor* in Ex. 25:31, 39). Moreover, the appliances of the *menorah* in the Tabernacle consisted of lamps, tongs, snuff dishes, and oil vessels (Ex. 25:37–39; Num. 4:9), the first three of which are mentioned in connection with the *menorot* in Solomon's Temple (I Kings 7:49–50).

The cultic use of the Temple *menorot,* especially those of the First Temple, is described in the Bible. The lamps were lit at dusk and trimmed in the morning by the high priest (Ex. 30:7–8), and burned "from evening to morning" (Lev. 24:3). Consequently, they are called *ner tamid,* or regular lamps (Ex. 27:20; Lev. 24:2). That the lamps burned only during the night is explicitly mentioned also in connection with the House of God at Shiloh (I Sam. 3:3).

Jachin and Boaz (fig.   38). Jachin and Boaz were two bronze pillars which stood in the inner court of Solomon's Temple, before the entry to the Sanctuary (I Kings 7:15–22, 41–42; II Kings 25:13,17; Jer. 52:17, 20ff.; Ezek. 40:49; II Chron. 3:15–17; 4:12–13). The form and nature of these pillars are uncertain, and many proposals have been advanced by scholars.

There is a detailed description of the pillars in I Kings 7:15–22, 41–42 and II Chronicles 3:15–17; 4:12–13. The pillars were composed of two major parts: the stem, 18 cubits (c. 30 ft.) in height, 5 cubits (c. 8 ft.) in circumference, and 1 cubit in diameter; and the capital of the pillar, 5 cubits in height. The size of the capital was apparently altered in one of the renovations of the Temple, undertaken after the time of Solomon. Thus, in II Kings 25 its height is given as only 3 cubits. During the renovation all the pillars were apparently recast, which probably explains the contradiction between the description of the construction of the pillars in Kings and that in Jeremiah. According to the former, the pillars and their capitals were cast from solid copper (I Kings 7:16, 46), while according to the latter, they were hollow (Jer. 52:21).

It is more difficult to discover the nature of the capitals, as the description of their construction is filled with unclear technical terms which do not appear elsewhere (cf. I Kings 7:17–20, 41–42; Jer. 52:22–23). Without going into detail, it may be said that the capitals were decorated with three varieties of ornamentation — "lilywork," "meshwork," and "pomegranates," crowned by an additional architectural design called *gullah*. The last item is usually interpreted as a round bowl (on the basis of the parallel Akk. *gullatu* and the description of the Temple lamp in Zech. 4:2–3). Scholars usually resort to archaeological parallels for reconstructing the meaning of the other three terms.

Rabbinic scholars and medieval Jewish exegetes held that the capital here is a double one (cf. I Kings 7:20). Indeed, double capitals are known from clay molds of cultic structures from Palestine and Cyprus dating to the period under consideration, i.e., the Iron Age. In these molds, as in the biblical descriptions, there is a capital of lily leaves, in the center of which is a semispherical bowl. Similar examples are found in ivory inlays from Palestine and Mesopotamia dating from the 8th to the 6th centuries B.C.E., which contain an additional element of a series of elongated objects shaped like pomegranates hanging below a capital decorated with lilywork. Some later scholars identified this capital with the square proto-Aeolian capitals characteristic of the architecture of the time of Solomon, which have been discovered in various locations in Palestine (in the royal palaces in Samaria, in the fortress of Ahab in Hazor, in the governor's house in Megiddo, Ramat Raḥel, Gezer, etc.). Others attempted to reconstruct the appearance of the capitals by comparison with incense stands discovered in Megiddo, Taanach, and Gezer. The closest example is that from Megiddo which, like the biblical model, contains three architectural designs — a bowl, rosette work (buds of flowers and lotuses), and pomegranates. In light of recent archaeological findings it has been suggested that "meshwork" (I Kings 7:17) should be explained as apertures in the bowl, like those found in incense stands (cf. II Kings 1:2, where the term refers to the "window bars"). This interpretation, however, is far from the literal meaning, and what is described here is a woven net which surrounded the capitals.

According to the Masoretic Version (I Kings 7:21 and II Chron. 3:17), it appears that the pillars stood in front of the Sanctuary, inside the entrance hall. Their size, however, gives rise to doubts concerning their structural function. Thus, few scholars maintain that the pillars fulfilled any function in supporting the roof of the portico (as in temples of the Iron Age period in Arad (fig. 45), Megiddo, and Tell Tainat (fig. 42)). Most scholars tend to the opinion that these were two freestanding pillars, one on each side of the entrance, like those found in the archaeological tradition of the ancient Near East and in references in classical literature. Thus, the clay molds from the Iron Age mentioned above have freestanding pillars in the entrance hall. A similar phenomenon was found in three temples (8th century B.C.E.) in Khorsabad in Assyria. Graphic representations of pillars standing outside the structure of a temple have been found on coins from the 1st century C.E. in Cyprus, Sardis, Pergamum, and Sidon. Finally, there are literary references to this type of pillar in descriptions of the temples of Herakles (Herodotus, 2:44), of the Tyrian Baal (Menander, quoted in Jos., Ant. 8:145), and of the Syrian goddess Atratah (Lucian, *De Syria Dea*, 16–27); one or two such pillars were constructed in honor of Heracles in the Tyrian settlement of Gadez (modern Cadiz) in Spain (Strabo, 3:170).

Even those scholars who agree that these pillars played no structural role in the Temple are divided in their opinions regarding their function. One suggestion is that they had a mythological significance, as "trees of life," or cosmic pillars; or perhaps they fulfilled a ritual function as cressets or incense lamps, like those found in a drawing of a tomb in Mareshah (Hellenistic period). Another possibility is that they symbolized the dwelling place of God in the Temple, like the monuments found in the temple in Shechem and the temple of Mekal in Beth-Shean (Canaanite period). Still another suggestion is that they might have been imitations of Egyptian obelisks.

The Molten Sea. One of the most amazing pieces of art described in the Bible is the "molten sea" constructed by King Solomon (I Kings 7:23–26; II Chron. 4:2–5). This was a bronze vessel about 15 ft. in diameter and about half that in height, which also stood in the inner court of the Temple. The rim was "wrought like the brim of a cup, like the flower of a lily," and it held about 10,000 gallons of water. It is not certain whether this huge container was cylindrical or hemispherical. According to rabbinic tradition it was square at the bottom and round at the top. It is estimated that when empty it weighed between 25 and 30 tons. It was supported by 12 cast bronze oxen, grouped in threes, facing the four directions of the compass. The purpose of the "sea" was to hold the water with which the priests washed their hands and feet during the Temple service.

No bowls of this size have been discovered by archaeological investigations, and it has been difficult to find any parallels in other cultures. The nearest is probably in an Assyrian relief dating from Sargon II (c. 722–705 B.C.E.) which depicts the temple in Musasir. Two huge cauldrons are shown at the temple entrance, standing on legs shaped like bull's feet.

In Cyprus, at Amatheus, a large bowl was discovered, measuring about 6 ft. in diameter and about 6 ft. in height. It had four handles on which bulls are carved in relief. Another vessel over 6 ft. high was found in the vicinity. Steps were used in order to reach the water in the bowl. These bowls differ from the molten sea of Solomon in two ways. They are less than half the size, and are not of bronze but of stone.

The huge dimensions of the "molten sea," as well as the two bronze pillars, Jachin and Boaz (see above), must have been outstanding feats of bronze metalwork. To appreciate this and to put Solomon's accomplishments in this field in proper perspective we have only to remember that Sennacherib, king of Assyria (705–681 B.C.E.), boasts of his invention for casting bronze in special molds. Solomon's "molten sea" and pillars had been cast some 250 years previously.

The Bronze Lavers. Solomon also made ten bronze lavers, with bases on wheels, for the Temple service. The bases were about 6½ ft. square and 5 ft. high. On top of each there was a "round compass" (probably a round rim) about 10 inches in height, which held the laver. The bases were decorated with reliefs of lions, oxen, cherubs, and palm trees. The lavers stood, with the molten sea, the sacrificial altar (see   p. 58), and the bronze pillars, in the inner court of the Temple.

In this instance archaeology has found a number of parallels which give us a good idea of what these bases and lavers must have looked like. From Ras Shamra (ancient Ugarit, on the Syrian coast) comes a laver with metal pomegranates hanging down from the brim, and from Megiddo comes a bronze openwork stand dated 1050–1000 B.C.E., which is shortly before Solomon's time. More interesting are examples of bronze bases from Cyprus. One is from Enkomi and has a rectangular frame with spiral ornamentation. In the center is a double "woman at the window" design (see p. 38). On top of the base is a circular socket, also with spiral ornamentation. The stand is dated to the 12th century B.C.E.

Yet another discovery was a carriage base from Larnaka. This is also rectangular but it has large wheels attached, reminiscent of the biblical bases. There was also a circular ring with a spiral design, for holding the basin. The decoration was similarly reminiscent of the biblical description; it showed sphinxes, with a stylized tree in relief on the sides of the carriage.

Similar to the above was another carriage base on wheels, with a frieze of animals on the ring and four different motifs on the sides (cf. the vision of Ezekiel's chariot, Ezek. 1:10), a winged sphinx, a lion, a chariot, and two figures approaching a king or god. These carriages were found in tombs and it is not quite certain what purpose they actually served. The ring on top must have held a bowl.

A lovely bronze bowl on an iron tripod stand was found in a late 8th century B.C.E. tomb at Salamis (Cyprus). The rim was decorated with eight griffins and four sphinx heads. And at Tell al-Saʿīdiyya in the Jordan Valley, a bronze tripod stand was discovered which had a bronze bowl riveted to three prongs at the top of the stand. This was found in a woman's tomb dating from the 12th century, which contained Cyprian, Mycenaean, and Egyptian objects.

Many more stands were found in Cyprus, but the above examples with the wheels, so similar to the biblical description of the stands made by Solomon for the Temple, provide a striking illustration of the type of work they must have exemplified.

Minor Utensils

In addition to the large utensils that were part of the Temple, a great many smaller, portable utensils were used by the priests in their ministrations, such as pots, shovels, basins and flesh-hooks (I Kings 7:40, 45; II Chron. 4:16), all made of brass. These brass utensils were used at the altar in the courtyard. The pots were used to cook those portions of the offerings which were permitted to be consumed; the shovels were used to remove the ashes from the altar and perhaps also to remove refuse from the courtyard; the basins were used to sprinkle the sacrificial blood on the altar (cf. Lev. 1:5).

The Bible does not provide a description of these utensils, and no brass tools of this type have been found in excavations in Ereẓ Israel. (Nor have shovels been found elsewhere in the Near East.) It has been suggested that the basins were beaker-like in shape, although no examples of such have been found.

The utensils used in the large hall of the Temple were made of gold and included lamps, tongs, snuffers, basins, pans, firepans, and hinges for the doors of the hall and the Holy of Holies (I Kings 7:49–50; II Chron. 4:20–22).

We are familiar with the usual shapes of clay lamps, and there is no reason to assume that the metal lamps differed in their form. Our knowledge of clay lamps derives solely from archaeological excavations. Essentially, the lamp consisted of an open clay bowl, with a lip-shaped edge in which the wick would be inserted. This was the basic lamp both in Canaanite and Israelite periods, and the innovations, over the passage of time, were limited to small variations in the lip, the opening of the bowl, or the base. A clay lamp was considered an item of practical daily use and no attempt was made to lend it a particularly esthetic form.

In the Early Bronze period, simple flat clay bowls served as lamps, and it is only through the signs of soot on the surface of the bowl that one can identify them as lamps. The lamp assumed a specific shape for the first time in the Middle Bronze I period; the sides of the bowl were pressed together in four places to provide four "lips" for wicks. The lamp had a flat or rounded bottom. This change in form was evidently connected with external influences current in the potteries of Erez Israel. When these influences disappeared, the four-cornered lamp also disappeared.

During the Middle Bronze II period the typical Canaanite lamp appeared in common use. It was made on a potter's wheel, had a plain opening that was slightly concave, and was pinched together lightly at one place to provide support for one wick. Its base was generally round in shape. The lamp of the Late Bronze period was distinguished by the sharp folds of its sides, and by the deep pinch at one end, forming a narrow and long lip for the wick. The opening of the lamp bowl turned slightly outward, and the base was rounded.

The lamp retained this basic form through the beginning of the Iron Age (12th century B.C.E.). The Israelites adopted the form of the Canaanite lamp without changes; only later in the Israelite period did many variations appear, although the basic form was retained. The lamp became smaller and shallower, the lip was widened, and the flat base was adopted. Here and there lamps with places for seven wicks appeared, at times standing on a high pedestal. Such a lamp spread more light and was probably used on special occasions, or perhaps for cultic purposes. In the 7th century B.C.E. the lamp in common use in Judah had one wide lip, a low bowl, and a heavy raised flat base; its workmanship was very poor. Occasionally lamps would stand on bases or on a figure of a man's head. This deviation from the standard form has been explained in terms of symbolic significance.

Lamps of the Persian period developed a wider opening, had a still lower bowl, and a sharply pinched lip in which the sides almost touch one another. At times the lamp was larger than earlier examples, its base flat and irregular, at times scraped with a knife. This lamp was unsteady and was also unserviceable because of its shallowness. Thus far only two bronze lamps of biblical times have been found, one from the end of the Israelite period, the other from the Persian period. Both copy the clay lamp in form.

The tongs were used for tending the lamps and inserting the wicks. Examples have been found in excavations.

The functions, and sometimes even the forms, of the remaining utensils mentioned in connection with the Temple service are not clear. The basins were probably medium-sized, and were used for libations and mixed offerings. Examples of such basins are the gold-colored brass bowls of the middle Israelite period, discovered at Tell Ziklag. The snuffers are more difficult to identify, and they remain an unanswered riddle. The spoons and the fire-pans were used in connection with the incense. Several broken incense-spoons have been found in various excavations, and the golden spoons used in the Temple undoubtedly were similar in shape. On the other end of the spoon was a mouthpiece in which a hollow reed would be inserted. The priest would hold the spoon by this "handle" and even blow through it to fan the coals for the incense. Thus far incense pans of the biblical period have not been found in Erez Israel, with the exception of one questionable specimen made of bronze that was found at Megiddo.

The flesh-hooks mentioned in II Chron. 4:16 (in place of the snuffers of I Kings 7:50) were used in the inner court while cooking the meat of the offerings (cf. I Sam. 2:14). Specimens have been found in excavations at Lachish, near Acco, and in Macalister's work at Gezer. These have been dated approximately to the 14th century B.C.E.

Stringed instruments (*kinnor* and *nevel;* see p. 246) were prepared by Solomon (I Kings 10:2; II Chron. 9:11), and probably had a place in the Temple services.

It must be assumed that utensils that were not part of the permanent furnishings of the Temple were stored in the Temple treasuries. Initially these treasuries were located in the three-story wing of the Temple compound, and probably contained the priestly vestments as well.

Priestly Vestments and Related Items
The priestly vestments were the special garments (see also pp. 224–28, and fig. 100) that were worn by the priests during divine worship, as was customary in cultic services in the ancient Near East and elsewhere (see e.g., II Kings 10:22). The priests are commanded to leave their priestly garments in the holy chambers after the service (Ezek. 42:14; 44:19), and to refrain

Figure 100:   Model of the high priest and common priest wearing their vestments. Left: (1) blue band; (2) miter; (3) gold plate; (4) onyx stones with names of the tribes (six on each stone); (5) robe of the ephod; (6) breastplate; (7) blue band; (8) band of the ephod; (9) ephod; (10) bells of gold and pomegranates of dyed wool and linen; (11) coat; (12) girdle. Right: (1) headdress; (2) coat; (3) girdle.

from carrying them into the outer court (Lev. 6:4). It is likewise stated: "He shall then take off his garments and put on other garments," the latter apparently referring to garments worn by the people, as in Ezekiel 42:14. In the Bible, the priestly garments are described only in Leviticus. Several of them are briefly referred to in Ezekiel 44:17–18; only the ephod is mentioned in other biblical sources.

Several features characterize the priestly vestments. Some of them are made "for splendor and for beauty" (Ex. 28:40); others, as is usual with cultic apparel, undoubtedly preserve vestiges of an old style, while some reflect cultic significance.

The priestly garments as a whole are frequently referred to as holy garments. A total of eight garments are enumerated, but only Aaron attired himself in all eight. Of these, the four undergarments are to be worn by the common priests too, but those of Aaron are somewhat more embellished. A special group of four other garments of simple linen were worn when acts of extraordinary holiness were performed.

The four undergarments are to be made of fine twined linen, that is, a superior quality of linen; an exception within this group is Aaron's girdle, made of a mixture of fine linen and wool. The four undergarments consist of:

(1) A coat. Of Aaron's coat it is said: "And you shall weave the coat in checkerwork of fine linen" (Ex. 28:39), and hence it is called "a coat of checkerwork" (28:4) (see also p. 214). No mention is made of checkerwork with respect to the coats of the common priests (Ex. 28:39–40).

(2) A girdle (see p. 225). The girdle, bound around the coat, is also regarded as a vestment of distinction (cf. Isa. 22:21). Whereas the girdles of the common priests were made exclusively of fine twined linen (Ex. 28:39), Aaron's was of fine linen and dyed wools and was of embroidered work (Ex. 28:39; 39:29).

(3) A headdress (see p. 225). For the common priests turbans or "decorated turbans" are prescribed, while Aaron wears a miter (Ex. 28:39–40; 39:28; cf. Ezek. 44:18). The "decorated turban" is considered an attire of beauty and distinction (cf. Isa. 3:20; 61:3,10; Ezek. 24:17), but more imposing is the miter, which is also used as a synonym for crown (Ezek. 21:31; cf. Isa. 62:3).

(4) Breeches. The breeches are worn "to cover the flesh of their nakedness; from the hips to the thighs" (Ex. 28:42; 39:28; Ezek. 44:18).

The four outer garments, which pertain specifically to the high priest, are of greater richness and splendor than the undergarments. They consist of a mixture of dyed wool and fine linen, and display "skillful workmanship." Some also contain threads of pure gold, while others are woven of gold filaments and yarn of a mixture of wool and linen. These costly substances indicate a high degree of holiness, as is also attested by the mixture of wool and linen. Such a mixture was generally prohibited in profane garments, as it was conducive to holiness (Lev. 19:19; Deut. 22:9–11). Precisely for this reason, however, it was preserved among the priests. In this respect, the priestly garments correspond to the curtains and the veil of the Tabernacle, which are also said to have been made of a mixture of wool and linen, and have displayed "skillful workmanship" (e.g., Ex. 26:1, 31).

The very wearing of the four outer garments is regarded as an act of worship and is connected with the other acts performed by the high priest inside the Temple. While it is nowhere specifically stated that the high priest wears the four outer garments when he enters the Temple to perform the daily cultic act in the morning and in the afternoon, they are too heavy, cumbersome, and splendid for the tasks performed at the outer altar.

The four outer garments have several features characteristic of royalty (the gold, the blue, and the purple, as well as the crown) and when combined with the miter and with the anointing oil poured on the high priest (e.g., Ex. 29:7) they give him a regal appearance. In Ezekiel's vision there is no mention of these garments; Ezekiel knows only the vestments of ordinary linen (Ezek. 44:17–18). The existence of the high priesthood itself is not mentioned by him.

The four outer priestly garments are the ephod, the breastplate, the robe, and the plate (or crown).

The ephod, made of gold and a mixture of wool and linen, displaying "skillful workmanship" (Ex. 18:6–12; 39:2–7), is the most distinguished of the priestly garments. It alone is mentioned in the Former and the Later Prophets (Judg. 8:17; 17:5;Josh. 3:4; et al.). The ephod served a unique purpose in the early history of Israel. The Israelite religion prohibited all soothsaying and all divination by means of auguries, but did permit, side by side with prophecy, the priestly ephod. Both prophecy and the ephod were seen as a means of seeking the counsel of God and of obtaining a revelation of His will. The technical term for consulting the ephod is "to seek guidance from the Lord" (I Chron. 10:14) or "to come before the Lord" (Ex. 28:30), that is, before the Ark in the Tabernacle (Judg. 20:27; I Chron. 21:30). In private sanctuaries, as well as high places outside of Jerusalem, where there were no scruples about effigies, use was made of an ephod, together with teraphim (Hos. 3:4; see p. 267) and a graven image, for approaching God (Judg. 17:4–5; 18:14,17,20; Isa. 30:22; cf. Judg. 8:27).

The Bible contains no detailed description of the shape of the ephod, nor does the Hebrew root of the word furnish any additional clues. The Hebrew root is connected with the Akkadian *epattu*, which signifies a garment in Cappadocian tablets. The word also appears in Ugaritic tablets, where it may have the same meaning.

The early Israelite ephod was engraved with the names of the Twelve Tribes, apparently to signify the totality of the nation (Ex. 28:9–12). Despite the honored place accorded the ephod in the Bible, its use in the Temple was evidently abandoned at an early period. After the time of David it is nowhere mentioned, although it continued to be a vestment of the high priest in the days of the Second Temple. Consultation of the ephod, in combination with teraphim (see below, pp. 267–68), was still prevalent in the countryside outside of Jerusalem (Hos. 3:4). It is probable that from the time of Samuel onward, the increasing influence of the prophets contributed to the eclipse of this method of divination.

It is not stated how the ephod was made in the days of the Judges (Judg. 8:27; 17:5; I Sam. 2:18). The Bible contains a description of the ephod of Aaron (Ex. ch. 18) and Eleazar (Num. 20:28; 27:21; cf. Josh. 14:1–2). It would seem to be a square, sleeveless garment falling from just below the armpits to the heels. It was embroidered "of gold, of blue, purple, and crimson yarns, and of fine twisted linen worked into designs." To its two ends were attached straps which fastened over the shoulders, and on each of the shoulder straps was set a *shoham* stone — identification uncertain — engraved with the names of the tribes of Israel. The breastpiece was bound to the ephod at the top by rings and chains and at the bottom by a cord of blue, while in the middle it was encircled by "the decorated band" which was also made "in the style of the ephod" and of the same materials.

The high priest used the ephod along with the breastplate and the Urim and Thummim (see below) as a means of divination. Ordinary priests, as well as others engaged in sacred ministrations (Samuel — I Sam. 2:18, and once even David — II Sam. 6:14; I Chron. 15:27), wore a simple ephod of linen, apparently during sacred services or at special celebrations (I Sam. 22:18).

The breastplate, measuring a span by a span, was attached to the ephod. It was either a square tablet or a pouch. In it were set 12 precious stones on which were engraved the names of the tribes of Israel. On the breastplate rested the Urim and the Thummim. The breastplate was made in the same manner as the ephod — that is, of gold and a mixture of wool and linen, and displayed "skillful workmanship" (Ex. 28:15–30; 29:8–21).

The Urim and Thummim were a priestly device for obtaining oracles from YHWH on behalf of the ruler (Num. 27:21). They were one of the three legitimate means of obtaining oracles in early Israel (Urim, dreams, prophets: I Sam. 28:6). The right to work this oracle was reserved for the priests (Deut. 33:8). Owing to the oracular character of the Urim, the breastpiece is called "the breastpiece of decision." This concept evokes the "Tablets of Destiny," in Babylonian mythology the symbol of supreme authority that lay on the breast of the chief god.

There is no biblical information about the appearance of the Urim-Thummim, the material out of which they were made, or the technique of their use. The most illuminating passage is the Greek of I Samuel 14:41: Saul said: "O YHWH God of Israel, why have You not answered Your servant this day? If the guilt be in me or in my son Jonathan, O YHWH God of Israel, give Urim. But if this guilt is in Your people Israel, give Thummim."

From the verbs used in connection with the Urim-Thummim (v. 41–42), it appears that they were a kind of lot ([marked] stones or sticks?), since these verbs occur with lot-casting (Isa. 34:17; I Sam. 10:20). The Urim were suitable for indicating which of two alternatives was right; hence, inquiries to be decided by them were designed to elicit "yes" or "no" answers (I Sam. 23:10–12; 30:8).

The etymology of the terms is obscure. From the Greek passage adduced above it seems that the two terms are the names of two objects. Hence the conjecture that Urim derives from "curse," and Thummim from "be whole," indicating negation and affirmation respectively.

The robe was worn under the ephod. The robe was probably longer than the ephod, and extended below it. It was made only of woolen threads, all of blue. On its hem hung bells (see p. 248) of gold and pomegranates made of a mixture of dyed wool and fine linen (Ex. 28:31–35; 39:22–26).

The plate was also called a crown. It hung on a blue thread in front of the miter. Made of pure gold, it had two Hebrew words engraved on it meaning "Holy to the Lord" (Ex. 28:36–38; 39:30–31).

Shoes are not listed among the priestly vestments and the priests evidently ministered barefoot, as was obligatory in a holy place (cf. Ex. 3:5; Josh. 5:15).

In four passages (Ex. 31:10; 35:19; 39:1, 41) all the priestly garments of Aaron and of his sons are referred to by the special designation "the garments of *serad*," the etymology of which may be related to a similar root designating the word for "service." According to the literal meaning of the text it seems that Aaron's eight garments, i.e., his four undergarments and the four outer ones that were specifically for him, are referred to not as "the garments of *serad*" but as "the holy garments for Aaron the priest" (see the references above, and also Ex. 28:4; 29:29; 40:13), while the four garments of the common priests are called "the garments of his sons, for their service as priests."

A third group of priestly garments consists of those made of ordinary, not fine, linen, which were used for officiating in the holiest of places. On the Day of Atonement, Aaron entered the Holy of Holies clothed in four garments of ordinary linen: a coat, breeches, a girdle, and a miter (Lev. 16:4), which were probably white in color. However, garments, including breeches, of ordinary linen were also worn by the common priest when he ascended the outer altar to remove the ashes (Lev. 6:3), and these are assumed to be similar to the former four garments. The simple garments of ordinary linen bear a holiness still greater than the vestments of gold and a mixture of wool and linen, and the text finds it necessary to emphasize that "they are the holy garments" (Lev. 16:4). In the Egyptian priesthood, too, garments of simple linen were regarded as holy.

Other Religious Artifacts

Teraphim. In the story of the flight of Jacob and his household from Laban's home, it is related that "Rachel had taken the teraphim, and put them in the saddle of the camel, and sat upon them. And Laban felt about all the tent, but found them not" (Gen. 31:34). Teraphim were household gods, and that they were small and portable is obvious from the fact that Rachel managed to hide them under the camel cushion. On the other hand, the fact that Michal could deceive her father's messengers by leading them to believe that the teraphim on the bed was David's figure, makes it seem that some were of considerable size (II Sam. 19:13). There is nothing in either incident to show conclusively whether such a figure represented an entire human form or simply a head or bust.

The teraphim are both condoned and condemned in biblical writing. From the story of Rachel's flight and her appropriation of her father's teraphim, it seems to have been the accepted custom among the people in Mesopotamia to have objects of worship in their house and to take them along when going abroad. Furthermore, in the story of Michal, teraphim seem to be a usual piece of household furnishings, and were most probably tolerated by the Israelite religion of that time.

The tablets from Nuzi have direct bearing on our knowledge of teraphim since the Akkadian term *ilāni*, "gods," was used in Nuzi legal texts in ways that closely paralleled some of the occurrences of the word *elohim* or its interchangeable partner *teraphim* in the narrative about Rachel (Gen. 31:30; cf. 31:19,34,36).

In an adoption contract from Nuzi it is stated that on the death of the adoptive father the adopted son shall be heir. If, however, a natural son is born, he shall be the primary heir and receive his father's *ilāni* (gods); otherwise, the *ilāni* go to the adopted son. In cases where a normal heir was lacking, the possessor of the *ilāni* was entitled to a large share of the inheritance. Thus, Rachel's theft of her father's teraphim may be viewed as an attempt to secure her own or her husband's share in her father's inheritance.

The idea that possession of the household gods was in some way connected with rights to property inheritance has found widespread acceptance. Greenberg, however, has cast serious doubts on the validity of this interpretation, and maintains that since both the adopted son and the legitimate heir divide the inheritance equally, the possession of these household gods does not determine a title to inheritance but rather leadership of the family, and a claim to paterfamilias. Thus, an alternate motivation for Rachel's theft of the teraphim may be that she wished to secure the right of paterfamilias for Jacob.

Apart from the household gods already discussed, a different sort of teraphim are encountered in the Bible; their place is not in the home, but in the sanctuary, where they were used by the Israelites in cultic ritual. The cult could not be indigenous to Israel, since both Laban the Aramean (Gen. 31:30) and the king of Babylon consulted teraphim (Ezek. 21:26). Teraphim were used in the Israelite cult as early as the period of the Judges (Judg. 17:5; 18:17) and evidently survived in later years in Judah (II Kings 23:24).

The use of teraphim in divination is particularly obvious in I Samuel 15:23, where the sin of teraphim is condemned and placed on a par with the sin of divination. Josiah, known for his far-reaching cultic reforms, did away with all the cultic objects of idolatry, including teraphim (II Kings 23:24). Zechariah further rejected the teraphim by including them among the sources of false protection (Zech. 10:2).

The Golden Calf. Exodus 32 relates that the Israelites, anxious about Moses' prolonged absence, demanded that Aaron provide a god to lead them. Complying, Aaron collected the golden ornaments of the people and fashioned the gold into the shape of a calf or a small bull. The image was immediately hailed as a representation of the God who had brought Israel out of Egypt. Aaron then built an altar, and on the following day sacrifices were offered and the people danced and played. Thereupon the Lord told Moses of the apostasy of the "stiff-necked people," whom He proposed to destroy. Moses, however, interceded on behalf of the Israelites and persuaded the Lord to renounce His intended punishment. Carrying the Tablets of the Covenant down from Mt. Sinai, Moses saw the people dancing around the golden calf. In great anger Moses smashed the Tablets, melted down the image of the calf, pulverized the precious metal, and cast the powdered gold into the water which he made the people drink.

Exodus 32 states that Moses then upbraided Aaron for having "brought great guilt" upon the people. The parallel account in Deuteronomy 9:20 relates that but for Moses' supplication for his brother, the Lord would have destroyed Aaron. Stern punishment was, however, meted out to the calf-worshipers, 3,000 of whom were slain by the Levites who had rallied to Moses. Henceforth the Levites were consecrated to the service of the Lord. Despite Moses' self-sacrificing prayer for divine forgiveness, the Lord threatened that punishment would overtake the people. Soon afterward the plague was inflicted upon the Israelites. In addition the Lord announced that He would no longer abide amid this "stiff-necked people." The Israelites mourned the departure of the divine presence and stripped themselves of their ornaments (Ex. 33:1–6).

The narrative of the golden calf cannot be understood without relating it to the erection of two golden calves in the temples of Beth-El and Dan by Jeroboam I of Israel (I Kings 12:26ff.). Not only are the general features of the story similar in both accounts, but the explanatory formula in Exodus 32:4,8 – "These are your gods, O Israel, who brought you up out of the land of Egypt" – is virtually identical to the one in I Kings 12:28b. The reason for the formula's plural phrasing, which is by no means appropriate in Exodus 32, is that in I Kings 12 Jeroboam I made two calves. Exodus 32 presupposes I Kings 12, at least in a fixed oral form. Its chief purpose, therefore, is to condemn the calf symbolism of the northern kingdom as apostasy and breach of the Covenant, by showing Moses breaking the Tablets of the Covenant when he saw the apostasy of the Israelites.

The bull played an important role in the art and religious texts of the ancient Near East. The Canaanite storm-god Hadad is frequently represented standing on a bull, and it is possible that Jeroboam's calves corresponded to the cherubim (see p. 249) of Solomon's Temple in being regarded as seats or pedestals upon which the Lord was thought to stand invisible to human eyes. M. Haran remarks that if Jeroboam's calves were considered pedestals, then they were not meant to be an exact replica of the Ark of the Covenant, because the Ark was kept in the publicly inaccessible Holy of Holies, while the calves were placed in the courts of the Temple where the people could see and kiss them (cf. Hos. 13:2). It is also possible that the calves were, from the beginning, meant to represent the Lord, like the images in the sanctuaries of Micah and Dan (Judg. 17:4; 18:14, 15−31).

In any event, Jeroboam's initiative must have had some basis in an old tradition, or he could not have succeeded in his enterprise. Jeroboam's bulls, contrary to the Ark symbolism, were meant to be a popular cult (cf. I Kings 12:27); thus they soon became popular representations of the Lord Himself (cf. e.g., II Kings 17:16; Hos. 8:5−6; 10:5; 13:2).

The Serpent Symbol. In his excavations at Timna, at the temple of the Egyptian goddess Hathor (see p. 194− 95), Rothenberg made a remarkable discovery. In a hoard of thousands of votive objects which had obviously been brought to the temple as offerings, he found a writhing serpent made of copper, some 5 inches long (fig. 101). The body was textured with scales, the head was gilded, and the eyes were of lead.

The snake symbol was well known in Egypt and in many of the ancient cultures. It is found as a motif on Canaanite pendants, together with the goddess Astarte. At Hazor a rectangular bronze standard 5 inches by 3 inches was found which dated from the last stages of the Late Bronze Age (c. 13th century B.C.E.). Plated with silver and worked both in relief and by incision, it depicts two snakes, and between them, a human face. A smaller example of the Timna serpent, a bronze serpent 3 5/8 inches long, was found by Macalister at Gezer at the beginning of the century. Macalister suggested at the time that this might be a votive model. A perfectly preserved bronze serpent, about 8 inches long, evidently a cobra, was found later at Gezer. It is from the 14th century B.C.E. Another model of a serpent was found at Lachish.

Figure 101:   Copper snake with gilded head found at Timna cult-place

These serpents are reminiscent of the biblical account of a plague of poisonous snakes which descended upon the Israelites in the wilderness, when they spoke against God and Moses. The Bible relates: "And Moses made a serpent of copper and set it upon the pole; and it came to pass that if a serpent had bitten any man, when he looked upon the serpent of copper, he lived" (Num. 21:9). This narrative would seem to imply that the serpent had cultic power, similar to that found in neighboring cultures.

The copper serpent made by Moses was preserved for many generations, but since, in the reign of King Hezekiah of Judah, it had become an object of idolatry, the king felt compelled to destroy it: ". . . and he broke in pieces the brazen serpent that Moses had made; for unto those days the Children of Israel did offer to it; and it was called Nehushtan [bronze]" (II Kings 18:4).

The destruction of the serpent met with the approval of the Sages, and it was one of the three specific actions for which they later praised Hezekiah (Pesaḥim 4:9). Nonetheless they were surprised at the use of the serpent symbol as a healing agent. Their view is set forth in the Mishnah: "Could the serpent kill or could the serpent keep alive? However, when Israel turned their thoughts on high and subjected their hearts to their Father in Heaven they were healed, but if not, they pined away" (Rosh ha-Shanah 3:8).

Asherah. The biblical term *asherah* (plural: *asherim*) – not to be confused with the Canaanite goddess bearing that name – refers to an object which can be built, planted, erected, or constructed; it is placed near the altar; and it is destroyed by chopping it down and burning it. It therefore seems that the *asherah* which is never described specifically in the Bible, is some cult object made out of wood (see Judg. 6:26). No evidence exists to help determine whether it was an image of the goddess Asherah that was placed near the altar, a sacred pole which represented her, or some other object. The traditional view that the *asherah* was a sacred grove can most probably be rejected on the grounds that it seems to have been man-made. Charred pieces of wood found in excavations at Qatna (in Syria), Megiddo, and Ai have been tentatively identified as *asherim,* but there is nothing to corroborate this hypothesis.

Asherim were in use in both the northern kingdom and the kingdom of Judah, where they were intimately connected with the cultic high places and the *mazzevot* (I Kings 14:23). Although it is probable that they derived from the worship of the goddess Asherah, Israelite use was most likely a syncretistic phenomenon, an addition of an element from the surrounding fertility religions to its own monotheistic belief. The prohibition against using the *asherah* at the altar of the Lord (Deut. 16:21) was more likely an attempt to purge pagan elements from Israelite worship, than an indication that Asherah was worshiped together with the Lord.

Mazzevah. According to the Bible, the *mazzevah* (plural: *mazzevot*) served various functions. The most obvious was its role as a memorial stone for the dead (Gen. 35:20; II Sam. 18:18). It also was a monument commemorating a treaty or marking a border agreement (Gen. 31:45—52; Josh. 4:4—9).

The connection between the *mazzevah* and the worship of the Lord is most clear in the narrative of Jacob at Beth-El. The Bible relates that Jacob took the stone from under his head, erected it as a *mazzevah*, anointed it with oil (Gen. 28:18), and vowed that if he would return safely from Aram-Naharaim the *mazzevah* would become a House of the Lord (*ibid.* v. 22). Indeed, when Jacob did return, he erected a *mazzevah* at Beth-El, offered a libation, and anointed it with oil (Gen. 35:14).

A similarly positive attitude toward the use of the sacred stone or *mazzevah* in the Israelite worship service is evident in Isaiah's messianic prophecy regarding the future reign of the Lord in Egypt. The signs of this future happening would be: an altar erected to the Lord inside the Land of Egypt, and a *mazzevah* to the Lord to stand at its border (Isa. 19:18—23).

In general, however, biblical references to *mazzevot* are not positive. The sacred stone was condemned as an object associated with the worship of other gods, particularly Baal (I Kings 14:23; II Kings 3:2), or as a borrowed cult object that was unfit for Israelite worship of the Lord. Thus, the Israelites are commanded to break the *mazzevot* of the local people (Ex. 23:24; 34:13; Deut. 7:5; 12:3). A specific prohibition against the use of the *mazzevah* in the Israelite service of the Lord is found in the Book of Deuteronomy which explains that the Lord hates it (Deut. 16:22). Similarly negative attitudes are voiced in the Books of Joshua (3:4; 10:1—3), Kings (II Kings 17:10; 18:4), Ezekiel (26:11), and Micah (5:12). These references do not differentiate between a *mazzevah* built for cultic worship, and one used in the service of the Lord.

The *mazzevah* is frequently mentioned together with other cultic objects: the altar (e.g., Ex. 24:4; 34:13; Deut. 7:5), the *asherah* (e.g., Ex. 34:13; Deut. 7:5), the high place (e.g., I Kings 14:23; II Kings 17:10), and the graven image (Lev. 26:1; Deut. 7:5; Micah 5:12).

Archaeologists tend to identify as *mazzevot* large stones or groups of stones (sometimes even if they had no specific form) which would appear to have served cultic purposes, to have marked a grave, to have been a boundary stone or some other monument. Such stones have been found throughout the ancient Near East. In Erez Israel *mazzevot* are generally found at sites associated with high places and temples, dating from the Neolithic period to the end of the period of the First Temple.

Many *mazzevot* of the Early and Middle Bronze I periods have been found in Moab. Others were found in the temple at Nahariyyah and in Megiddo. Two *mazzevot* which stand at the entrance to the "tower temple" of Shechem (fig. 43), and a larger *mazzevah* that stands in its courtyard, are ascribed to the end of the Middle Bronze period. These *mazzevot* stood on pedestals.

Among the finds of the Late Bronze Age is an elaborate group of ten large *mazzevot* (up to 10 ft. in height) found at Gezer. They were lined up in three rows, running north-south, and in the center of one row stood a kind of altar. By analogy to *mazzevot* found in Byblos and Ashur, these may be identified as memorials to notables. A basalt *mazzevah* standing on a

Figure 102:   *Mazzevot* in a small temple of the 13th cent. B.C.E. in the lower city (area H) at Hazor. One of them is engraved with a pair of hands upraised in a gesture of pleading towards a disc, probably symbolizing the moon

pedestal, with a basalt basin sunken into the ground nearby, was found in the courtyard of the temple in Beth-Shean (14th century B.C.E.). The temple of Hazor (upper city, III; c. 13th century B.C.E.) also had ten basalt *mazzevot*. One was engraved with a pair of hands upraised in a gesture of pleading toward the moon, and symbols of the moon-god (fig. 102).

Excavations at Timna have revealed a structure which was identified by Rothenberg as a temple, in which five large stones stood. A cultic building (end of the 10th century B.C.E.) at Taanach contained three *mazzevot*, with a larger one standing not far away. A *mazzevah* stood in the Holy of Holies, probably behind the altar, in the temple at Arad (9th century B.C.E.); it bore traces of a red color, and was probably of Canaanite origin, reused by the Israelites. Two small flint stones were plastered and inserted into the wall of that temple, and may also have served as *mazzevot*. Additional *mazzevot* from the end of the Israelite period were found in northern Tell al-Far'ah and Jerusalem.

Graven Images. The biblical term *pesel* (plural: *pesilim*) refers to a graven image of a deity, or his sacred symbol (Hab. 2:18). The variety of biblical terms associated with sculptors and imagemakers attests to the fact that these images were made of many materials and in a variety of techniques. Our knowledge that they were made of stone and wood derives from several biblical verses (Hab. 2:18–19; Isa. 40:19; 45:20). Isaiah's detailed description of how graven images were made (chapter 44), and the description of their destruction by fire or by hewing down (Deut. 7:25; 12:3) also adds to our knowledge.

Some images were made of iron (Isa. 44:12), or gold or silver (Judg. 17:4; Isa. 30:22). Sometimes the wooden or stone image was overlaid with precious metal (Isa. 40:19; 44:13–17). Among archaeological finds are images with a core of brass or bronze, overlaid with silver or gold. The most commonly found images in Erez Israel, however, are made of clay, and are evidently the work of potters (cf. Isa. 45:9).

In general, the image stood in a temple or cultic site (II Chron. 33:7), but on occasion it was made too large (see hint of this in I Sam. 5:3–5). It was a holy symbol, formed in the image of the god or of one of the animals sacred to him or serving as his chariot. Thus some had human form (male or female) while others were made in the shape of an animal, bird, reptile, or fish (Deut. 4:15–18; 5:8). The temple also housed other symbolic objects, such as a picture or mask.

Since the image was the sacred symbol of the god, it was the object of cultic rituals; it was bowed down to and served (Deut. 5:9; II Kings 17:41), it was worshiped and prayed to (Isa. 44:17; 45:20); offerings were brought to it and incense was burned before it (Hosea 11:2; II Chron. 33:22).

While archaeological finds have helped clarify our knowledge about these cultic artifacts which had a specific function, such as the altar, the *mazzevah*, and the ephod, the symbolic artifacts, such as the graven image, the mask, the picture, and the idol, remain veiled in mystery and subject to various interpretations.

Many small images have been found in Erez Israel, but because of climatic conditions wooden images have not survived. Judging, however, from finds in Egypt, where the climate is dry, wooden images were common. The earliest images found in Erez Israel date to prehistoric times. Most were made in human or animal form, and were either fertility symbols or figures of the animals which were associated with the gods; they have been found in the Carmel caves, the Judean Desert, and elsewhere. Generally speaking they were made of pebbles on which a schematic drawing of a man or a face was engraved; images of this type were found in Shaar ha-Golan, and Hurvat Minhah in the north of the Jordan Valley.

Specimens of locally worked stone images are lacking in the Chalcolithic, Early and Middle Canaanite periods, but small images of Pharaohs or of Egyptian administrators, clearly Egyptian in style (and origin?) have been unearthed. In addition, some local attempts at sculpturing lions, gazelles, cows, etc. in clay and stone have been found.

Graven images flourished throughout Erez Israel and Transjordan at the close of the Late Canaanite period. Some undoubtedly were imported from Egypt, northern Syria or Cyprus, but most reflect the work of local Canaanite craftsmen seeking to imitate these styles. They have been found at three main sites: Tell Abu-Hawam, Beth-Shean, and Hazor. At Tell Abu-Hawam, the images are Cyprian-Mycenaean in style. At Beth-Shean, Egyptian reliefs and images were found, plus a large number of Canaanite reliefs carved in the same style. One *mazzevah* found here shows a mythological picture, in north Syrian or Hittite style, of a battle between a lion and a dog. At Hazor, numerous graven images of north-Syrian or Hittite style show gods sitting on thrones. Two other images of seated gods were found here in the Canaanite temple in stratum VIII, together with a statue of a god standing on the back of a cow. Another group of finds from Hazor includes three orthostats engraved with lions. Dating from the same period are remains of some stone images (evidently imported from Egypt). Mention must also be made of an image of a goddess seated on her throne (Tell Zippor) and a small image of a lion (Tell Beit Mirsim).

The Late Canaanite period was undoubtedly a time in which stone sculpture and wood-carving flourished, and rich finds of images and reliefs are spread throughout the ancient Middle East. Particular mention must be made of the abundant artifacts discovered at Ugarit; they include images of many gods in the Canaanite pantheon. In Syria images copied the Phoenician style, but a Neo-Hittite and Aramean style was also developed. Groups of small stone images depicting the heads of kings were found at Amman.

In contrast, stone images almost disappear in Erez Israel during the Israelite period, and the few that have been found are frequently of Egyptian import. These images had no cultic function, but were part of the palaces. A group of proto-Greek capital was found in Hazor, Megiddo, Samaria, Jerusalem, and Ramat Raḥel (see p. 24).

During the transition between the Israelite and Persion periods (6th century B.C.E.), many stone images were imported from Cyprus. These are obviously Cyprian in style, with carved fronts and flat backs. They have been found mainly in temples or in temple treasuries, at Tell al-Ṣāfī, Tell Erani, Tell Jamma, etc. Some few images are probably of Egyptian origin.

Ivory images dating to the Chalcolithic period have been excavated in Erez Israel. A unique group was found in a site near Beer-Sheba; it consisted of several male figures and one image of the goddess of fertility.

Excavations of the Early Canaanite period have yielded several ivory pieces shaped like cow heads; their origin is either Mesopotamia or Asia Minor. Three other ivory images were found at Jericho, Ai, and Beth-Yerah. After this period, ivory images disappear completely, reappearing in Erez Israel only at the end of the Middle Canaanite and particularly in the Late Canaanite and Israelite periods. Almost all of the ivories of these periods were made by Phoenician craftsmen. Particularly large finds of ivories have been uncovered in Canaanite excavations at Megiddo (see p. 205), Lachish, Tell al-Far'ah, Beth-El, and in Israelite excavations at Samaria, Hazor, Lachish, and Beth-Zur. Among these ivory images are several depicting Hittite and Egyptian deities or mythological creatures like griffons, sphinxes, and cherubs, but they appear to have served decorative, cosmetic, or gaming purposes, and to have had no cultic function.

Small metal images have been found in Erez Israel, dating back to the Middle Canaanite period; an important group was found in the temple at Nahariyyah. Like the other images, these also appear more frequently in the Late Canaanite period. Many small metal sculptures of that period were found at Megiddo, Hazor, Beth-Shean, Beth-Shemesh, and elsewhere in Erez Israel, as well as in Byblos and Ugarit in Syria.

Most of the Canaanite metalwork copies Egyptian, north Syrian, and Hittite styles; some shows Aegean or Cyprian influence. The small statues are mainly made of bronze; some are silver, gold, or lead; and only a few are made of iron. This last fact may reflect the disintegration of iron through oxidation and rust, rather than a lack of iron images. Some bronze-core images overlaid with gold or silver have been found at Megiddo and Beth-Shean.

As the Israelite period progresses, the number of metal images found in excavations dwindles. A group of bronze statues (some gold-plated), dating from the Persian period, was found at Ashkelon. Another group, found at Gibeon, depicts gods, sacred animals, and priests. Despite the Egyptian influence visible in these images, scholars hold that they were made by metalworkers in Ashkelon. As noted above, in all periods most of the images found in Erez Israel continued to be made of clay.

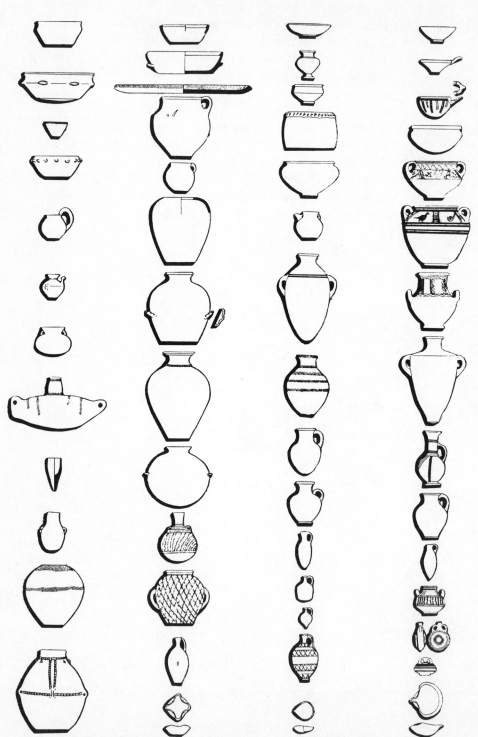

CHALCOLITHIC AGE	EARLY BRONZE AGE	MIDDLE BRONZE AGE	LATE BRONZE AGE
4000 — 3100 B. C. E.	3100 — 2100 B. C. E.	2100 — 1550 B. C. E.	1550 — 1200 B. C. E

Pottery types characteristic of the various archeological periods

IRON AGE I	IRON AGE II	PERSIAN PERIOD	HELLENISTIC PERIOD
1200 — 930 B.C.E.	930 — 586 B.C.E	586 — 330 B.C.E.	330 — 63 B.C.E.

SUGGESTIONS FOR FURTHER READING

Y. Aharoni, *The Land of the Bible* (1967).

Y. Aharoni and M. Avi-Yonah, *The Macmillan Bible Atlas* (1968).

W.F. Albright, *The Archaeology of Palestine* (1960[4]);
    idem., *Archaeology and the Religion of Israel* (1956);
    idem., *From Stone Age to Christianity* (1957).

R. Amiran, *Ancient Pottery of the Holy Land* (1970).

Archaeological Discoveries in the Holy Land (Archaeological Institue of
    America, 1969).

G.E. Wright, D.N. Freedman, and E.F. Cambell (ed.), *The Biblical Archae-
    ologist Reader*, 1 (1961), 2 (1964), 3 (1970).

M. Burrows, *What Mean These Stones? The Significance of Archaeology for
    Biblical Studies* (1957).

Everyday Life in Bible Times (National Geographic Society, 1970).

J. Finegan, *Light from the Ancient Past, the Archaeological Background of
    Judaism and Christianity* (1959).

H.J. Franken and C.A. Franken-Battershill, *A Primer of Old Testament
    Archaeology* (1969).

H. Frankfort, *The Art and Architecture of the Ancient Orient* (1954).

D.N. Freedman and J.C. Greenfield (eds.), *New Directions in Biblical
    Archaeology* (1969).

N. Glueck, *The River Jordan* (1968).

J. Gray, *Archaeology and Old Testament World* (1962).

L.H. Grollenberg, *Atlas of the Bible* (1956).

K.M. Kenyon, *Beginning in Archaeology* (1952);
    idem., *Archaeology in the Holy Land* (1965[2]);
    idem., *Royal Cities of the Old Testament* (1971).

P.W. Lapp, *Biblical Archaeology and History* (1969).

M. Noth, *The Old Testament World* (1966).

J.B. Pritchard (ed.), *Archaeological Discoveries in the Holy Land* (1967);
    idem. (ed.), *The Ancient Near East in Pictures Relating to the Old
    Testament* (1954, 1969[2]);
    idem., *Archaeology and the Old Testament* (1958).

Ch. Singer et al. (eds.), *A History of Technology*, 1 (1954).

R. de Vaux, *Ancient Israel, Its Life and Institutions* (1961).

M. Wheeler, *Archaeology from the Earth* (1950).

D. Winton-Thomas (ed.), *Archaeology and Old Testament Study* (1967).

G.E. Wright, *Biblical Archaeology* (1963);
    idem., *An Introduction to Biblical Archaeology* (1960).

Y. Yadin, *The Art of Warfare in Biblical Lands* (1963).

Sh. Yeivin, *A Decade of Archaeology in Israel, 1948-1958* (1960).

ILLUSTRATION CREDITS

Jerusalem, Israel Museum: Figs. 1a, 10, 30, 44, 45, 68; 72 ,78 (replicas);
Israel Department of Antiquities Collection: Figs. 1b, 19, 38, 102.

Israel Department of Antiquities and Museums: Figs. 2, 8, 14, 15, 16, 20,
36, 37, 59, 61, 62, 63, 67a, 79, 86, 88a, 89, 92, 93, 97b, 97d, and cover:
Photo David Harris.

London, British Museum: Figs. 21, 22, 90, 97e.

Government Press Office, Tel Aviv: Figs. 4, 33, 75.

David Eisenberg, Jerusalem: Figs. 12, 51, 65, 66, 69, 84, 91.

Werner Braun, Jerusalem: Figs. 3, 32, 70.

Richard Cleave: Fig. 47.

R. Amiran, P. Beck, and U. Zevulun, *The Ancient Pottery of Eretz Israel*
(Hebrew Edition), The Bialik Institute and the Israel Exploration Society,
Jerusalem 1963, pl. 77, no. 4: Fig. 6.

Encyclopaedia Judaica, vol. V, Jerusalem 1971, col. 593: Fig. 7.

Qadmoniot, Quarterly for the Antiquities of Eretz Israel and Israel Exploration Society, vol. IV, no. 1 (13), 1971. Figs. 11, 55; vol. III, no. 2 (10),
1970, p. 44: Figs. 52, 53, 54.

C.R. Lepsius, *Denkmaeler aus Aegypten und Aethiopien,* Berlin, 1849:
Figs. 17, 81, 95.

M. Levin, *Mlechet Hamishkan,* Tel Aviv, 1968: Figs. 34, 100.

G.E. Wright, *Shechem, The Biography of a Biblical City,* Gerald-Duckworth
and Co, Ltd., London, 1965: Figs. 23, 29a, 43, 50.

By Courtesy of Y. Yadin, Jerusalem: Figs. 31, 48.

C.W. McEwan, *American Journal of Archaeology,* Archaeological Institute
of America, vol. 41 (1937), pp. 8–13: Fig. 41.

Haifa, Dagon Collection, Archaeological Museum of Grain Handling in
Israel: Figs. 80, 87.

Eretz Israel, Archaeological, Historical and Geographical Studies. Published
by the Israel Exploration Society and the Hebrew University, vol. V,
Jerusalem, 1958: Fig. 24.

Encyclopaedia of Archaeological Excavations in the Holy Land, Israel
Exploration Society and Massada Press Ltd., Jerusalem, 1970: Figs. 13, 25,
26, 27, 29b, 35, 49, 56, 67b, 73, 74.

Ha'aretz Museum, Tell Qasila Excavations. Photo Prior, Tel Aviv: Fig. 28.

According to C. Watzinger, *Denkmaeler Palaestinas*, Leipzig, 1933: Fig. 39.

T.A. Busink, *Der Tempel von Jerusalem*, I: *Der Tempel Salomos*, Copyright by Nederlands Instituut for the Nabije Oosten Noordeindsplein 4–6, pl. 49, 52, Leiden, 1970: Fig. 40.

Sir L. Wooley, *A Forgotten Kingdom*, Harmondsworth, Middlesex, Penguin Books, London 1953, pp. 101–164: Fig. 42.

Based on L. Henneguin, *Fouilles et champs de fouilles en Palestine et en Phénicie*, extrait du "Supplement au Dictionnaire de la Bible", Letouzey et ané, Paris, 1936, Fig. 289, p. 434: Fig. 46.

H. Torczyner, *Lachish I*, second frontispiece, Oxford University Press, New York – Toronto, 1938: Fig. 57.

Y. Yadin, *The Art of Warfare in Biblical Times in the Light of Archaeological Discovery*, Weidenfeld and Nicolson, London, 1963: Fig. 58.

Based on N. Avigad, *Israel Exploration Journal*, vol. 20, 1970, p. 129 ff. fig. 3: Fig. 60.

Drawn by E.J.H. Mackay and L.H. Vincent, 1932, in *Sefer Hevron:* Fig. 64.

Based on D. Bahat, *Carta's Historical Atlas of Jerusalem*, 1973: Fig. 71.

W. Wreszinski, *Atlas zur Altaegyptischen Kulturgeschichte*, vol. 2, Leipzig, 1923: Fig. 77.

Views of the Biblical World, The International Publishing Co. Ltd., Jerusalem – Ramat Gan, 1961: Fig. 82.

W.M. Petrie, *Bet Pelet I*, British School of Archaeology in Egypt, University College, London 1930, pl. LV: Fig. 96.

R.S. Lamon and G.M. Shipton, *Megiddo I*, Chicago, 1939, pl. 77: Fig. 97a.

C. Shaeffer, in *Syria, Revue d'Art Oriental et d'Archéologie*, publiée par l'Institut Français d'Archéologie de Beyrouth, Librairie Orientaliste Paul Geuthener, Paris, vol. 31, 1954, p. 62: Fig. 97c.

Hebrew University, Institute of Archaeology, Excavations in the Jewish Quarter: Fig. 99.

Benno Rothenberg, Tel Aviv University, Institute of Archaeology: Fig. 101.

By courtesy of W.G. Dever, Hebrew Union College, Biblical and Archaeological School, Jerusalem: Fig. 76.

Based on survey map in C.C. McCown et. al., *Tel en-Nasbeh I*, Palestine Institute of the Pacific School of Religion, Berkley, and the American School of Oriental Research, New Haven, 1947: Fig. 9.

INDEX

283

SKOKIE PUBLIC LIBRARY

31232001826181

SEP   2005

WHAT'S THE TRICK?

by Caroline Walsh

SKOKIE PUBLIC LIBRARY

Cover Illustration: Laura J. Bryant
Inside Illustration: Laura J. Bryant

For Arlo, Audrey, and Jackie

Text © 1999 by Perfection Learning® Corporation.
All rights reserved. No part of this book may be used or reproduced in
any manner whatsoever without written permission from the publisher.

Printed in the United States of America. For information, contact
Perfection Learning® Corporation
1000 North Second Avenue, P.O. Box 500
Logan, Iowa 51546-1099.
Phone: 1-800-831-4190
Fax: 1-712-644-2392
Paperback ISBN 0-7891-2379-7
CoverCraft® ISBN 0-7807-7745-x
Printed in the U.S.A.
5 6 7 8 9 10 PP 08 07 06 05 04 03